A Personality Portrait

A Personality Portrait

Sixteen Biblical Leaders Who Identify Your Traits

EARL A. JONES

WIPF & STOCK · Eugene, Oregon

A PERSONALITY PORTRAIT
Sixteen Biblical Leaders Who Identify Your Traits

Wipf & Stock
An Imprint of Wipf and Stock Publishers
199 W. 8th Ave., Suite 3
Eugene, OR 97401

www.wipfandstock.com

PAPERBACK ISBN: 978-1-5326-6410-6
HARDCOVER ISBN: 978-1-5326-6411-3
EBOOK ISBN:978-1-5326-6412-0

Manufactured in the U.S.A.   11/05/18

Contents

Disclaimer

THIS BOOK IS NOT in any way intended to be an explicitly scientific analysis of biblical characters. Neither the author nor this book, *A Personality Portrait,* are in any way affiliated with: Consulting Psychologists Press, Inc. (CPP), Myers-Briggs, or the MBTI trademarked brand. The analysis of the biblical characters was completed by the author using *Introduction to Type* by Isabel Briggs Myers only as reference material. Additionally, the author used his knowledge of the holy Bible, Bible characters, and human psychology as outlined in the pages of this book.

As discussed in the book, the biblical leaders mentioned did not participate in the actual MBTI (Myers-Briggs Type Indicator) testing instrument. Nor did they receive concrete MBTI test results. They could not, did not, and will not take an MBTI test instrument.

The author simply reviewed the interactions of the biblical leaders described as they appear in the holy Bible and used the characteristics described in *Introduction to Type* in order to, in the opinion of the author, describe where each biblical leader discussed in this book most closely aligned with the actual MBTI Personality Types. These types are described in *Introduction to Type.* All personality profiles created by the author are based on the author's opinion. They were derived based on a reading of their actions and interactions, and then compared to the MBTI Personality Traits described in *Introduction to Type.*

In order to obtain the most precise MBTI and associated trademark brand test results, the author recommends that you take an actual MBTI test instrument as administered by an official representative of CPP and obtain official test results. For additional details on CPP and Myers-Briggs, please contact CPP or visit these websites: www.cpp.com or http://www.myersbriggs.org.

Myers-Briggs Type Indicator, Myers-Briggs, MBTI Step I,-III, *Introduction to Type,* and the MBTI logo are trademarks or registered

1

Introduction: Why Bible MBTI?

GROUP PHOTOS

TAKE A LOOK AT a group photo that you are a part of. Is it a nice photo? What makes it nice? Is it a bad picture? What makes it bad? Is this subjective assessment of the photograph wholly contingent upon how you look in the photo? If so, you are not alone; do not feel badly about yourself. You should not begin to believe that you have more narcissistic and vain tendencies than you used to think you possessed.

Everyone does this with group pictures. It is how counselors and psychologists make a living. Counselors, advisors, psychologists, as well as people who just enjoy listening to and helping other people with their problems use introspection to help the person see where they have been and where they are going in a particular area of their life.

WHAT IS MBTI?

The Myers-Briggs Type Indicator (MBTI) is a personality-type identifier which helps people to describe the normal differences that exist within and between psychologically healthy people.[1] There are many different tests that psychologists have developed to help them to help us. They use these tests to describe the simple differences in people's God-given inherent personalities.

You do not have to believe in the biblical creation story in order to enjoy this book. However, if you believe that all people are wonderfully

1. Myers, *Introduction to Type.*

complex in their construction, as the biblical book of Psalms states[2], you also believe that we are made in the very likeness and image of God in order to reflect his nature or personality as well as his characteristics and inherent integrity.[3] Thus, you have a unique personality type that is as distinctly your own as your fingerprints.

I want to show you that there were some people who have similar personalities though none are exactly the same. You will find yourself and similar personality traits in many different people. You will see that you are similar to some people who are called introverts, and to some who are called extroverts. Neither of those words, in reference to a personality type, means the same thing that they mean when they are used in general conversation.

WHY BIBLICAL LEADERS MBTI?

Why am I discussing such a complex topic as personality type by analyzing people who I never met, i.e. biblical leaders? It sounds like I am about to play "Wheel of Fortune" with personality types. Personality types express themselves in many ways that are observable to the trained eye. It is not my aim to write a technical manual on the finer psychological points of the MBTI, because I do not like to read and I definitely would not enjoy reading a book like that.

However, I have always enjoyed reading about my personality. During down times I would do internet searches about ENTJs. Some of these personality profiles yielded by my internet search were based on characters from my favorite television shows. Some were based on people who appeared in movies that I had watched. The author of the profile would analyze the character and place them in the MBTI where they believed that person would fit. In short, they had fun and they could not be "wrong or incorrect" in their analysis because they had never met the fictional character.

My goal in writing this book is for you to not only find yourself in the group photo but to like the photo. Then I would like to have you look at some of the other people in the photo and consider the idea that the picture may be nice or not so nice because of the others who are also represented in the picture as distinctly unique individuals. We like to look

---

2. Ps 139:14.

3. See Gen 1:26–27.

at ourselves. By looking at ourselves through personality types, we can also learn to enjoy looking at and possibly gain a better understanding of ourselves and others because we see similar and different personality traits between ourselves and others.

I will use sixteen real biblical leaders to illustrate this point. But I cannot be incorrect in my analysis of these people because I have never met them nor have I asked them to take the official MBTI personality test. I am just looking at four simple personality preferences and combining them to create a picture of that person as they exist in the group photo.

COUNSELING CLASSES

When I was in my doctoral program, I was enrolled in a counseling class geared toward learning crisis intervention techniques. I was an "Educational Leadership and Higher Educational Administration" degree candidate, but I had worked as an academic advisor or higher educational student counselor for many years, particularly dealing with academically at-risk college students.

During those meetings we discussed many of the issues that arose in their personal lives that negatively impacted their academic performance. We also discussed ways and methods that would help them to eliminate the distractions and to focus more attention on studying. Thus when it came time for me to take a couple of electives, I sought out a greater depth of knowledge in the area of counseling.

My master's program introduced me to many different counseling theories as a "Student Affairs in Higher Education" degree candidate. We studied college student development theory, or as I jokingly called it: "school counseling for the 13th grade." Later I came to teach Christian counseling classes for a university that offered degree programs and facilitated college courses through local churches. The students' favorite class in the Christian counseling major was called "An Introduction to Behavioral Analysis." They loved to look at themselves in that group photo!

The course offered two textbooks as reference material in order to guide the learning process: one focused on the DISC model[4] and the other on Personality Plus.[5] The students loved this material. They wanted

4. Rohm, *Positive Personality Profiles*.

5. Littauer, *Personality Plus*.

to run right out and try the material out at home on their relatives and friends, just as a mother in an episode of one of my favorite TV programs did.

I don't suggest that you run out and try to get people to look for you or for themselves in the group photograph, try to help them analyze themselves, or even worse, try to analyze the personalities of all of your family members. I would suggest that you buy this book for them and have them take the MBTI test referenced at the end of the book.

My students in that behavioral analysis class liked the topic of personality typology so much that the teacher from the biblical studies class, which was operating in the classroom next door, used to come over and sit in on our class, perhaps looking for herself in the group photo. I even did a workshop based on the Personality Plus material for the administrative staff at her community college. That group loved it too! People just love to look for themselves in the group photo.

While teaching that class, much to the chagrin of my students, I added a third personality typology text to the other two assigned textbooks: the Myers-Briggs Personality Type Indicator (MBTI). They enjoyed the MBTI too, though not as much as the first two personality theories. The book was a bit too technical and advanced for their particular level of expertise, although they still enjoyed the group photo.

I personally favor MBTI because it highlights as well as combines four different preferences that people lean toward as they express their personality and interact with others. It distinguishes between four distinct and discernable personality preference zones. It docs not just combine all four preferences, relative to specifically discrete parts of the personality analysis, into one of four zones. You lose the explicit characteristics relative to the person in the group photo if you combine them in such a generalized fashion.

The outcome of the MBTI is that it differentiates sixteen distinct personality types based on the person's individual preferences. MBTI places a finer point on the separable personality types. Speaking metaphorically, it uses a higher digital photograph pixel count when developing the group photograph.

WE ARE ALL INDIVIDUALS

Some people hate being around a large group of people, much less speaking in front of them. Other people love this and seem to gather more steam the longer they are in front of the crowd: they are right at home in front of a huge room full of people. Some people find a room full of people to be a totally draining experience for them: they feel as if all of the eyeballs in the room are attached to their skin. However, if these people can get alone with just one person, they are energized by the ideas that are interpersonally exchanged during that conversation. These images describes the differences between introverts and extroverts.

MBTI also helps people to find themselves in the group photo based on their preferred method of processing information. This personality type indicator also helps people to discover their preferred method for decision making. Finally, MBTI helps people discover how they distinctly and uniquely organize and make sense of their world. Based on these four preferences, MBTI helps people to see how unique they are and where they fit within a combination of four preferences. There are a total of sixteen distinct personality types according to MBTI.

LEADERSHIP ATTRIBUTES

In writing this book, I was able to identify many of the leadership attributes that were present, if not always obviously so, in the biblical leaders who are used to exemplify the personality type. Leaders come in all shapes, sizes, and come with vastly different personality traits. Popular opinion may lean toward the idea that extroverts make better leaders than introverts because they are outspoken and more comfortable speaking in front of crowds; this book demonstrates that assertion to be incorrect.

Inspired leaders can be extroverts or introverts. They may organize information using a "Sensing" preference which focuses more on the real, rational, and tangible aspects of the information. Or they may exercise an "iNtuitive" approach, employing their imaginative and linguistically creative nature to serve as their guide. These examples will be explored further later on in this book.

The point is that a good leader is exactly that: a gifted leader. Their personality does not dictate their gifting. Their personality provides the vehicle through which that gift is expressed and executed, relative to those who they will lead. All sixteen of the biblical leaders and their leadership traits are quantified via their MBTI personality profiles.

BIBLICAL LEADERS

Back to the question: why I am using Biblical Leaders to demonstrate MBTI personality types?

In the counseling class that was taken as a part of my doctoral program, we analyzed movie characters. We used different crisis intervention techniques to help the fictional character. It was a lot of fun! You couldn't be wrong. You didn't really know these people anyway; they were fictional movie characters. I chose characters from one movie about the Revolutionary War and one dramatic comedy.

All you had to do was watch your favorite movies. Movies always have some character in crisis, as a part of the dramatic element present in all of them. We were assigned to analyze the character's crisis. We looked at what situations and circumstances led them to the particular crisis. Then we described the steps that would have helped them to avert the crisis, as well as some steps that could have prevented the crisis from occurring. In short, we helped the person in crisis.

I began to use this same model in my Christian counseling classes. They would analyze a biblical leader as a part of their final project, then, depending on the specific counseling topic for that course, we could fit the leader into the theories and help the leader overcome life's challenges.

My purpose in writing this book was to help people to learn more about their individual personality type by learning something that may be new or possibly less than familiar to them, like MBTI. My plan was to accomplish this goal by presenting the sixteen personality types to the reader by taking a look at something more familiar, i.e. the personality types of biblical character. I wanted the readers to enjoy learning about personality typology and the Bible by noticing the similarities and nuanced differences in personality types. I also wanted readers to learn more about the personality types of our family members and friends, via using biblical characters. Our comparable familiarity with biblical characters may help us to better understand the personalities of those we interact with on a daily basis.

People express their uniquely individualistic personality types in all areas of life and human interaction. Biblical leaders also interacted with the real world as it existed during their time. Some of them enjoyed being in a crowd, and some appeared to prefer to engage people, or God, in a one-on-one setting. Biblical leaders also appeared to each process information differently. This impacted how they chose to face many critical life decisions. They were very similar to us in that way. Thus, we can take a look at sixteen people that we have never met and combine four preferences in order to create a picture of the leader's personality as they exist in the group photo called the Bible. Then we will hopefully be able to find ourselves in our own group photo of life through looking at their portraits.

2

Biblical Preferences

PREFERENCES

PEOPLE HAVE PREFERENCES. SOME like Italian food, but for others it is too spicy; they prefer a less complicated and less acidic meal. As these same people interact with the world they demonstrate certain preferences and tendencies.

Good counselors "pattern people." I have some knowledge of human psychology, or as I say, "I have a good sense about what goes on behind people's eyes." Thus, I am always people-watching. I watch as they interact with others in professional settings and in more relaxed social settings, as well as in individual conversations. Also, if I am privileged enough to see them go from a professional setting to a social setting or recreational gathering, I watch and observe any changes in their behaviors, demeanor, and mannerisms. Some call this "putting on a face."

People have public faces and private ones. Many people who know me from social settings, professional settings, and/or from recreational activities would argue that I am extremely extroverted. But I am not. Many times, I have to draw myself away from the crowd in order to re-charge. The floor show comes easily to me because of my "Extroverted" MBTI personality preference, but it also takes a lot of energy for me to sustain that expression over long periods of time because I am simultaneously watching and reading the crowd in order to identify the people that I would like to help. It's just my personality; I cannot shut it off. I am also a borderline MBTI "Introvert," though many who think that they know m would completely disagree with my MBTI assessment.

8

EXTROVERSION VERSUS INTROVERSION PREFERENCE

The first preference area that I would like to discuss in easy-to-read terms is the concept of "Introversion" and "Extroversion" as preferences.[1] Let me begin by telling you what Introversion and Extraversion, as they relate to MBTI, are not.

Introverts may have self-esteem issues that contribute to them appearing "shy" to the naked ey, but that is not what defines their Introverted personality type. Their personality type preference is to engage people in a one-to-one setting as opposed to engaging an entire crowd, like the Extroverts.

Extroverts are not considered Extroverts simply because they "talk loud and draw a crowd." They may do that, but it is not what defines their personality as Extroverted. They are likely just loud people. They may have self-esteem issues, but that's another book.

Introverts and Extroverts, as they relate to our MBTI personality types, are associated with the ways that we relate to and connect with the people who are in our outer world every day. We encounter people on a daily basis. Some of these people may be our family members, some of them could be our work colleagues, and some can be friends, but we generally engage and interact with them quite often (too often in some cases). However, the quality of the interaction is the essence of the Introvert's and the Extrovert's personality preference. We can feel energized during and after these interactions, or we can feel quite drained and become weary from these encounters, based on our perception of the quality of the interaction and our personality preference.

They are called personality preferences because much like a preferred food choice (Soul Food, Italian, Chinese, Thai, Indian, Mexican, Jamaican, etc.), people's personality preferences are not rigidly static choices; rather they are simply the places that we like to visit and eat at most frequently.

The first preferences that we will discuss are the Extrovert's personality preferences. Extroverts prefer a crowd; they are perfectly comfortable taking a microphone and heading for the center of the stage and expressing themselves. Some may be more emotional and artistic, some may be more bookish and intellectual, but Extroverts prefer the stage.

1. Myers, *Introduction to Type*, 9.

That part of them is irrepressible; if it does not get out, they become a bit more miserable inside. They are energized by the crowd and by the show.

Muhammad Ali, the famous boxer, comes to mind. He was loud, but he became more energized the more he interacted with the crowd and put on his show. I am certain that he was very different in private but when the lights came on, so did Ali.

Introverts are different. You may find them with an opaque look on their faces when they are in the midst of a crowd. The introvert prefers to go into a quiet part of the room and talk to a close friend, or just sip an iced tea alone and quietly reflect on their inner thoughts. Introverts are funny to me because their true preference in that scenario is: "you really do not have to feel compelled to come over to me and talk. I am fine over here, alone. Actually, I am quite enjoying myself."

However, this is not to say that Introverts do not make great public speakers (many do). But they are drained by the experience of something like a press conference, whereas an Extrovert would say, "let's do that again!" The Introvert would do the second presser well, yet they would be twice as drained by the experience.

Extreme Extroverts may tend to see themselves in everyone in the group photo. They might say to themselves: "That poor person must be so sad that they are all alone over there in the corner by themselves. Let me go talk to them!" Meanwhile, the beloved Introvert is praying that the "life of the party" would just let them be. The Introvert might say to themselves: "Please don't let them come over here. Oh no, here they come . . ." The beloved Introvert will become quickly drained by Ms. "life of the party" on her mercy mission of doom.

Each type draws energy in a different way. Introverts draw energy from being alone or having a really meaningful conversation with one person. Extroverts draw energy from being center stage and from being the life of the party. Thus, each type has a preference. Neither is right or wrong. Each is different and that is a good thing. Life would be no fun if everyone in the group photo looked alike, on the inside or on the outside.

SENSING VERSUS INTUITION PREFERENCE

The second type of personality preference according to MBTI is based on how people take in, process, and organize information. We take in information all of the time. We take in information on our jobs, in our homes, through various forms of entertainment, and in our life's travels.

People who have a Sensing preference[2] process information in an "as is" format. If you write 2+2=4 on a piece of paper and give it to a person with a Sensing preference, they will accept your mathematical equation for what it is, and then move on with their lives to the next piece of information to process.

People who have an iNtuition preference[3] (the "N" becomes the primary letter that represents this preference in MBTI because the "I" has already been used for my beloved Introverts), will look for the "thing behind the thing." They use insight and a gut instinct to guide the way that they process information. They may ask themselves, "What is the purpose of the person writing the 2+2=4 equation on the paper and giving it to me?" They may also ask, "Are there any places where 2+2 does not =4?"

I had a student once who was a math major. She came to me and told me that they had given her a job as a graduate assistant working on a research grant. On this research project, they were trying to find some other number that equaled zero. I have a strong N preference. I tell people that I always look at and can see "the thing behind the thing" or the action and what went into the action behind the observable activity. I do this instinctively, as opposed to just looking at the action itself. I believe that my student was also an N, but we were not in agreement on this one. As I mentioned, these are preference zones, not rigid personality mandates. I thought like a Sensing person in this instance, and said, "A zero is a zero. Why are they paying you guys to look for a zero that is not a zero?" It seemed like a huge waste of time. However, when she told me how much money she was making on the project as a graduate student, I again reacted like the Sensing person and said, "Carry on!"

INtuition preference people look for the future possibilities in a piece of information. They are curious about the future possibilities and think about the information in creative ways as they assimilate the information. They look for the "thing behind the thing."

Sensing people take the information for what it is and how it is presented to them. They take their information for what it is worth and accept things at face value. Their world would be flipped upside down if

2. Myers, *Introduction to Type*, 9.

3. Myers, *Introduction to Type*, 10.

they were forced to figure out if 2+2=4 meant anything other than what it says!

THINKING VERSUS FEELING PREFERENCE

As we gather information, we generally store that information in the human mind and retrieve it on demand in order to make appropriate decisions. These decisions affect our lives. Thus, our decision-making process, or as the academics call it, the development of our critical thinking skill sets, are invaluable to us. People have preferences when it comes to the process of decision-making.

People who have a "Thinking" preference, according to MBTI,[4] prefer to make decisions by being as objective about the situation as possible. They prefer to remove themselves from the situation and remove their emotional attachment to the situation in order to make the best and most concrete decision possible. Researchers would call this causal or cause-and-effect decision making. If I pour motor oil on the ground, will it leave a stain? To the Thinking preference person, the answer is: Of course it will; thus, if I do not want a stain here, then I had better not pour oil here.

This process can become a bit radical or extreme for the Thinker if they are not careful. They can become, like me, a perfectionist. My mother always told me: "You will have a hard way to go in life, because you are such a perfectionist!" But I have also found this preference useful in my work as a higher educational, and often times as personal counselor and advisor. The Thinking preference allows me to become and remain totally emotionally detached from the person and the situation that we are discussing. Now, I can hear you in my head saying, "No one is totally detached," but remember, I am also a perfectionist. I am emotionally detached when I am helping someone with a problem. I am personally shocked when I am not totally detached, and my emotional connections begin to impact my decision-making process.

"Feeling" preference[5] people are rather the opposite of their Thinking preference counterparts. They want to become emotionally involved in their decision-making process. They feel ill at ease when they cannot place themselves in someone else's shoes or consider the other guy's point

4. Myers, *Introduction to Type*, 10.
5. Myers, *Introduction to Type*, 10.

of view. They are compassionate and fair in their decision-making process. They always consider the feelings of others when making a decision. They want to know: How will this affect everyone in the group photo? Is this a good time to take the picture? What if Cousin Emma is running late or having a bad day, then is she going to hate the picture? So maybe we should take it tomorrow?

To the Thinker, taking the picture at any point other than right now is a huge waste of time. But to the Feeling person, they must consider the entire group before arriving at a decision. They have opposite preferences.

Problems begin to exist when the Thinker cannot relent and accommodate the desires or at least the expressions of the Feeling person's desire in order to include everyone's potential feelings in the decision making process. Problems can also exist when the Feeling person cannot let it go, move on, and just take the picture because not everyone will be here tomorrow or Cousin Elisa may be feeling terrible tomorrow, too. Thinkers and Feelers can become extreme or perfectionists in their decision-making processes if they are not careful to keep their preference type in check.

JUDGING VERSUS PERCEIVING PREFERENCE

The final preference types involve the manner in which people like to consider, visualize, and organize their life as well as the world around them. This impacts how they function in the first three preference arenas.

I am sure that you have heard people say: "I can't think amidst all of this clutter! How do you do it?" To that person, the organization of the things around them impacts how they can function within and interact with the world around them. Organization impacts how effectively they may interact with others and with whom, and the quality of the decision that they can make regarding the day's activities. All because clutter confuses them and they are not able to be at their best in the middle of a junky room or at a junky desk.

"Judging" preference[6] people are not "judgmental finger-waggers" who hate everything from college football to the lilies growing wild in the field. The Judging preference according to MBTI is one preferred way that some people organize things and make sense of their world. Some Judging people write outlines and strictly adhere to them. The back seat

6. Myers, *Introduction to Type*, 10.

of their car is as clutter free as the trunk or cargo area. To describe them in one sentence: Judging preference people are creatures of habit.

My young cousin used to come to my house during the summer along with her siblings. She told her grandmother once: "Earl's house is always clean." It was true, and I would not have it any other way. I do not even face the challenge of not being able to think in clutter because things in my life never become junky. Clutter drives me crazy! So I start cleaning it; for example, I will unplug the phone cord in your house or office if I am left alone in there for a long enough period of time. The rat's nest cord drives me crazy! I will look in your cupboards for sanitizing wipes if I go to use your restroom and will never tell you. If I find a can of disinfectant spray and a piece of toilet paper instead, and that's my only option, it is good enough! At times, I'm just cleaning your sink. I am who I am.

But I also tell people "don't live like me." I do that stuff, but you do not have to become that obsessive about trying to accommodate me when I come over. Thankfully they love me and try to clean to a level that is close to my standards when they know that I am coming to their house. It's just a preference, while others may prefer to live another way.

Perceiving preference[7] people live in a very different world. They are very spontaneous regarding their organization; they can operate within certain measures of clutter because they can overlook it in order to live in the moment. They fly by the seat of their pants in the way they organize their world, uncaring of the current state of the room or their desk.

Perceiving people are much more interested in enjoying the process and working toward the beautiful outcome than they are engaged in, as opposed to paying attention to what the phone cord looks like. They just want to talk to the person on the other end of it and exchange ideas that will lead to a glorious outcome. As a matter of fact, they feel confined and constrained by too much organization. These people need an open-ended situation so they can change courses in the middle of the process with the unspoken expectation that they will achieve the best outcome.

For example, organizing things perfectly and washing every dish as you use it before you move on to the next phase of cooking stifles their creative process and will make the food taste horrible to them. However, if they are allowed to make their magic and leave the clutter there because they cannot stop their creative muse, they will make a delicious meal. But that meal will taste great to them because they were "free to be me" while

7. Myers, *Introduction to Type*, 10.

making it. They may clean up later, depending on how attuned they are to the potential negative effects of their Perceiving preference.

The Perceiving person can leave a mess if things are not kept in check, if they are not self-aware, or if this preference is taken to an extreme place. Likewise, the Judging preference person can just flat out get on everyone's nerves because they are always organizing and fixing things.

Judging preference people find it very difficult to just sit there. They believe in the Golden Rule as well as Newton's Law. In other words, for them what comes out is a result of what goes in to the process.

For the Perceiving person, what comes out is a result of all of the creativity that they just poured in, without respect to what the room looks like. As long as the cake tastes good, they are Machiavellian in their conceptions: the end justifies the means!

BRINGING THE FOUR PREFERENCES TOGETHER TO MAKE ONE BIBLICAL LEADER'S MBTI

When you combine those four distinct preferences, remembering to always keep each of them in check, you will develop a good portrait of a person's personality as they exist within the group personality photograph. The group photograph that I will look at is the Bible.

The MBTI personality types can be observed by watching the way that the people in the Bible interact with others. I call myself a "highly trained observer of the human condition." Thus, as a "highly trained observer of the human condition" I can tell if they love being in front of a crowd, or at least do not mind that one bit. We can tell if they prefer to be alone or interact with people in an individual and interpersonally-intimate setting. We can look at the ways that they absorb the information that is presented to them. We can also look at the decisions that they make relative to that information.

For example, Jonah in the Bible was told by God to go to Nineveh and preach, obviously in front of a crowd, against the land and their evil activities. Jonah was given information by God Almighty himself.[8] He took it in, processed it, and decided "I'm going to Tarshish!" which just happened to be in the opposite direction from Nineveh. He likely did not feel that he either wanted to or could clean up the Ninevites' world. When

8. Jonah 1:1–3.

he found himself in the belly of a great fish, I wonder if he pulled out the sanitization wipes and started cleaning, orr if Jonah just lived in the moment and thought to himself, "Lord, I tried to pull a fast one and run away from You. You caught me, but if you get me out of this fish, I will go and clean up the Ninevites' world as you instructed."

Through the expressed personalities of these people in the Bible we can see if they like organization in their world or if they could function well in a disorderly environment.

PERSONALITY EXTREMES

Jesus sat everyone down in groups before he performed the miracle with the five loaves of bread and two fish.[9] In my opinion, Jesus represents perfect balance between all personality sides. However, there were times that he decided that order was not as important relative to the process and outcome, such as when he created a whip from ropes, turned over tables, spilling coins everywhere, and drove the money-changers out of the temple during Passover.[10]

What we can learn from this is that we cannot become too extreme in or rigidly attached to the expression of any of the four personality preferences that contribute to our MBTI personality make-up. We have to work to keep everything in check and create a balance. For example, we all have preferences, but we Extroverts do not have a carte blanche mandate to always be the life of the party. Eventually people will see that person as obnoxious and likely not invite them to the party in the first place. Similarly, people may perceive the extreme Introvert as being aloof, standoffish, sullen, remote, or just no fun to be around if the Introvert is not careful to at times engage other people and allow them into their world.

Finally, before we begin to discuss the individual Biblical Leaders and their MBTI personality profiles, we need to keep in mind that we are not rigidly predisposed to functioning exclusively in any specific personality preference area unless we allow ourselves to take our personality preferences to the extreme end of the scale. Thus, we should not be extreme in the combination of the four preference zones which are brought together to make one MBTI personality profile for us.

9. Luke 9:12–17.
10. John 2:13–17.

As I have mentioned, I am by no means an extreme MBTI Extrovert. I have taken the free MBTI test referenced at the end of this book, many, many times. I am a borderline MBTI Introvert: 51 percent–49 percent. That's why I am a hopeless romantic who often watches Hallmark channel movies when some might expect me to be watching college football or basketball. This also demonstrates my ability to regularly visit my Feeling decision-making preference. I could be extreme in the iNtuitive manner in which I process information, and begin to chase waterfalls, shadows, and ghosts, always looking for the "thing behind the thing," though in some instances, things are exactly as they appear to be. I could be extreme in the Thinking manner that I use to make decisions and completely ignore the Feelings of others. I could also exercise a heretical desire to have and maintain perfect order in my home, office, and car, in connection with my Judging preference. But I am self-aware enough to know that, even though I could have tested on the high end of the final three preference zones of my ENTJ personality type, I have to maintain balance. This will enable me to be sensitive to how my part in the group photo may positively or negatively impact others in the picture. I have to remember that I am a part of the group photo, not the whole thing, but also keep in mind that my role in that photo will make an important contribution to the whole, if I build a bridge and not a wall, which extreme behavior does not do.

PERSONAL APPLICATIONS AND DEVELOPMENT WITH MBTI

We will explore some explicit aspects of and applications for your individual MBTI personality profile at the end of each of the sixteen chapters. There are ways to more appropriately apply your personality to your: work life, home life, and personal relationships. These directly correlate with how effectively you will interact with others within each of these arenas.

My attempt regarding the development of each of the definitive personality profiles associated with the sixteen biblical leaders who were examined, specifically as it relates to those who have a biblical worldview is to demonstrate how these leaders were selected by God in order to accomplish the unique tasks that he created them to accomplish. My belief and understanding is that when God created us, including our distinctively individual personalities, God knew precisely how he would make us. Although God does not exist in time, he matched our personality traits with the callings that he would place on our lives, so we could execute and live out those callings via our gifts and talents in the world, within the timeframe that he set for us to exist.

YOU WILL ENJOY THIS BOOK, BIBLICAL WORLDVIEW OR NOT

If you are not one who has adopted that particular biblical worldview, this book will still provide you with a deeper understanding of your own personality type, as well as those of your family members, friends, and colleagues. You can speed through the portions that speak from a certain biblical worldview and still obtain a more enlightened and profound understanding relative to the fact that we are all individuals and thus we all have individually distinctive personality types. These personality portraits are all placed along a continuum which influences how each person behaves and interacts with others (in very different ways). Therefore, developing a deeper understanding of ourselves as well as a more profound understanding of others helps us all proceed through life with a more balanced and healthy perspective. The personality types are what they are, irrespective of your belief system or philosophy of life.

Most people of a certain biblical worldview and belief system accept as true that God knew exactly where and how He planned to use us, as well as where on his created earth that he would place us in order to be used for a set purpose. For example, God knew that he would need to use Queen Esther for this exact time and season as her cousin Mordecai mentioned to her while trying to persuade her to go to her husband the king on behalf of her people.[11] Though God is eternal and thus does not exist in tim, he knows that we do.[12] Thus he knew that he would need Esther to become queen, at that exact time in history in order to use her, including her specific personality, to advocate on behalf of the Hebrew people. He knew every hair on her head[13] as well as exactly what her personality would need to be, in this case an ESFJ, in order to use her gifts

---

11. Esth 4:14.

12. See Ps 90:2; 103:17.

13. See Luke 12:7.

and calling to accomplish his purpose, which was to prevent the exiled Hebrews who were in the kingdom of Persia from being destroyed.

Similarly, I believe that God uses us to accomplish his purposes in this time in which we live. He knows exactly where we belong and who we will interact with from day to day. God knows what our time is to be used in order to most impactfully influence others and accomplish not only his purpose as it relates to our world but also to his kingdom. We will explore those relationships and connections relative to how our personalities apply to our lives, as well as to our gifts and callings.

PERSONALITY EXTREMES AND CONNECTIONS WITHIN MBTI

I discussed how to manage your personality extremes. Your specific and set personality that I believe is given to you by God is placed along a continuum. As I have mentioned, I am an Extrovert, but I am also a borderline Introvert. Thus, I can be used by God to function as an Extrovert, regarding how I interact with the world around me. However, I can easily function just as effectively in one-on-one settings, such as in the area of advising and counseling, thereby employing my Introversion personality traits. If I allow myself to shift along that continuum to an extreme end in the Extroversion zone, I would not be as effective when I am used by God to discuss personal issues with my students or when functioning in an advising and personal counseling setting.

I have to avoid extremes relative to each of my four personality trait zones, as well as how the four combine to make my one true personality, in order to ensure that I am remaining in the correct position to affect positive change. I also have to avoid extremes so I can achieve my purpose.

As an example, I cannot visit the Creole restaurant to the exclusion of the seafood restaurant, because I love fish as well as most types of seafood. All they have at the Creole restaurant is catfish and crawfish, and I do not like crawfish, nor the idea of eating a crawfish, at all. But some people love crawfish. However, they are missing out if they never try a good ole' fried cod sandwich from time to time. Gotta avoid those fried food extremes, Jones! In similar fashion, I need to manage my personality zones where they are set, and not allow any of them or my overall personality type to go to the far extreme end of the continuum, because

I will be missing out on some great things. I will also hurt many people and we definitely have to avoid those situations.

While developing this book there were some connections between the personality zones that became abundantly obvious to me. We have to manage each individual personality zone, ensuring that we do not allow ourselves to become an overbearing Extrovert or a reclusive Introvert. However, we should also ensure that we notice the ways that our Extroversion-Introversion personality zone preference, or how we interact with the world and the people around us, has a direct connection relative to the Judging-Perceiving preferences, or how we organize and make sense of the world around us.

I also believe that there are obvious connections relative to our information-gathering functions (the Sensing-INtuitive zones), connecting with the decision-making functions (the Thinking-Feeling zones).[14] All of the zones are interconnected.

The entire INFP personality type is interconnected and each of the four personality zones are placed on a continuum, almost never placed at the extreme end of any specific zone, and these connections make up our personality portrait. However, the information-gathering function has a direct impact on the decisions that we make relative to the information that we gathered and stored in our brains. This information is available for recall and use on demand. Thus, the connection between these two personality zones have an apparent and influential connection within the overall functioning of our complete MBTI personality.

We will also examine the specific S-N to T-F connections, understanding that there are interrelated connections between each of the four personality zones as well as within your explicit MBTI personality type.[15] These two types of connections, the E-I to J-P, as well as the S-N to T-F connections are simply more obvious and relevant, regarding their direct interaction and impact on our relationships and growth, than the other combined connections. However, each of these connection explorations are directly impacted by the entire and distinctly-individual personality type functioning as a whole, and also impact the two connections explored within each of these expository discussions.

14. Myers, *Introduction to Type*, 9–10, 32–33.

15. Myers, *Introduction to Type*, 9–10, 32–33..

GROWTH OPPORTUNITIES AND THREATS
TO YOUR MBTI

The last application that we will discuss at the end of each of the sixteen biblical leaders personality profiles is the idea related to learning how to grow, considering the inherent strengths and weaknesses (or opportunities and threats) associated with each MBTI personality profile.

In addition to all of my experiences which I have already discussed in reference to academia, I was also a marketing major as an undergrad, and functioned as a marketing professor for a couple of sections of the "Principles of Marketing" course for non-business majors at one university where I worked. This afforded me the opportunity to encounter students from many different majors, who behaved differently and probably had different personality profiles from their business major counterparts.

I believe that in a fashion, similar to the way that God selects us with the appropriate personality profile, he matches that personality profile to the exact kingdom assignment that he has chosen us to fulfill. We have a tendency to be aligned in a loosely-observable way with our personality profile and our major or career choice. If their personality profile does not align at all with their major, most students, in my experience, tend to struggle in that major.

Most people who are destined to become accountants do not generally do very well as English or art majors and vice versa. There are exceptions to this but it generally holds true. Therefore, if the personality type does not align in any relationship to the major or career choice, then the concepts discussed within the classes for that chosen major fit the student like a tight shirt. They simply cannot move and breathe very well within the misaligned major. They are not "free to be me," as I mentioned when I was discussing my Perceiving preference folks.

As a marketing major and later marketing professor, I learned to perform what we called a Strengths-Weaknesses-Opportunities-Threats (SWOT) analysis, regarding the manner in which the product, service, or idea that you are comporting to sell interacts with and places within the specific business environment where you are planning to sell it. Now, I can once again hear you in my head saying, "How can this man, who knows as much as he does about human psychology, also function as an ENTJ and a marketing professor? Those two subjects seem as far afield as the art major attempting become a business accounting major." As I have mentioned, we are not statically locked into one set and intransigent personality type.

Some Extroverts are very bookish and intellectual as they relate to, engage with, and interact with their world and the people in that world. Some are more emotional and artistic. However, both people are still Extroverts. The modifications come in relative to the interaction with the other three personality zones.

That does not even include the times when that Extroverted ENTJ visits his Introverted preference! For example, I can seem more closely aligned with the personality traits and characteristic that are usually connected with those of a business marketing and management major and professor, because I have various interests and many layers to my personality type (that of an ENTJ MBTI). However, when I feel like visiting a different restaurant, so to speak, I can easily take off my ENTJ hat for a while, and put on an ENFJ hat, which more closely aligns me with my counseling and advising brethren. All of this can occur while I continue to remain one who exhibits the traits of an ENTJ most often. But my personality type makes me ill-suited with those who have personalities that align most closely with people who major in nursing or engineering science.

Some personality types, when all four zones are combined, are never going to make an artist into a quantitative finance major. I know of an artist who knows absolutely nothing about sports, while that same person's sibling is a sports talk radio and tv personality. They often compare notes and make fun of each other's lack of knowledge about the other sibling's chosen fields of study and occupation.

My point is that we generally have both Opportunities and Threats that are associated with our specific personality type as we interact with other people in our daily lives. These Opportunities and Threats will also impact our ability to grow and develop; this growth and development arc will also influence those of us who have a biblical worldview.

The reason that I discussed my marketing background is related to that SWOT analysis. I prefer to use the words Opportunities and Threats as opposed to Strengths and Weaknesses when discussing personality types. We as humans can allow our personality zones or the entire MBTI personality type to go to an extreme place. That place, extreme or not, directly impacts how effectively or ineffectively we can interact with the people in our world.

It also directly impacts how efficiently or inefficiently we grow and develop such as was the case concerning Enoch.[16] Enoch walked with God. He became so effective, efficient, and proficient at growing in God and at keeping pace with God's ordained steps that Enoch was taken from the earth by God and transported into heaven! It only took 300 years of walking with God before he was taken away.

Using the word "weaknesses" puts us into a more negative mindset than I prefer for us to carry around with us from day to day. We have inherent weakness in our general human existence after the fall of man.[17] But as some of us choose to walk with God, our "strengths" should become more dominant as we simultaneously die daily to our flesh, our self, and to our humanity.[18] We do have continuous opportunities for growth and development, specifically relative to a daily walk with God, as well as in our daily interactions with people in the world around us. Additionally, there are Threats or extremes that we must learn to avoid as some of us attempt to develop a closer and more fruitful walk with God.

What we do in marketing is to perform a SWOT analysis as previously discussed. Following that SWOT analysis, we analyze each of the four individual elements of SWOT as they interrelate to the business environment, and we attempt to convert the Weakness into Strengths. We also attempt to convert our Threats in the marketing environment into market Opportunities.

Similarly, we can and will explore those Opportunities and Threats as they relate to our MBTI personality type, how they can impact our daily interactions, and how they can impact our proper development. We will also discuss how we should attempt to convert the Threats into Opportunities so that the outcome of these converted Threats produce more positive, effective, and healthy interpersonal interactions, as well as impactful development. We should transform our Threats into our Opportunities for growth and development, irrespective of how the other people in our world are behaving.

16. Gen 5:23–27; Heb 11:5–6 .

17. Gen 3:1–24.

18. 1 Cor 15:31.

FUN WITH BIBLICAL LEADERS' MBTI TRAITS

My biblical leader analysis is in no way intended to be a completely scientific exercise. I could have just as easily used fictitious movie or TV characters. My real intention is to help us to look at biblical leaders as people in a group photo and to clearly identify the biblical character or characters that we are most like. However, I also hope that we will see ourselves and different parts of our personalities in many different aspects of the personalities represented in many of these biblical leaders.

No one should be extremely placed on the far end of the INTP personality. There are subtleties that exist in each preference zone. Just like my experience with my math major and her zero, we can slide back and forth into other personality preference traits.

We have to learn to balance the extremities on each end. If you are a borderline Introvert, be careful not to seclude yourself too often. If you have a firmly entrenched Thinking preference, relative to decision making, be sure that you consider the feelings of others before you render your brilliant decision.

ONE SUGGESTION

The teacher in me abhors the idea of telling people how to think and process the information that I present to them. I prefer to allow people to draw conclusions for themselves. I simply provide the water. However, in this instance I will offer one suggestion regarding how to take in the information presented in this book. You may wish to consider reading two of the groupings of personality profile chapters together and then reflect on what you have read before you move on to the next set. For example, read the ESTJ and ISTJ chapters together, and then take some time to digest the information associated with those two related personality portraits before you move on to the next set of two.

This will allow you to more easily absorb all of the information presented, particularly if you are unfamiliar with MBTI. If you are a binge reader, by all means, GO FOR IT! But this may help those who are learning some new or unfamiliar concepts to better understand what they are reading.

ANALYSIS APPROACH

In my analysis of the biblical leaders MBTI personality traits, I simply decided to select the leaders from the Bible who most closely resembled the personality traits that are associated with each of the four preference zones, combining to make one MBTI personality profile. Specifically, I used the generalized bullet points associated with each preference zone[19] in order to analyze the behaviors associated with each of the distinctive biblical leader's MBTI personality as I perceived it to be expressed through their actions and interactions. It was a fun exercise for me.

After completing my analysis of the particular biblical leader's personality traits, deciding if they fit the characteristics associated with an MBTI Introvert or Extrovert, I selected the appropriate preference area. Then I moved on to the next preference zone. When I completed assigning that leader to all four preference zones, I compared the results of my analysis to the thumbnail sketch.[20] You can find all sixteen MBTI personality type thumbnail sketches in *Introduction to Type*.

I give comparisons at the end of each of the biblical character's MBTI personality description and how each of the four preference zones combined to make one MBTI personality type. I tried to demonstrate how well-represented the personality traits associated with, for example, an ISTP, were represented in the Biblical Leader that I selected and analyzed, in comparison to the Myers thumbnail sketch of personality traits.

I did not read the MBTI brief description of that explicit personality type, much less read the detailed descriptions of each of the sixteen types in the Myers booklet until after completing the profiles for each biblical leader. I used the detailed personality profiles,[21] as well as other information in Myers, only after developing each completed Biblical character's MBTI profile in order to prepare for the Life Applications and Growth sections of this book. Those sections were completed after all personality profiles were finished.

In order to complete the discussion on relevant connections between personality zones, I had to briefly consider the appropriate section to my discussion, Using Preference Type Combinations.[22] All of these concepts related to MBTI are relative to my interpretation of the work on

19. Myers, *Introduction to Type*, 9–10.

20. Myers, *Introduction to Type*, 13.

21. Myers, *Introduction to Type*, 14–29.

22. Myers, *Introduction to Type*, 32–35.

MBTI as represented in the *Introduction to Type* booklet. However, I used it only as a reference foundation.

Relative to each individual MBTI personality analysis, I simply completed my analysis of the leader. Then, I used the thumbnail sketch to compare the completed results of my assessment of their combined personality type.[23]

I wanted to use my "people-watching" skill-set to analyze the biblical leader without bias or preconception. I wanted to empty my mind of all preconceptions about personality types. I wanted to consider the biblical leader and what I knew about them based on my knowledge of the Bible as well as what it says about that specific leader as they traveled their real-life journey. I believed that a self-proclaimed "highly trained observer of the human condition" could use the preference zones to make an accurate analysis of sixteen biblical leaders' MBTI personality traits.

As I mentioned, there is so much material in publication and other sources relative to MBTI that I did not want to engage any bias prior to writing this book. Thus I put this book away for about two years prior to assessing the leaders. I did not look at anything related to MBTI during that time period, by choice and because I was so familiar with the material, particularly as it related to my MBTI personality: the Extroverted, iNtuitive, Thinking, Judging (ENTJ) personality preference.

Hopefully that explanation was not too technical. My hope and desire is that people enjoy looking for themselves and others in the group photo as much as I do.

STRAIGHT DOWN THE COLUMNS

I decided to go straight down the list of preference traits. Thus, we will begin our journey with the ESTJs, who occupy the left-side of the MBTI preferences column. We will conclude our journey with the INFPs who occupy the right-side of the MBTI preferences column. We will not explore the Jungian relationships or the Myers Types Dynamics and Development-Dynamics Theory, i.e.; the Dominant function, the Auxiliary function, the Tertiary function, and the Inferior function hierarchy, in order to keep things as simple as possible.[24]

23. Myers, *Introduction to Type*, 13.
24. Myers, *Introduction to Type*, 4, 7, 35.

3

ESTJ: Noah, An Organized Man for the Job

NOAH, AN ORGANIZED MAN FOR THE JOB

THE STORY OF NOAH is found in the book of Genesis (6:1–9:29). Things around him were unfolding during a time that the world was considered to be growing into an intolerably wicked place by God. But Noah was not considered wicked; rather, Noah and likely his personality pleased God.

I say that his personality pleased God because of the way that God first selected Noah for the job that he was going to ask Noah to complete. God wanted Noah to build an ark before God himself was planning to destroy all life on earth via a flood that would cover the whole earth for many days.[1] God knew how best to present information to Noah so that Noah could finish the task of building an ark, and so his family as well as animals of all kinds could be spared extinction as a result of the pending flood.[2]

NOAH'S EXTROVERT PREFERENCE

Rather than start at the beginning of the story of Noah, I will, after presenting some brief background information on Noah for context, go to the end of his journey in order to illustrate one example of his preference

1. Gen 6:5–18.
2. Gen 6:19–22.

toward Extroversion. Remember, Extroversion refers to the manner in which these people interact with their world and how they become energized through interpersonal interactions. We will try to discover why Noah was more likely an Extrovert than an Introvert.

The Bible does not mention specific interactions with the wicked people of his day.[3] However, as God began to instruct Noah and told him why he had been selected, God told Noah to take his entire family onto the ark with him. God said that he was going to use Noah and those he allowed Noah to take with him to preserve and ultimately repopulate the human race, after the flood destroyed all of the others who lived on earth at the time.[4]

God could have told Noah the Introvert, had he been one, to "just take your wife. You and she can do the work of repopulation." Noah's righteousness was extended to cover his family, including his wife, sons, and daughters-in-law. God allowed all of these people join Noah on the ark and to repopulate the earth. Had Noah been an Introvert, who drew energy best from one-to-one interactions, God could have allowed Noah and his wife to repopulate the planet without his children. Noah was instructed to only take two of each kind of animal for the purposes of repopulation.[5] These people were in very close quarters with many animals. They also had to be organized in order to keep the ark clean. They would not be able to get back to solid ground for many days.[6] The people on the ark would not be able to go to their own little corners of the ship and recharge like the Introvert would need to do. This would have been particularly hard on Noah who was the leader of this little cruise and the captain of the ark. Noah was an Extrovert and could handle the jobs that God gave him in every respect because of his Extroverted personality preference.

Now for the story at the end of Noah's journey: after the flood was over, Noah planted a vineyard and began to make the grapes into wine. He became quite drunk. He was apparently a bit of a partier. His youngest son Ham mocked his nakedness, and then proceeded outside to tell his two older brothers, Shem and Japheth. The older two boys backed into their father's tent with a large garment over their shoulders and covered

3. Gen 6:5–6.

4. Gen 6:8–22.

5. Gen 6:18–20.

6. Gen 3:8–14.

him without looking at his nakedness. Noah blessed Shem and Japheth for honoring their father by covering his shame. However, Noah cursed Ham's son Canaan because his father Ham had mocked him for being passed out, drunk, and naked.[7]

Noah did not have an issue confronting people, even his children. At times, Introverts may have to achieve balance in that area. At the same time, Extroverts may have to learn to restrain themselves from being too harsh in their specific dispensation of justice. Noah was an Extrovert.

NOAH'S SENSING PREFERENCE

God first judged Noah to be a righteous man who was worth sparing from the flood.[8] He also judged Noah to be a man capable of carrying out his divine task to the letter of the mandate. God gave Noah very specific instructions regarding the rational for destroying the earth by flood, the materials to use in construction of the ark, the dimensions of the ark, the total number of animals to take for the purposes of repopulation of the species, and the total numbers of the unclean as well as clean animals to take on the trip. Finally, he was instructed regarding the collection and storage of food. The Bible repeatedly says that Noah did everything that he was commanded to do by God.[9]

Noah was a capable person regarding the assimilation of information. I have met only a few people who, as I say, "can keep up with me." I am becoming more long-winded the older that I get and the longer that I function as a professor. I tend to send very lengthy emails and text messages. Many people balk at the length of my messages. I also have to keep an eye on the clock while I am teaching. But some amazing people, or at least they are amazing to me, can take large and at times random quantities of information that I present to them and condense all of it into a few short sentences. I often ask the question "Make sense?" to people when I am giving instruction. These Sensing people, like Noah, just say "yes" and proceed to carry out the task to the letter every time. Noah had a Sensing preference regarding his ability to absorb and assimilate information.

7. Gen 9:18–29.

8. Gen 6:8–22; 7:1–3.

9. Gen 6:22; 7:9.

NOAH'S THINKING PREFERENCE

You might say that this task was easy for Noah to complete: God did all of the thinking and heavy lifting for him, so Noah did not have to be much of a Thinker in order to accomplish the tasks given to him by God. I beg to differ with you if you are thinking this way.

Noah could not just randomly run out after constructing the ark to God's standards and collect the first set of two elephants, rhinoceros, or hippopotamus that he found. He had to discern the best place to collect the cypress wood so that the job could be completed in as timely a manner as possible.[10] He then had to collect the animals in a logical manner.

In spite of the Sunday school stories, they did not just line up at his newly-constructed ark door in order of entry. He had to get the big boys in first, most likely, and then he could collect a few rodents and snakes and stick them in the smaller cages at the end.

Finally, Noah had to decide how to find out if the flood waters had receded. First he sent out a raven. Next he sent out one dove on three separate occasions before discerning that the ground had begun to reappear.

The first time he sent the dove out, it returned to the ark. He knew, based on this information, that the dove could not find a landing place and water still covered the whole earth. The second dove, likely to his elation, returned with a freshly-picked olive branch in its beak. This information required no interpretation and the Sensing Noah knew what the straightforward information meant. There was some dry land, though maybe not enough. He used his Thinking preference and decided to wait seven more days before sending the dove for a third time; that time the dove did not return and he knew that dry land had appeared. Noah used a cause-and-effect decision-making process.[11]

Noah was presented by God with the information regarding the specific parameters associated with the task at hand. Noah was then left to decide exactly how the process would unfold, in order to complete the task in an efficient and effective manner. Noah had a Thinking preference regarding making the decisions required to complete a task.

10. Gen 6:8–22.

11. Gen 8:6–14.

NOAH'S JUDGING PREFERENCE

Noah was obviously a very organized person. God gave him very explicit and neat instructions.[12] He told him where to build the animal pins and cages. God also told Noah exactly how to complete the door. He gave Noah detailed instructions regarding the dimensions of the ship and the food to bring along for the journey. Noah organized the ship. Noah organized his family. Noah organized the animals. Noah organized the food. Noah led them all onto the ark before the flood came.

When the trip was over and Noah and the family left the ark, Noah presumably went back to his initial occupation: farming. He was not a ship-builder by trade from what I can tell. Plus I think he lived in a desert. But as soon as he landed he started a vineyard and rejoined the previous organization of his world.[13] Noah was a man of sound judgment regarding the organization of his world.

ESTJ

MBTI considers people who are ESTJs to be practical and realistic thinkers. They are decisive people who can quickly take action in order to complete a task, such as building an ark and collecting pairs of animals to live on the ark for a couple of years with their family. ESTJs are people who quickly organize projects and can focus their attention in a single-minded fashion in order to achieve the most efficient and effective results.

ESTJs have a clear sense of integrity and possess a set of standards that they expect their family members (in Noah's instance, family members who were invited on the ark) to live by. Most ESTJs like Noahcan be forceful when implementing their plans and their judgements. This was a lesson that Noah's son Ham and grandson Canaan learned after Ham mocked Noah for being drunk and naked.

12. Gen 6:8–22; 7:1–3.

13. Gen 8:15–19; 9:18–19.

ESTJ: THE ORCHESTRATERS

APPLICATIONS FOR ESTJS

At his best, Noah was a man dedicated to the plan of God. Noah accomplished the purpose and task that God set before him by completing the journey from the construction of the ark to landing safely on dry ground with his family. He effectively held his family together during the trip.[14] All of them, as a result of his positive influence, reestablished their lives after the flood occurred.

ESTJs should strive to use their personality to their advantage. They can very effectively dedicate themselves to the plan of God if they subscribe to that particular biblical worldview because of their given personality. Those of that ilk believe that they are chosen by God to administer those plans to the letter because, as a result of their ESTJ personality type, they can become a benefit to everyone that they are connected to by organizing, communicating, and executing God's plans.

Noah the ESTJ had to learn to get everyone to buy into the plan that God laid out for him. He accepted the plan and thus the purpose of God right away. He also did everything that God told him to do.[15] However, Noah likely had to do a bit more of an extensive sales job on his family, who could not all have been ESTJs, in order for them to buy in as well.

ESTJs are apt to develop and follow plans to the letter.[16] They make great administrators of tasks. When they can also effectively communicate these plans to the team, they will be capable of more successfully getting everyone to come together and to buy into their vision, thus making it into a shared vision for the entire group.

Developing As An ESTJ

Noah was a man who could easily buy into the plan of God based on his ESTJ personality type. He was also good at organizing and administering that plan. God shows us the plans and purposes that he has designed for our lives.[17] In my experience, he reveals those plans to us in short segments, or snapshots, if you will.

14. Gen 6:9.
15. Gen 6:13–22.
16. Myers, *Introduction to Type*, 24.
17. See Jer 29:11.

That can be quite frustrating for some of us, but particularly so for the ESTJs. ESTJs like to gather information in a straightforward manner.[18] They want to know exactly what will transpire in and through their lives. And the sooner the better! "Give it to me fast and give it to me straight" is the name of the game for the typical ESTJ. The ability to pre-plan is a strength for ESTJs, or the ability to plan the order of execution of their plan and purpose.[19] However, God almost never gives it to us fast *or* straight. He reveals as much as we need to know in small segments so that we will continue to seek his face.[20]

This will actually force some of us to continue to walk by faith and in step with God at his designed pace,[21] instead of allowing us to just check in with God from time to time while the ESTJ is off executing the revealed master's plan. After receiving the plan for that season we can go off and execute it without Him or with minimal conversation with him. I believe that Christ died so that we could reenter an interpersonal communion and relationship with God via his holy spirit living inside, directing and walking with us.

Thus, he reveals his plans and purposes to them in stages or in snapshots as opposed to all at once. The ESTJs among us need to learn to slow down and learn to remain in close fellowship with God, as some of us walk at his desired pace toward the completion of his master plan and purpose for our lives as well as for the lives of those who are connected to us.

PERSONALITY EXTREMES FOR ESTJS

At times if an ESTJ allows themselves to take their ESTJ personality type to an extreme (relative to any of the four zones, as they combine to make up one personality) the ESTJ can come off as overly self-assured, while not effectively embracing and managing the natural concerns of the other people that they are working with.[22] They must be careful to ensure that, as an Extrovert who can easily address the whole group, they not only effectively communicate the vision but also ensure that they can have

18. Myers, *Introduction to Type*, 24.

19. Myers, *Introduction to Type*, 24.

20. See 2 Chr 7:14; Ps 27:8.

21. See 2 Cor 5:7.

22. Myers, *Introduction to Type*, 24.

well-formed and effective communication with each member of the group in a one-on-one format.

CONNECTIONS FOR ESTJS

The Extroverted manner in which ESTJs relate to and interact with their world is connected to the Judging preference manner in which they organize and make sense of the world. Also, ESTJs like to take in information in a straightforward no-nonsense format using their Sensing preference. That Sensing preference has a direct correlation to the manner in which they make decisions. We can learn a lot from these connections.

Connections Between The E-J Functions

I would consider Noah to be more of a bookish and intellectual Extrovert, although as I mentioned I think that he was also a bit of a partier. He liked to interact directly with the people in his world and according to his Judging preference, he was a man of distinctive order regarding the organization of that world. Thus, when he was made responsible for the clear communication of the plans that God had given him for constructing the ark, getting each animal onto and caged in the ark, and for how to function together as a family unit on the ark before, during, and after the flood, Noah probably decided to communicate his plans to them so that they would function as a team in as efficient and effective a manner as possible.

The fact that their journey was a success, even though no one on earth had ever seen or experienced anything like the great flood, was a testimony to Noah's effectiveness as an Extroverted-Judging preference leader. He obviously got the family to buy into God's plan as well as getting them to agree with Noah's administration of that plan before, during, and after the great flood. Noah was an effective communicator as an Extroverted-Judging preference leader of his family. We as E-Js must also strive for such clear and effective communication when organizing those around us to execute God's plans as one unit.

Connections Between The S-T Functions

Noah also had to make many decisions based on the information that God had given him. Then he had to marshal his family to execute those decisions according to God's plan, in order for the entire group to accomplish God's purpose regarding the flood and those who God chose to spare from that flood. When the Bible states that "Noah did everything that God commanded him to do,"[23] it could say that Noah and the family did everything that God told Noah to do. However, between God's revelation of the plan and the entire family's execution of that plan, from construction of the ark in the middle of a desert to landing safely again on dry ground atop Mt. Ararat, Noah had to make many decisions that the family was tasked to carry out.

Noah was able to successfully receive the information in the straightforward format that God communicated it to him because of his Sensing preference. Noah was then able to use that information to make effective decisions which made the entire journey a safe and prosperous one for the entire family. ESTJs must learn to manage this S-T (information-gathering to decision-making) connection according to their distinctive personality preferences in order to make the plans and purposes of God into a common goal for all concerned, and to succinctly execute those decisions that ESTJs make using that information to ensure prosperity for all concerned parties.

GROWTH OPPORTUNITIES AND THREATS AS AN ESTJ

ESTJs are logical and analytical people who create very practical as well as functional systems. They can be tremendous organizers and leaders if they remain in balance. Others derive a sense of confidence and comfort from being around well-balanced ESTJs because of the effect that their personality can have on people, as well as how people view and perceive them.[24]

There are tremendous opportunities for the balanced and effective ESTJs to use that personality, as well as the effect that they can have on people in order to aid those people. ESTJs are very good at developing a plan and marshaling others to execute their well-thought-out plans

---

23. Gen 6:22; 7:9.

24. Myers, *Introduction to Type,* 24.

and decisions. When the ESTJ learns to grow within that personality, understanding that they cannot be too overbearing, or set expectations of themselves or of others too high (as some Extroverted-ESTJs can do when they allow their personality to go to an extreme place), the ESTJ has a great opportunity to be a very effective administrative leader and communicator.

However, if they allow their expectations of themselves or their high expectations of others to go to extreme places, they can become a burden to everyone that they work with. They have to manage those expectations, learn to make room for one-on-one communication, and to provide reassurance to people who are in their charge or to their colleagues as they make their grand decisions and execute their well-informed and forthright plans.

4

ISTJ: Daniel, The Faithful Judge

DANIEL, THE FAITHFUL JUDGE

DANIEL, WHOSE NAME MEANS "judge of God" in Hebrew, appears to demonstrate the personality traits and preferences associated with those who test as ISTJs. Daniel's story can be found in the book of Daniel in the Bible. Daniel was taken into captivity as a child and survived four kings and the rule of two different countries during his tenure as a servant in the administrations of his captors.[1] He continued to pray three times per day no matter the tasks before him, and remained dedicated to the mandates of his God while he sojourned in a foreign land. He was a prophet of God, an interpreter of dreams, a high-ranking government administrator, and an ISTJ.

DANIEL'S INTROVERSION PREFERENCE

Daniel followed the laws in the Hebrew Scriptures irrespective to the captivity status of his Judean people. King Nebuchadnezzar and the Babylonians were the first to capture Daniel's people when he was just a boy. Later, Daniel demonstrated his penchant toward Introversion, as he would sequester himself to pray regardless of his daily activities as a leading government official.[2]

1. Dan 1:1–12:13.
2. Dan 1:1–6; 6:10–13.

Although it is not always easy for an MBTI Introvert to confront people, Daniel had to do so at a very early age and stage of his captivity. Daniel and three friends, who were also Judeans, were taken captive by the Babylonians at a young age. In spite of their enslavement, they continued to follow the mandates of their God. At one point, Daniel had to confront the guard who had been given charge over them in order to request that he and his friends be permitted to only eat fruits and vegetables and drink only water for ten days.[3] They did not want to eat foods that were forbidden by their culture. Daniel requested that their health be observed after ten days to see if they were not as healthy, if not healthier, than the other young men who did eat the foods that were given to them, foods which were expressly forbidden for Hebrews to eat.

Daniel, as a likely Introvert, had to consider how he would approach the guard with his plan. They were slaves of the Babylonians and the Babylonians could have easily refused his plan. Extroverts, if not wise about the expression of their personality preference, might have just launched into the guard with verbal guns blazing, demanding that they not eat forbidden foods. But Daniel, in his fully expressed Introversion, likely did not consult his three friends (Hananiah, Mishael, and Azariah) prior to going to the guard with his plan. The Bible at least does not suggest that he consulted his buddies. Daniel approached the guard man-to-man, one-on-one, slave to captor. His measured approach worked. The guard allowed them to eat their food. After the ten-day fast concluded, they appeared healthy, fit for the job, and better in all of their abilities than any of the other young men.[4] Daniel approached the potentially contentious situation as an Introvert, with a measured plan in a non-verbose, one-on-one manner. It worked for him and his friends. Daniel was an Introvert.

DANIEL'S SENSING PREFERENCE

The Bible says that Daniel and his young cohort of friends had wisdom as well as the ability to assimilate and learn information about many things related to the Babylonian and later Persian kingdoms. They were assigned to study the literature of those cultures. Daniel demonstrated an ability not only to study and assimilate information that pertained to his own Hebrew culture, as well as information associated with the cultures of his

3. Dan 1:3–20.
4. Dan 1:3–20.

captors, but also information given to him by God.[5] He used all of this information to inform a logical and straightforward decision-making process as a Sensing preference person would.

King Nebuchadnezzar once had a dream. He wanted to know the meaning of the dream, but he also wanted to be sure that anyone of his wise men who would translate dreams for him were telling him the true meaning of his dream. He asked them to tell him what he dreamed, and then to tell him the meaning of the dream that he would not first reveal to them. All of the wise men begged the king to tell them the dream first, and then they would then interpret it. He refused. Thus they could not tell him what the dream entailed. Nebuchadnezzar ordered that all of the wise men in his kingdom be killed, because the useless sluggards could not meet the king's seemingly unreasonable demand regarding dream interpretation. This execution order included Daniel and his friends too, although they were not present for the initial request regarding dream interpretation. Daniel asked his friends to pray, demonstrating that Introverts make excellent leaders. During the night, God showed Daniel King Nebuchadnezzar's dream in a vision. Daniel went to the executioner (chosen by the king) of the wise men in Babylon and told him not to put the wise men in the kingdom, including himself and his buddies, to death. The dream that the king had was revealed to him during the night. He could also interpret the dream for the king.[6]

Daniel could receive information from various sources and via different methods. He could also assimilate and translate that information. Daniel had a Sensing preference.

DANIEL'S THINKING PREFERENCE

Daniel had to make many decisions during the course of his career. On one occasion, Daniel translated both a vision and the occurrence of a hand appearing out of nowhere and writing on a wall in Hebrew (Daniel's native language). This made King Belshazzar so pleased with Daniel that he made Daniel the third-highest ruler in the kingdom.[7] This was obviously a position that came with many responsibilities, as well as the authority to render decisions that would help to govern the kingdom.

5. Dan 1:3–20.

6. Dan 2:1–49.

7. Dan 5:1–31.

Unfortunately the position did not last long. The translation of the dream mandated that Belshazzar would soon be killed and be deposed by the new rulers, the Medes. The same night that Daniel was promoted, before he made any of those Thinker-like, analytical, cause-and-effect, decisions, Belshazzar was killed and King Darius took over.[8] But have no fear: once a Thinker, always a Thinker.

King Darius reorganized the administrative structure of his new kingdom. Darius chose 120 governors to rule the land. Then he chose three supervisors to have rule and oversight over the governors. Daniel was chosen as one of those three supervisors over presumably forty or so governors.[9]

Daniel the Thinker demonstrated that he was the best of the three supervisors regarding decision-making. He was so good that he became the chief executive administrative officer over the other two supervisors, the 120 governors, and over the whole kingdom of the Medes. The other two supervisors as well as the governors all tried to discredit Daniel as a leader. His work and decision-making were impeccable because of his reasonable Thinking man's approach.

Daniel ended up being thrown into the lion's den because of his devotion to detail and his tough-minded determination to sequester himself and pray to his God three times per day. However, God delivered him and Daniel was very successful during the remaining days of King Darius and during Cyrus the Persian king's rule after Darius.[10] Daniel was a Thinker.

DANIEL'S JUDGING PREFERENCE

As mentioned previously, Daniel's name literally means "judge of God" in Hebrew, but Daniel also demonstrated a preference toward operating in a MBTI Judging manner regarding how he organized things in his world. Daniel quickly rose to power in every administration he lived under, although he was one of the captured people in those kingdoms. Daniel was very organized and systematic. That is why he was promoted from one of three supervisors to the position of leading administrative head over the

8. Dan 5:30–31.
9. Dan 6:1–28.
10. Dan 6:28.

entire kingdom of Darius.[11] Daniel was also the third most powerful man in the previous kingdom, even if it only lasted less than a day.[12]

The Bible says that he was promoted because of his organizational skills (Judging), his ability to assimilate information (Sensing), and his ability to render effective decisions (Thinking). He had a devoted and methodical structure when it came to approaching a problem or crisis (Introvert). Daniel was a thinking man's chief administrator and an ISTJ.

ISTJ

MBTI describes ISTJs like Daniel as people who are quiet and who have a serious demeanor. We never saw an occasion where Daniel was telling uproarious jokes to the kings who he served in order to curry their favor. He let his work speak for itself. When he faced an issue or crisis, he confronted it head-on and in a serious and face-to-face manner. Daniel demonstrated practicality, logic, and reason in his leadership.

Daniel definitely valued his Hebrew traditions, but he remained a loyal civil servant in the administrations of four kings from two different countries. Daniel was loyal to the kings that he served under, but above of all Daniel was loyal to his God. Daniel was an ISTJ.

ISTJ: THE ELEVATORS

APPLICATIONS FOR ISTJS

ISTJs like Daniel are excellent at serving as the thinker and most useful helper in any group. Daniel rose to a position of administrative leadership in each setting where he was placed by his God. He served multiple kings in the role of leader, thinker, and helper. Daniel, like most ISTJs, kept a wealth of knowledge and straightforward information stored inside of himself. ISTJs use that information to make their decisions that will advance the mission of any group they're in.[13]

Many people who subscribe to a biblical worldview are of the belief that when God shows an ISTJ like Daniel the purpose for their work and lays out a plan via the revelation of straightforward information, that will

11. Dan 6:1–3.

12. Dan 5:29–31.

13. Myers, *Introduction to Type*, 14.

be used by the ISTJ to inform their decisions. They will make entire organizations or families operate at peak levels of efficiency and effectiveness. They are the proverbial rising tide that floats all boats. But that is when they are at their best.

When ISTJs cannot clearly see the purpose or when all of the information relative to the plan is not made abundantly clear for them in advance, an extreme ISTJ can begin to panic.[14] They may begin to devalue themselves or their contribution to the accomplishment of the larger mission of the organization or family.

In this instance, the ISTJ needs to pause and reevaluate. They need to refocus their attention on the God of the purpose. Instead of allowing themselves to become frustrated by the as-yet-undiscovered parts of his purpose, they will rejoin the team and function in their designed role as effective thinker and helper to the team.

Developing As An ISTJ

ISTJs need to learn to attune themselves to the parts of the plan that has been revealed and then learn to trust the process for the rest of the information to become clear for them. Some know that this will occur according to God's perfect timing. They also need to learn to manage their expectations of themselves and others, if they have allowed themselves to take part or all of their personality as represented within the four individual zones to an extreme place. ISTJs have a tendency in such instances to begin to distrust others on the team and they can then begin to detach and isolate themselves from the group, preferring to do it all themselves for fear of the others doing it wrong.[15]

ISTJs do this because they feel duty-bound to ensure that the task is done right and to the satisfaction of their unrealistically high standards. ISTJs need to learn to manage these expectations of themselves. They need to learn to patiently wait and do things according to the correct timing in order for them, as the recipient of the plan, to accomplish everything that they were purposed and designed to accomplish.[16]

14. Myers, *Introduction to Type*, 14.

15. Myers, *Introduction to Type*, 14.

16. See Isa 64:8.

PERSONALITY EXTREMES FOR ISTJS

ISTJs need to ensure that they remain available to others. They may have to force themselves, if they are already at the extremes, to share themselves with and reveal themselves to other people. If not, they can become isolated and secluded.[17]

ISTJs have to remember to let others in or they can become lost in the vast world of their own thoughts about the massive amounts of information that they store within themselves. They use this information to inform and make excellent decisions, but when the ISTJ goes inside of themselves as opposed to remaining vigilant about sharing themselves with others, they damage their opportunity to grow and can become dulled as a result of not allowing other irons to sharpen their iron.[18]

CONNECTIONS FOR ISTJS

The Introverted manner in which ISTJs relate to and interact with their world is connected to the Judging preference that they use to organize and make sense of everything. Also, ISTJs like to gather information in a straightforward, no-nonsense, format using their Sensing preference. That Sensing preference regarding the storage and retrieval of information is used to inform the ISTJ's Thinking preference, which is their decision-making function. We can learn a lot from these connections.

Connections Between The I-J Functions

ISTJs are primarily Introverted in how they relate to the people around them. As mentioned above, they organize and make sense of their world in a very orderly fashion using their Judging preference as a guide. As a result, ISTJs can become very organized in their mind and in their ability to effectively manage the world around them.

However, they may not realize that the only one who understands what they are doing is them! They tend to internalize the rationale behind their observable actions, in regards to their inherent need to remain organized. They may not realize or remember to allow others into their world for long enough periods of time in order for other people to discover

17. Myers, *Introduction to Type,* 14.
18. Prov 27:17.

or understand why the ISTJ is doing what they're doing. My advice to ISTJs is to draw back the curtain and let some light in, or in other words, remember to let some other people into the intricate thoughts relative to how you organize and make sense of your world.[19]

Connections Between The S-T Functions

ISTJs store vast amounts of information within the confines of that wonderful brain of theirs. That information is recalled on demand, as well as or better than any other personality type, because of their ISTJ personality and the impact that the Sensing function has on their information storage and retrieval ability.[20] That well of knowledge is used to effectuate well-conceived and highly-organized decisions. The ISTJ then goes about the task of executing their decision and plan with flawless precision, based on their Thinking decision-making preference.

This seamless connection can become a tremendous benefit to an organization if they can get a well-balanced ISTJ on the team. ISTJs will receive and process information in a straightforward manner, as occurred with Daniel. And when the well-balanced Daniel executed his assigned duties, he was able to become the leader of the leaders and the governor of governors in King Darius's court.[21] ISTJs can be an invaluable resource to those around them and they can be used to advance entire kingdoms or organizations.

GROWTH OPPORTUNITIES AND THREATS AS AN ISTJ

ISTJs also have to learn to embrace differences in the opinions and thoughts of others.[22] I would venture to say that ISTJs, more than any of the other fifteen personality types, feel that they are the primary purveyors of "right." I always say that right is a dangerous thing to have or be, because we tend to wave around the conceptualization of being "right" in a situation or about a circumstance like the mighty Thor wields his hammer Mjolnir. They use the hammer of "rightness," pointing it to the sky and drawing lightning from the heavens, to shoot that lightning at

19. Myers, *Introduction to Type*, 14.

20. Myers, *Introduction to Type*, 9–10.

21. Dan 6:1–3.

22. Myers, *Introduction to Type*, 14.

their opponent. That opponent being: anyone who dares to oppose their "rightness," anyone who they want to come to their side, or anyone who they want to get out of the way of their "rightness!" As a last resort, they might just throw the hammer itself.

ISTJs are particularly susceptible to this specific personality Threat, often allowing it to proceed to an extreme place within the construct of their personality type. We are all susceptible to this issue with "right" in one form or another. However, ISTJs can become particularly afflicted as a personality Threat by the use of their concept of "right."

As mentioned previously, ISTJs store vast amounts of information inside of themselves.[23] They draw upon that reserve to inform their appropriately conceived decisions, like Daniel did on many occasions. However, if they are not careful they can shoot the lightning of correctness at all who oppose their well-conceived plans and decisions, thereby possibly harming the other people.

Those with a Feeling preference or with a Perceiving preference can tend to make decisions and view the world in a completely different manner than the ISTJs would use that worldview to help them make decisions or make sense of their world. ISTJs know a lot. However, they do not know everything.

ISTJs must learn that other people with different personality types view the world and make decisions very differently than they do. A different perspective may do the extreme ISTJ a lot of good if they can embrace it and use that different perspective as an Opportunity for growth, and they just might obtain some previously unrealized information because it came through a person that did not make sense at first to the "right" ISTJ.

---

23. Myers, *Introduction to Type*, 14.

5

ENTJ: Joseph, The Dreamer, The Prime Minister

JOSEPH, THE DREAMER, THE PRIME MINISTER

JOSEPH IS ONE OF my two favorite biblical leaders because he and I share the same MBTI personality profile, ENTJ. Therefore, I will try to keep myself in check as I discuss this leader in reference to his personality type.

Joseph demonstrated his personality type from the beginning of his life to the end. He demonstrated his Extroverted interpersonal nature in many ways and through many interactions with everyone, from his family members to the people in the kingdom of Egypt.[1] During Joseph's sojourn in Egypt he served as a slave and was thrown into prison. However, he was eventually named the equivalent of prime minister. Joseph demonstrated his ability to organize information in a logical and insightfully iNtuitive manner.

He was a rational cause-and-effect decision-maker as well as an insightful and iNtuitive dream interpreter. He could take the interpretations of those dreams and help people, including the pharaoh of Egypt who he helped to make decisions that would save the entire kingdom and surrounding lands. Finally, Joseph was always placed in a position of leadership no matter where life led him because of his ability to organize, manage things, and direct as well as lead people. He was appointed to

1. Gen 37:1–36; 39:1–50:26.

a leadership position whether he was in his father's house, serving as a slave, in prison, or in the king's palace.[2] Joseph always rose to the top. Joseph was an ENTJ.

JOSEPH'S EXTROVERSION PREFERENCE

Joseph was always in charge. Joseph wore a coat that demonstrated that he had been placed in a position of authority in his father's house and in regards to his father's family shepherding business. He rose to his position in the family business even though he was the next to last of twelve sons born.

Joseph worked under some of his brothers in the beginning. However, he reported to his father about some of their lazy activities. As an Extrovert he did not have any problem with or remorse about confronting his brothers about their negative behaviors. Joseph also told the whole family when he had been given two dreams from God about his future and God's plans for him to function as a leader.

Some people who have recounted Joseph's story have mused that Joseph was impetuous and a braggart. I do not believe that at all. If you understand the true nature of an Extroverted ENTJ, you know that they love big jobs and do not have any issue whatsoever with saying what's on their mind. They seek out and thrive in positions of authority. They view leadership as a very natural part of their existence.

So when they have a dream or two about leadership, they believe that everyone else knows what they already know about themselves. They assume that everyone recognizes that they were destined to be in charge. Joseph's brothers probably thought him a bit hasty and likely considered him glory-hungry. Instead of letting his dreams come true, they decided to kill him, although they settled for throwing him in a pit and selling him into slavery.

During his enslavement, Joseph once again demonstrated his inherent Extroverted leadership abilities and became the chief administrator for the entire household of the captain of the palace guard, and Pharaoh's chief executioner, Potiphar. Joseph was eventually thrown in jail due to a mishap that occurred with Potiphar's wife and her unrequited affection for Joseph.[3]

2. Gen 37:1–36; 39:1–50:26.
3. Gen 39:1–23.

Joseph was subsequently released from prison after some years to interpret a dream for the king of Egypt.[4] However, he was not released until he had interpreted the dreams of two of his fellow prisoners and he was placed in charge of all of the prisoners by the warden.[5] In each instance Joseph had no problem speaking to and at times leading the other servants, his brothers, the other prisoners, or the king of Egypt. Joseph was an Extrovert and a natural and gifted leader.

JOSEPH'S INTUITIVE PREFERENCE

Joseph could manage large amounts of information and he was able to iNtuitively look into any hidden meaning within that information in order to help the people that he served. His father would send him on errands to oversee his older brothers as they managed the herd. He would then report back to his father Israel about the brother's activities. Joseph would gather the intel, assimilate it, and bring it back to dear old dad in an organized format, noting his brothers' often times poor patterns of behavior.[6]

If he did a poor job gathering or interpreting this information, or if he could be talked out of being a man of integrity by his brothers, who were usually up to no good, he would likely have falsified the reports to his father. Then his brothers would have loved him. Conversely, his father would not allow him to continue to serve as a leader in the family business. The brothers did not love him because he did not behave as they did. Joseph was great with information and had an ability to stay on task.

Joseph rose to leadership positions in every arena of life that he was placed in: Potiphar's house, the prison, and ultimately in the prime minister's position in Egypt. Through it all he continued to assimilate, correctly interpret, and effectively communicate that information to his superiors or to those who he helped. He was quite proficient at the interpretation of dreams as well because he could find and communicate their hidden meaning.

He interpreted his own two dreams to mean that he would eventually be a great leader and that his brothers would bow down to him.[7] His

4. Gen 41:1–56.

5. Gen 40:1–23.

6. Gen 37:1–36.

7. Gen 37:1–36; 41:1–56.

dream came to pass, although not until he was in Egypt as prime ,inister and famine ravaged the region.

He interpreted the dreams of his fellow prisoners while serving as their supervisor. It happened just as he interpreted because Joseph trusted his insights and instincts. One of the prisoners, the baker, was hanged and impaled on a pole. The butler was restored to his position in the king's palace. Both happened in three days, after Joseph correctly interpreted the meaning of their dreams to each person.

Finally Joseph was called out of his jail cell to interpret a dream for the pharaoh, a dream that none of the wise men could interpret. He correctly explained the meaning of the information to the pharaoh revealed through the dream. He told Pharaoh exactly how long the period of prosperity would last: seven years. Then Joseph correctly told Pharaoh that those seven years would be followed by seven years of famine. He then told Pharaoh what to do with the information and how to save the entire kingdom of Egypt from the famine years.[8] Joseph was iNtuitive regarding the assimilation and the insightful interpretation of information.

JOSEPH'S THINKING PREFERENCE

Joseph was a strong Thinker regarding his ability to make the decisions required of a person in a leadership position. Joseph organized Potiphar's house so well that all the chief of the palace guard had to think about was what he wanted for dinner.[9] He was eventually thrown in jail after being falsely accused by Potiphar's wife. She accused him of attempted rape, but in truth, she attacked Joseph. However, he behaved with integrity and refused to sleep with her.[10]

When he left Potiphar's home, he became the leader over the prisoners in jail, appointed by the prison warden. Once again, all the prison warden had to think about was what he wanted for dinner. Joseph handled everything else.[11] Every other decision was correctly made by Joseph. Everywhere Joseph went, he was placed in charge and the place prospered under his leadership because of his ability to render sound decisions.

8. Gen 41:1–56.

9. Gen 39:5–6.

10. Gen 39:6–20.

11. Gen 39:21–23.

When Joseph came before the pharaoh and was told the dreams that he wanted Joseph to interpret, Joseph not only accurately translated the dreams, but he also told the pharaoh how to respond to the prophecy within the dream. This enabled the pharoah to put policies in place that would allow the kingdom and the rest of the world in that region to survive the predicted pending famine that would follow the first seven years of plentiful harvests.[12]

Joseph, a prisoner only a few hours before, reorganized the entire kingdom of Egypt. For this, of course he was made the kingdom's chief executive officer and second in command to Pharaoh himself. Pharaoh also gave him a wife. It seems like a good deal, if you could get it! Joseph was a great Thinker and decision-maker. It caused people to promote him to positions of prominent leadership everywhere he went.[13]

JOSEPH'S JUDGING PREFERENCE

One of the issues that I have found during my journey through many different types, forms, and functions of organizations is that many people become imbalanced and develop a bent toward either management or leadership.

Managers become preoccupied with the system or things that they are managing. They tend to place less importance on leading the people in the organization in a manner that will permit everyone to succeed in the accomplishment of a common goal. Consequently, the people under the manager may be harmed due to the manager's focus on the process.

Imbalanced leaders can demonstrate the same qualities on the opposite end of the spectrum. They can become overly preoccupied with how the people will feel or on the people in general. They overuse their Feeling preference regarding decision-making. These leaders forget all about the efficiency and effectiveness of the process and system. Therefore the mission and goals of the organization are not able to be effectively attained.

The goal of any effective leader is to marry the two and maintain equilibrium between them in order to function as a well-balanced organizational leader. Joseph was an excellent organizational leader. Joseph was a man of sound judgement who demonstrated excellent organizational leadership abilities. He did this at each stop along his journey.

12. Gen 41:1–36.
13. Gen 41:37–57.

This allowed him to rise to the most prominent positions of leadership, regardless of the organization that he was placed in to serve.

ENTJ

MBTI describes ENTJs like Joseph as demonstrating an innate ability to readily assume leadership roles in organizations. ENTJs like Joseph are quick to identify inefficient or ineffective practices which will hinder both the people working in the organization as well as prevent the organization from accomplishing its stated mission and goals.

ENTJs like Joseph enjoy creating short, medium, and long range plans, strategies, and goals for themselves and for their organizations. They can be forceful in the presentation of their ideas. However, they are usually very well informed on many subjects. They are quick and insightful decision-makers who quickly follow their instincts. They love big jobs. They believe that they are in the right place and will excel in the job when they become the leader. Joseph was an ENTJ.

ENTJ: THE CONQUERORS

APPLICATIONS FOR ENTJS

Joseph and all ENTJs are fascinating to me. Yes, that is a result of our shared MBTI personality profile; however, it is also a result of the INtuitive function operating at a very high level within this ENTJ. ENTJs love to solve complex problems. We love to look inside of complexities and find "the thing behind the thing."[14]

We love to find complexities, investigate them, and then solve them. Once ENTJs implement a plan, we discover that finding the solution and implementing it is one of the greatest joys that we can experience. We do this in every situation and circumstance. But then we cannot wait to move on to the next challenge.

This discovery process ending in elation can occur because of the vast mystery that is human psychology and the functioning of the mind. This is why personality typology is among the things that have caught and held my attention for years. This can also measure relative to attempting to master the intricate and complicated operations of a Fortune

14. Myers, *Introduction to Type*, 25.

500 company. ENTJs love to master and conquer the vastly complex and previously unsolvable mysteries. After we find, implement, and watch that solution work to perfection, we do not want to linger. Rather we are ready to move on to the next challenge. Thus, when we engage this process, and due to our natural charisma, we expect everyone to "get on board."

ENTJs need to learn to pay more attention to the "small stuff." They are so iNtuitively insightful, especially when relative to their information-gathering function, that at times they can overlook how the people inside of the thing that they are mastering will feel relative to the great plan that the ENTJ has just concocted and then immediately moved to implementation. This brings up another point; ENTJs need to take the time to ask themselves and others with different personalities: "Will this work?" They need to do this in order to gather some additional, Sensing Preference-oriented, and straightforward information so they can see if they missed anything when they performed their insightful interpretation of the information. Joseph did both of these very well. However, other ENTJs may not be as balanced.

ENTJs are movers and shakers. But they can neglect to acknowledge that the other people involved may be completely overwhelmed by the workload that they are about to ask them to complete, or that they may have other thoughts and goals in mind based on their different personality types.For example, Michael Jordan was the best basketball player on the court during the time that he played. But if he did not realize that everyone on the court could not do all of the things that he could do, yet they were good at playing their roles, he would not be effective at marshaling the entire team to win the game or ultimately the championship.

Similarly, ENTJs like to win and will find the path of least resistance almost instantaneously. But if they cannot find the corresponding solution instantly, that is not a problem for the ENTJ because they love a challenge and they love to overcome obstacles. However, others may possess some information that the ENTJ missed. If the ENTJ never asks, they will never know, and then become frustrated when their grand plan becomes stymied during the implementation phase.

Developing As An ENTJ

ENTJs have many challenges to overcome regarding their proper development, considering the active functioning of their personality. ENTJs love to see and make things work. They also enjoy making them work perfectly or as perfectly as possible. However, those who choose a life path that includes walking with God know or will soon learn that the path does not occur in a straight line, on a well-lit street, with no blind alleys present, and with no unforeseen or unanticipated stumbling blocks on the path. ENTJs love to anticipate disaster and to plan excellent contingencies designed to thwart potential disaster. This idea of learning to diligently and patiently walk along the correct path can frustrate the ENTJ to no end.

Learning to walk along the correct path-system that, as some believe, God himself has set up occurs as it does because God wants to teach all of us to learn to walk by faith while we are here on earth.[15] ENTJs can struggle with this because they can be so accustomed to using their human mind to gain insight into the information that is presented to them via their iNtuitive preference. Making the Thinking and well-organized decision becomes easy to the ENTJ because, concurrently employing their Judging preference, they have already organized and made sense of the world around them.

The Extrovert in them is accustomed to having people follow them into any battle because they are naturally magnetic people and others tend to think that ENTJs have it all together. Thus, when the ENTJ chooses to walk with a God who is first, last, and always in charge of everything the ENTJ can be a little ill at ease. If they believe, then they must learn to listen to God and get all of his instructions pertaining to the situation and circumstance that they are presently analyzing and moving swiftly toward solving. Additionally, they must submit themselves entirely to God's timing. Many times ENTJ believers might pray: "God, I've already figured this one out! Let's advance to the implementation phase, and get this sucker wrapped up, so we can move on to conquering the next challenge!"

In short, the ENTJ believer can at times think, "God, I got this!" God will at this point along the path stand still and wait for the ENTJ to realize, "Oops I just walked ahead of God. I have to double back to the

---

15. See 2 Cor 5:7.

point where he stopped walking with me and ask him, "What do we do next?"'"

These are some very difficult challenges for the classic ENTJ to learn to overcome. However, if they learn patience and keep in mind that the Almighty created them and therefore he is always going to be incalculably more brilliant than they are or could ever be, then they will grow effectively and accomplish fabulous things. However, keep in mind that the great things will occur in the correct time and season.

Joseph remained in balance and he saved the entire world from famine because he was able to use this principle when he came before Pharaoh. Yet Joseph learned via the things that he suffered: in jail, with his brothers, and with good ole Potiphar's wife.[16]

PERSONALITY EXTREMES FOR ENTJS

I do not think that I am employing hyperbole when I say that ENTJs are or can be extreme. Thus, when examining how they can in some instances allow their personality to go to extreme places, I am describing a relatively short trip for many in this ENTJ group. ENTJs can become overwhelming for many people if they allow themselves to become too rigidly attached to their well-crafted plan. They may implement that plan too quickly without gaining useful insight and information from others with different personalities and different perspectives on the situation.[17]

ENTJs are likely to be the person in the room who looks at the "poor little Introvert" over there in the corner, sipping on their iced tea, and assume that everyone must be like the ENTJ. They think to themselves: "That person must be so lonely and could not possibly be enjoying themselves in such dreadful isolation within a room full of people. Let me go and help them by talking to them." They go over to talk to the horrified Introvert. They engage the Introvert in one of their patented, challenging debates, intended to generate thought and perspective previously unconsidered by the ENTJ.[18] Meanwhile, the Introvert has to either figure out a way to make their cell phone ring or find an excuse well beyond "I must go powder my nose" in order to get out of there! The iced tea that they are drinking could help spur their "exit stage left" in this example.

16. Gen 37:2–36; 39:1–41:57; Heb 5:8.

17. Myers, *Introduction to Type*, 25.

18. Myers, *Introduction to Type*, 25.

The ENTJ like all of us must learn that all creatures and people are made differently, and thus they may also have useful thoughts that could contribute to the decision that is pending implementation. Non-ENTJs may, as some Feeling preference and Perceiving preference people that I have worked with, just be holding onto the "horrible way" (in the ENTJ's never so humble opinion) that the organization is being run; they simply cannot bear the thought of firing the 69-year-old person who is on retirement's doorstep just because it will make them feel bad, even though that employee is the slowest and least productive worker in the office. This is totally nuts and a horrible reason to make a decision not to fire someone to the well-organized, obstacle-overcoming, and Thinking decision-making ENTJ. "Get them a gold watch, a bucket of chicken, a three-liter bottle of grape soda, throw them a party, and get them the heck outta here! They're messin' up my plans," as some extreme ENTJ might say. They may not just say this to themselves; they may say it to their Assistant Manager! ENTJs do not tolerate inefficiency, not very well anyway.[19] But the ENTJ must realize that one man's trash is another man's treasure." I guarantee you that an ENTJ did not come up with that previous statement.

CONNECTIONS FOR ENTJS

The Extroverted manner in which ENTJs relate to and interact with their world is connected to the Judging preference which they use to organize and make sense of their world. Also, ENTJs love to look deeply into and behind the information that they receive, using their iNtuitive preference. That iNtuitive preference, regarding the manner in which the ENTJ processes information, is not only their favorite thing to use in their analysis of information; they also love to use the interpreted data, to inform their Thinking preference which is their highly structured, decision-making function. We can learn a lot from these connections.

Connections Between The E-J Functions

Because of their Extrovert function, ENTJs love to engage the entire world. They rely upon their natural charismatic magnetism when it comes to heading center stage and engaging the people in order to get

19. Myers, *Introduction to Type*, 25.

them on board with their master plan. It was no accident at all that Joseph was able to step out of prison into the pharaoh of Egypt's court and win over the entire room inside of five minutes. Particularly when the pharaoh did most of the talking.[20] The point is that Extroverted ENTJs use that inherent charisma to their advantage and rely on it to help them to win the room.

This manner of engaging the room is seamlessly connected to their Judging functioning. When ENTJs head to the center of that room and start talking to the crowd, they present a well thought-out, sensible, and well-organized plan that everyone should be able to clearly understand. Thus, everyone should be able to buy into the vision that the ENTJ has just laid out. If the ENTJ can learn the old salesman trick of overcoming objections while selling their plan,or the used car, then the Extroverted ENTJ has just captivatingly engaged the entire room, while the Judging ENTJ has simultaneously bedazzled them via their marvelously constructed plans.

Of course, we all know that the best laid plans of mice and men, often go awry. But the point of this discussion on the connection between the E-J personality preference zones for the ENTJ is that a balanced ENTJ will use both zones to their advantage and expect both to work in concert, and to perfection.

Connections Between The N-T Functions

There are also definitive and noticeable connections between the N-T functions as relative to the ENTJ. ENTJs look for the "thing behind the thing." They do this iNtuitively every time they receive new information. They investigate and interpret the information presented to them as they simultaneously search the present information for new and as yet unrealized possibilities.[21] Following the collection and successful interpretation of the information, the Thinking function as relative to decision-making takes that information and turns it into a well-organized plan of action, intended to derive maximum success.

The only thing that is left for the ENTJ is to gain "buy in" from everyone that will work to execute their plan. Hopefully the ENTJ does not overlook the functioning of their Feeling decision-making counterparts

---

20. Gen 41:1–46.

21. Myers, *Introduction to Type*, 9–10.

at this point in the implementation phase. As an aside, I always say that "feelings (not the Feeling preference zone) are like city mass transit busses; there will be another one coming along in fifteen minutes! Please do not catch the first feelings bus." Also, "you cannot think with your heart, because your heart does not have a brain." These two little idioms intimate that you cannot use your randomly varying feelings, which derive from your thoughts, past experiences, and temporary mood, to make effective decisions. You have to look for real, tangible, and concrete information. Then allow yourself to be led prior to deciding which bus is the right bus to catch.

Back to the N-T connection: if the ENTJ does not overlook any of the small details (which they tend to do quite often if they are not well-balanced), if they are sure to seek out additional information as well as request additional opinions from their Introverted, Sensing, Feeling, and Perceiving preference counterparts, and if ENTJs thoughtfully consider that new information, they will arrive at a well-informed decision that should achieve the attainment of a common goal.

GROWTH OPPORTUNITIES AND THREATS AS AN ENTJ

I have mentioned quite often during this examination of the areas and ways in which ENTJs can grow and develop that ENTJs have a tendency to become overly absorbed with their own brilliant interpretations. They can often overlook many small details, as well as other people, on their way to attaining success.[22] This is likely the biggest Threat faced by ENTJs in regards to developing a well-balanced personality portrait, one that I believe God can use to overwhelm and fully possess the kingdom.[23] ENTJs love the very sound of the phrase, "Overwhelm and fully possess!"

ENTJs will be presented with many Opportunities to take time and notice the color purple, so to speak, as it is painted on the tulips and bell-flowers growing wild in the field. They will also be afforded opportunities to pay closer attention to what people think and feel.

Additionally, I believe ENTJs will have many Opportunities to learn that any decision worth implementing which does not accomplish a higher purpose and that does not lead others into a closer relationship with God is not a decision that they want to implement. Nor should they

22. Myers, *Introduction to Type*, 25.

23. Matt 11:12.

attempt to get people to buy into their decision just because that decision came from the ENTJ. In short, the one thing that ENTJs need to learn more than anything else is to listen and to allow themselves to be led in all that they presume to accomplish.

6

INTJ: Elisha, The Prophetic Advisor to Kings

ELISHA, THE PROPHETIC ADVISOR TO KINGS

ELISHA WAS AN EXAMPLE of an INTJ. He served as a mentor, a mentee, a servant, a leader, and a prophet to the kings of Israel, Judah, Aram, and Edom, during his lifetime.[1] Elisha happens to be another of my favorite biblical leaders. Thus, I will once again restrain myself and stick to the facts, as a true Thinking preference person would. However, I would like to point out that I am a borderline Extrovert, and this likely creates my attraction to Elisha who is an INTJ; the only difference between us being his Introversion preference as opposed to Extroversion.

Elisha was a direct mentee of Elijah the prophet. Elisha often interacted one-on-one with Elijah. He then became the leader of the sons of the prophets, a group of prophetic advisors in many cities in Israel. Elisha became their leader after Elijah was taken away in a chariot of fire, thus abandoning his post.[2] He served and walked among the kings of four nations including Israel, his nation. Elisha was an example of an INTJ.

1. 1 Kgs 19:17–21; 2 Kgs 2:1–13:21.
2. 2 Kgs 2:1–25.

ELISHA'S INTROVERSION PREFERENCE

Elisha was a true Introvert in his interactions with other people and had times when he needed to be alone or have his nerves calmed. He was from the nation of Israel and primarily functioned as a prophet to Israel. Once when the kings of Judah, Israel, and Edom came before him for prophetic advice, he expressed his intense disdain for the king of Israel because his monarchy had begun a practice of worshiping gods other than Jehovah, whom Elisha, the Israelited, and Judeans worshiped.[3]

Elisha directly confronted the king of Israel and told him to go ask one of the stone idols that the king's mother and father called gods, instead of coming to Elisha for prophetic advice from Jehovah. Introverts can confidently confront negative circumstances as easily as their Extroverted counterparts. After scolding the king, he told a friend to bring him someone who plays the harp so that he could relax and find some inner peace.[4] He needed moment of solitude before providing prophetic advice to the kings, as any Introvert would. Introverts are capable of engaging large audiences with depth and alacrity, however this activity drains their energy and they seek a place where they can privately go inside of themselves, reflect, and recover. Elisha was an Introvert.

He also developed a very close friendship with a married woman from the town of Shunem. Elisha would stop by the house and eat with her and her husband. She eventually made him his own room with a private entrance, where she welcomed him to rest each time he was in town.[5]

Although Elisha, serving as Elijah's replacement as prophet in Israel, functioned as the leader of the sons of the prophets (the group of prophetic advisors in Israel), he was generally only found with his servant and mentee, Gehazi. Introverts can gain a lot of energy by being alone with their thoughts or by engaging in meaningful interactions with just one other person and exchanging ideas with them. Elisha was an Introvert.

3. 2 Kgs 3:1–27.
4. 2 Kgs 3:13–15.
5. 2 Kgs 4:8–37.

ELISHA'S INTUITIVE PREFERENCE

Elisha received the information from God that he was required to dispense in the form of prophetic advice to kings and others. When Elisha advised the three kings of Israel, Judah, and Edom, he provided them with very explicit and detailed instruction regarding how they should approach their pending battle with the Moabites. He insightfully instructed them to dig holes and told them that the Lord would fill the holes with water so the armies of the three countries would have fresh water to drink. Then he told them that the Lord would hand the Moabites over to them in battle so that they would utterly decimate the kingdom of Moab.[6]

Elisha was able to take in and process specific information. Then he was able to translate it into a user-friendly format for those who he was advising. He functioned as an iNtuitive.

In another instance, Elisha gave precise information to the woman from Shunem regarding the birth of her first child. He told her that she would have a child one year from the day that he was speaking with her. This would occur despite her difficult history regarding becoming pregnant. Her son was born one year later. Many years after the child's birth, he died, likely of a brain aneurism.[7] Elisha demonstrated what any iNtuitive person should do in the face of a lack of information. Remain silent until you get some. He told his servant Gehazi that he knew the Shunammite woman was troubled but that God, Elisha's source of information, had not revealed to him why the woman was so deeply troubled. Once he found out what was bothering her, he was able to take action.[8] Elisha was an iNtuitive person regarding the iNtuitive use and dispensation of information.

ELISHA'S THINKING PREFERENCE

Elisha also had a Thinking preference. Elisha took the information about the Shunammite woman and once he understood the problem, he made well-informed decisions. He told his servant Gehazi how to handle the situation, as well as what he should do while he is traveling to the Shunammite woman's home (not to speak with anyone during the journey).

6. 2 Kgs 3:16–27.

7. 2 Kgs 4:11–37.

8. 2 Kgs 4:25–30.

He engaged a well-thought-out plan. However, the woman said that she would not leave Elisha unless he personally went to her home to check on the dead child, whom she laid on his bed in the room that she had given him.

So Elisha altered his plan, displaying a Perceiving function although he was primarily of a Judging preference, and went home with her. He was used by God to bring the child back to life because of the decisions that he made within the context of a crisis situation. When Elisha did not have enough information to make an initial decision or plan a course of action, he did nothing.[9]

Another time, Elisha demonstrated the ability to effectively use the information-gathering function of his iNtuitive preference, along with the Thinking function relative to decision-making. A woman who was a widow of one of the deceased sons of the prophets came to Elisha with a crisis situation. She told him that the creditors were about to take her two sons and turn them into slaves because of the deceased husband's debts. Elisha asked for information and mused how he might help her. Then he followed up that question by asking what she had in her house. He did not tell her that he was planning to perform a miraculous act. He just asked his information-gathering question. She told him that she of course had next to nothing; she only had a pot of oil. So he told her to borrow more empty pots. He provided her with explicitly-detailed instructions regarding her next steps. He told her to go borrow as many pots as she could find, go into the house with her sons, and close the door behind them. Then they were instructed to pour the oil from that one pot into each of the borrowed pots. When they ran out of pots, the oil stopped flowing from the first pot. The lady came and told Elisha what happened. He revealed the final stage of his plan: "Go and sell the oil, pay the debts, keep your sons, and live off of the rest." He gave her a short-term and long-term plan for debt freedom and fiscal security.[10] Elisha was a Thinker.

9. 2 Kgs 4:25–37.
10. 2 Kgs 4:1–7.

ELISHA'S JUDGING PREFERENCE

Elisha was a very systematic organizer. He told the widow how to orga-nize and execute his plan for financial independence.[11] He also told the ings of the three nations how to win their battle by using a step-by-step organized process.[12]

Elisha understood the principles of organization. When Elijah was taken from him in a chariot of fire, Elisha demonstrated this principle with the sons of the prophets. They could see that the succession of lead-ership had occurred and Elisha was now their leader. They asked Elisha, who had witnessed the chariot taking away Elisha's mentor, if he wanted them to go and look for Elijah. They mused that maybe the chariot had dropped him off somewhere within walking distance. He told them not to go. He understood that this was all part of God's plan. They begged him and Elisha allowed them to go, knowing that they would find noth-ing. They returned without Elijah. He told them that he had said they should not go.[13] Elisha understood that the organizational structure was being changed and that he was now going to have to fill Elijah's shoes and accept the responsibility of providing prophetic leadership. Elisha was an organized and process-oriented leader.

Later, as he served the king of Aram by prophetically advising the commander of his army (Naaman) to go to the Jordan River, dip him-self in it seven times and he would be miraculously healed of leprosy, a dreaded skin disease. The army commander Naaman did not want to follow the plan. He judged the advice by his own perception of the water in the Jordan River. He figured that there were much cleaner rivers in his country. He was also upset that Elisha would not come down to per-sonally speak with him; Elisha sent General Naaman messages that were relayed between them through Gehazi.

Naaman's servant encouraged him to obediently follow the explicit instructions of the man of God, Elisha. The cause-and-effect nature of Elisha's plan produced the desired outcome. Naaman was healed of his skin disease after he dipped seven times in the Jordan River., even though the water was dirty.[14]

11. 2 Kgs 4:1–7.
12. 2 Kgs 3:16–27.
13. 2 Kgs 2:1–18.
14. 2 Kgs 5:1–27

Elisha was a man with a plan and he knew how to organize information effectively. He also knew how to make productive decisions using that information. He knew when he needed to regain his energy required to do his job. He also knew the value of organization. He clearly understood that by following step-by-step instructions people would achieve the desired goal. He is one of the most seamless examples of the connection between the four preference zones demonstrated in one biblical leader. Elisha was an INTJ.

INTJ

Elisha had a unique mind and vision for how things fit together. He demonstrated that distinctive gift through the miracles that he was used by God to perform. He demonstrated the ability to create a plan and put it into action. And if those who he led and served followed his prophetic advice, they achieved a marvelous, desired, and needed miraculous outcome.

Elisha was also a very independent thinker, such as when he prophetically advised the king of Israel about the troop movements of the Arameans. Elisha was very skeptical of the king of Israel. He would warn the king where the Arameans would set up camp long before they got to their eventual destination.

Elisha held the king of Israel and his servant Gehazi to a very high standard. This was a standard to which he also held himself in accountability. Elisha once asked Gehazi, when he took wealth and gifts from Naaman against Elisha's orders in exchange for the miraculous healing, did not his prophetic insight and high standard go with Gehazi when he went down to collect your bounty from Naaman? He held Gehazi to such a high standard that Elisha prophetically ordered that the skin disease which Naaman was healed from be inflicted upon Gehazi for his act of selfishness, greed, and disobedience.[15] Elisha was an example of a seamlessly-expressed INTJ.

15. 2 Kgs 5:19–27.

INTJ: THE INGENIOUS ONES

APPLICATIONS FOR INTJS

INTJs can be detached based on their Thinking preference as it interacts with their overall INTJ personality type.[16] It is easier for the iNtuitive-Thinking and well-organized decision-maker to remain detached while engaging in information-gathering and decision-making as a result of the Introverted manner in which they interact with the world that they just detached from. Detachment is easier for most INTJs than it is for their Extroverted cousins, who love to engage the room and get all the people in it to "buy in." This makes sense because INTJs can be very creative, but they rarely share those creative thoughts in the imaginative ways in which the INTJ conceives them. Rather, somewhere between formulating the creative thought about a subject and translating that notion into a discussion point, the INTJ's conceptualization will become transformed. Thus, that creative idea becomes a very well-conceived and rational thought,[17] i.e., it becomes boring! It is amazing to me how wonderfully complex that we were Created, where one seemingly-small change in manner in which we engage and interact with the world can make an entire personality type very different from another.[18]

INTJs like Elisha seek out complex concepts to which they can apply themselves to solving. They generally display an Introverted and seemingly aloof manner while they are working to investigate the problem and arrive at a detailed and poignant decision. They can become easily bored by anything that does not challenge their intellect, which they value very highly. INTJs are also very hard on themselves.[19]

INTJs can show a disregard for authority when those in authority are not as adept as they are at solving problems. They can become disengaged when they are involved in what the INTJ considers to be useless chicanery.[20] Elisha had no patience whatsoever for the king of Israel. He only permitted King Joram into his presence because Joram was accompanied

---

16. Myers, *Introduction to Type*, 18.

17. Myers, *Introduction to Type*, 18.

18. See Ps 139:14.

19. Myers, *Introduction to Type*, 18.

20. Myers, *Introduction to Type*, 18.

by King Jehoshaphat of Judah, who Elisha did not regard as a useless, idol-worshiping,oaf.[21]

INTJs need to attune themselves to their work style because they can almost become lost in a world of their complex thoughts. If they get to that point, they will not come off very well to others. This will not allow them to properly communicate their wonderful decisions, which they have so insightfully derived based on their interpretation of widely-presented information. They need to learn the best ways to convey to others the wonderful knowledge that they possess by remembering to remain engaged with that external world.[22] They are a major asset to any organization that they become a part of because they are able to see things in a very clear and iNtuitive manner. They can also translate the information that was given to them, as Elisha believed, by God. This means of communicating information occurred very often with the prophet Elisha. But at times the information was given to Elisha by man. INTJs, upon receipt of information, can use their God-given insight to provide everyone with a solution that will benefit the accomplishment of goals. They are swift and conclusive decision-makers, as well as determined, well-organized individuals.

Developing As An INTJ

INTJs need to remain consistent. If they hold to a biblical worldview, they can do this by remaining engaged with the Holy Spirit in order to ensure that they are using Godly wisdom and insight. This is in order to help them to translate all of the information that they are receiving and to render Godly decisions based on their correct interpretation of the presented information. They remain highly-organized and orderly persons; those who use modern-day football vernacular would call them "students of the game" and educators would call them "lifelong learners."

INTJs have to be vigilant in their efforts to not go inside of themselves because they are very entertained by formulating complex thoughts and ideas relative to the information that they have just received. According to biblical exegesis, the goal of every God-inspired thought or

21. 2 Kgs 3:1–15.

22. Myers, *Introduction to Type,* 18.

God-breathed idea relative to that thought is to benefit the kingdom of heaven.[23]

INTJs have to remember the old axiom:, "if a tree falls in the forest, and no one is around to see or hear it, does it make a sound?" Answer: of course it does. What a narcissistic proverb! Similiarly, if an INTJ conceives a wonderfully complex thought, a thought as indiscernible as the heavens themselves, but they never let it out for anyone to ever hear or see, that conceptualization will have no impact on the world around them. INTJs have beautiful minds that they must use and exercise by informing others of all of the creative complexity stored up inside of them.

PERSONALITY EXTREMES FOR INTJS

Extreme INTJs can become easily frustrated. It is not difficult for them to avoid interacting with the world around them. Based on their Judging preference, they have already pre-organized and made perfect sense of the world around them (at least, according to them). Being Introverts who are iNtuitive thinkers about information (taking it in all of the time), they can become reclusive if they are not careful because they are so entertained by looking for the possibilities behind the information, and by searching for solutions to the complex problems that were presented to them.[24] If they are believers, they should remain cautious and intimately connected with God, who will remind them to open themselves up to the others to whom God has sent them, as well as help them to interpret how he wants them to use that information in order to render his decisions.

I believe that God has strategically placed the INTJs in the world to be a creatively useful benefit to so many, as was Elisha. I am going to attempt to assuage the INTJs from becoming too extreme, relative to any temptation to become isolationist in their interactions, by encouraging them to remain vigilant and stay engaged. If you believe similarly to me, then you will likely desire to avoid extremes in interactions with others and continue to be a blessing to both God and man.

23. 2 Tim 4:7.

24. Myers, *Introduction to Type*, 18.

CONNECTIONS FOR INTJS

The Introverted manner in which INTJs relate to and interact with their world is connected to the Judging preference which they use to organize and make sense of their world. INTJs like to take in information and interpret it to solve complex problems, with wonderfully creative and insightful solutions, using their iNtuitive preference. That iNtuitive preference, regarding the assimilation and interpretation of information, is used to inform the INTJ's Thinking preference and decision-making function. We can learn a lot from these connections.

Connections Between The I-J Functions

The connection between the I-J functions for the INTJ is critical for them. They must remain engaged with the rest of the world, a world that they believe they have already organized. This is so they can remain a useful enhancement to others. Introverts like smaller groups and generally like to remain in one-on-one conversational settings.

INTJs particularly like to get lost in the recesses of their minds because there is so much going on in there. But the Introverted INTJ has to remember to get out and live a little in order to achieve maximum impact. They also have to maintain a small ego, relative to their big brains.

INTJs are very curious people. They already believe that they have systematized their world. However, it is erroneous to believe that the world, which the Judging preference INTJ has organized to their satisfaction, will remain in their pre-prescribed, orderly, and digestible state.

In one of my favorite science fiction television shows, the ship's engineer tells a spaceship design and mechanical engineer, regarding the construction and flying of the spaceship that she had designed: "They fly differently in outer space!"[25] In other words: it does not matter what the INTJ concocts in the laboratory of their mind, because once that idea is test-piloted in the real world it will function differently, no matter what lengths the INTJ goes to in order to control and account for all variables and contingencies. One with a biblical worldview will most likely come to realize that the world is beyond the INTJ's control, and learning that

---

25. *The Next Generation,* "Galaxy's Child."

God is beyond the INTJ's encapsulation is the beginning of wisdom and positive growth for the INTJ.[26]

Connections Between The N-T Functions

INTJs probably interpret and iNtuitively analyze information better than any of the other MBTI personality types because they are very insightful and do not mind brooding over the data for extended periods of time. There is no need to satiate their desires for lots of stimulating human interaction with large groups of people like their Extroverted cousins. The Introverted person with an iNtuitive function regarding information-gathering will stay with the process until it is resolved.

This information assimilation process is what makes the N-T connection into a boom or bust scenario for the INTJ. In the boom scenario, the INTJ will deftly use that information (if correctly interpreted) by allowing God to give them insight, but also by allowing God to create and determine for them the best decisions possible relative to that correctly-interpreted data. This applies if you hold to a specific biblical worldview. These decisions will derive from the previously interpreted data. Under the bust scenario, INTJs could disconnect from God and mankind, become overly intrigued by the information in their mind, and render an incorrect decision. One that they made sans any input from God.

If the INTJ believer remains connected to the true vine and remembers that we are all mere branches, then they will be able to render kingdom-altering decisions.[27]

GROWTH OPPORTUNITIES AND THREATS AS AN INTJ

The opportunities for growth for the INTJ believer revolves around the INTJ applying themselves to their most unsolvable mystery: their personal relationship with Christ. This is not the most natural thing for the INTJ to do. But we are all trying to grow past our naturally egocentric tendencies, whatever they may happen to be. That is, if we consider ourselves to be those who possess a biblical worldview. I said that making Christ the best and most unsolvable mystery for the INTJ is difficult for the INTJ because their inclination is to believe that they can, based on

26. See Prov 9:10; Isa 55:9.

27. See John 15:1, 5–7.

their God-given insight and derived via their iNtuitive function, solve any mystery. Yet God is unsearchable for his creation.[28] There is always so much to God that we do not and will never be able to fully comprehend. This is a humbling reality if you subscribe to this biblical worldview.

However, this conundrum also works to the advantage of the INTJ. They love to try to solve things. They spend countless hours trying to insightfully interpret data and information in order to enlighten their complex decisions to the benefit of their organization, family, and friends. Getting wrapped up in God and trying to understand him as they pray and seek without ceasing is the best way to remain humbly yet intimately engaged with the master,[29] and to ensure that INTJs are most effectively using their beautifully ingenious minds.

28. See Ps 103:11; Isa 55:9; 2 Pet 3:8.

29. See 1 Thess 5:16–18.

7

ESFJ: Queen Esther

QUEEN ESTHER

HADASSAH, OR ESTHER AS she was called, demonstrates the preferences and traits associated with ESFJs. Esther was from the tribe of Benjamin, along with her cousin Mordecai, who took care of her like a father after her parents died during their captivity under King Xerxes of Media.[1] She received and successfully processed information that would become crucial to her life. Later, that information would help her regarding a decision that would not only impact her life but the lives of all of her people. She would filter that straightforward information and use her Feelings preference to make an appropriate decision for all concerned.

Esther was a very attractive woman, so when she was selected to become one of the women who might be chosen by Xerxes as his next queen, Mordecai told her not to tell anyone that she was a Hebrew. One of the King's eunuchs, named Hegai, liked Esther and helped her out during her training and preparation phase for the possible chance to become Queen Esther.[2] She also came under the care of another eunuch, Shaashgaz, who cared for the king's wives in the palace.

She gladly received all of the information provided by Hegai, Shaashgaz, and the other eunuchs. Her ease of interaction and ability to comfortably receive that information, processing it in a forthright manner,

1. Esth 1:1–2:7.
2. Esth 2:7–20.

demonstrated her Extroverted nature. She also had great compassion relative to the plight of her cousin and the rest of her fellow Hebrews. She organized a plan of action and executed that risky plan in order to help save her people.

ESTHER'S EXTROVERSION PREFERENCE

Hadassah would ultimately become known as Queen Esther. She expressed her Extroverted preference in social situations; she interacted comfortably with strangers, eunuchs, servants, and her cousin Mordecai. She also interrelated well with her own people the other Hebrew captives.

She was relatively fearless as she went through the beauty treatment process that lasted for over a year as she was being prepared to spend time with the king and possibly become his next wife.[3] The king was a hard man. He was famous for deposing his former wife, Queen Vashti, from her royal position. King Xerxes banished Vashti because she did not appear at a banquet as he requested. Yet Esther went through the process required to possibly become the next queen undaunted by the rumors and innuendos surrounding Vashti's demise. She willingly obeyed her cousin Mordecai when he told her not to tell anyone that she was a Hebrew by birth so that it would not reflect negatively on her chances to become the new queen of the Persian king. She interacted successfully with his eunuchs who prepared her for her big day. They showed her special favor knowing that the day for her time with the king fast approached. She ultimately met and spent time with King Xerxes. He favored Esther more than any of the other virgins. Hadassah became Queen Esther.[4]

When the Hebrew people ran into a plot by one member of the royal court named Haman to destroy all of the Jews in the kingdom, Esther exchanged messages with her cousin Mordecai via one of her eunuchs named Hathach.[5] She had to communicate with him via letter, not because she was an Introvert and this was her preferred method of communication; far from it. She used letters because she was now a queen and he was just a captive citizen of the Persian Empire. Mordecai often sat at the king's gate. Queen Esther discussed the plans to approach the king about the plot enacted by Haman to kill all Jews in the kingdom,

3. Esth 1:1–2:23.

4. Esth 2:1–20.

5. Esth 2:19–4:17.

even though no one was able to gain an audience with the king unless they were summoned to him. Not even his queen. Breaking the rule that prevented anyone from having audience with King Xerxes unless invited by the king could result in the penalty of death. When Esther decided to seek audience with the king in order to plead for mercy for the Hebrews regarding Haman's new law, she asked the Hebrews to fast for three days on their own behalf. Then she would go fearlessly before the king and present her case to save the Jewish people from death.[6] Esther was a logical but fearless Extrovert.

ESTHER'S SENSING PREFERENCE

Esther knew that even as queen, she was not allowed to gain an audience with King Xerxes without being summoned.

Her cousin Mordecai was at the king's gate on that fateful morning that Haman had handed down a ruling which would cause the deaths of all of the Hebrews in captivity in the Mede kingdom.[7] Queen Esther discovered that her cousin was in mourning at the king's gate because of the plight of his fellow Hebrews. The ruling, which ultimately included a payoff from Haman to the king, stated that all of the Jews must bow down to Haman, who the king promoted to become the highest-ranking ruler in the kingdom. Esther sent Mordecai some clothing and other supplies, and then learned why he was in mourning.[8]

Haman the Agagite,[9] an enemy of the Jewish people, was particularly angry because Mordecai would never bow down to him.[10] He asked that the king issue a ruling that would have the soldiers in the kingdom kill all of the Jews scattered throughout the kingdom of the Medes.[11] The payoff was designed to pay the soldiers for this task.[12] The king agreed to Haman's suggestion and issued the order, not knowing that his queen Esther was a Hebrew. Xerxes also did not know that the people that Haman was specifically targeting were the Hebrews in the kingdom.

---

6. Esth 4:1–17.

7. Esth 3:1–4:17.

8. Esth 4:1.

9. See 1 Sam 15:8–33.

10. Esth 3:1–10.

11. Esth 3:11–15.

12. Esth 3:9.

Mordecai asked Esther to go and speak with the king on behalf of their people.[13] This is the same Esther that Mordecai, who was like a father to her, told never to tell the king that she was a Hebrew. Now he wants and needs her to reveal her true national identity in order to save her people. She understood that doing this might help her people but the reality was that even as queen, she was not able to freely go and see the king whenever she wanted to see him. Her presence had to be requested by him in order for her to gain audience with King Xerxes.

After a few back-and-forth messages exchanged between Esther and Mordecai, he sent her one final message imploring her to go speak with the king. He based his message on the fact that her crown would not protect her. Ultimately someone would find out that she was a Jew and her fate would be the same as her people's if she did not put a stop to the order.

She took all of the information into consideration. Esther weighed the reality of the laws that governed her ability to see the king versus her desire to save her people. She told Mordecai and her servants as well as the other Hebrews in the kingdom to fast for three days. Then she would go before the king, uninvited, and if that decision resulted in her death then so be it.[14] Esther was a Sensing and straightforward processor of information.

ESTHER'S FEELING PREFERENCE

Esther had a preference toward Feeling regarding her decision-making procedures. She was guided by information, but her compassion and personal values helped to shape her decision to go before the king even though that decision could have resulted in her death.

Queen Esther and her cousin Mordecai ended up in a disagreement over the decision to go and see the king. She knew the laws of the land. She understood how that specific law also governed her actions, even as queen. Mordecai knew that Esther was made queen for exactly this moment, time, and reason.[15] He knew that God wanted to use her to save her people. But she had the final decision. Though she was engaged in a logical thought process which forced her to weigh all options, she used

13. Esth 4:1–17.
14. Esth 4:1–17.
15. Esth 4:14.

her tenderhearted affection for her people to inform her final decision to take her life into her own hands and go before the king uninvited.

Her decision followed a logical and necessary process to make this bold move, demonstrating how her Sensing preference interacted with her Feeling preference. She also demonstrated how we are not statically locked into one personality zone, because the logical process that she asked her people to engage in, prior to going before the king uninvited, demonstrated that she visited and engaged a Thinking preference while her primary motivation remained attached to her Feeling preference. She asked for the help of all of the Hebrews in the kingdom. She wanted them to fast and pray with her for three days prior to going before the king. With their help, she received the inner strength and courage to go in front of the king and plead her case for her people and against Haman's unjust law. Queen Esther was a Feeling-oriented decision-maker.

ESTHER'S JUDGING PREFERENCE

Queen Esther used a Judging preference and a logical thought process to guide and make sense of her life as well as to make her rule as queen an impactful and well-organized one. She knew exactly how long she needed all of the Jews to fast with her before she went to see the king and possibly meet with death. She was methodical in her organization of the world around her, both regarding her preparation to become queen as well as in the process to exercise what authority that she had associated with her crown. She lived in a well-organized world which positively impacted her outcomes.

King Xerxes was pleased with Queen Esther from their very first meeting. She knew that. Esther was organized in her approach and stuck to her plan. She could use the favor that the king had shown toward his queen to her advantage. She could use that kindness to help her spare her own life and the lives of her countrymen. She would not haphazardly go before the king upon finding out that her father figure was outside of the king's gate in mourning. She needed to gather more information, and to create an organized plan of action in order to avoid last-minute stress as she took her life into her own hands and sought audience with the king. Esther was a wise and organized leader with a Judging preference.

ESFJ

Queen Esther is a portrait of a person who demonstrated ESFJ traits and predilections. She was caring and conscientious. She was generally co-operative. Her Sensing ability, which allowed her to process information in a logical way, caused her to gather additional impetus and weigh all options before she made a final decision.

Queen Esther worked with all of the Hebrews in order to fast and gain the inner strength required to take her life into her own hands by going before her husband the king so that she could plead the case for sparing the Hebrew people. She really demonstrated a care and concern for her cousin as he sat in mourning for his people at the king's gate. She also demonstrated extraordinary empathy for her Hebrew people's plight.

Her plan ultimately worked. Esther gained a favorable audience with King Xerxes. Haman was hanged and Mordecai was promoted for a prior act where he and Queen Esther saved the king from a plot to kill him by a couple of the palace guards,[16] Mordecai was subsequently used by Esther to issue an order, under the authority of the king, to override and fight against Haman's previous directive, thus saving their people.[17] She enjoyed the favor and appreciation of the king during her entire tenure as queen. Esther was the portrait of an ESFJ.

ESFJ: THE DIPLOMATS

APPLICATIONS FOR ESFJS

Queen Esther may not serve as the best example when it comes to finding personality extremes for the ESFJs. However, she does lend a pretty good template for life applications as well as instructing some on how to develop within the ESFJ personality type. ESFJs like to live in harmony and peace with all mankind when they are appropriately balanced in their personality type.[18] They, more than many other personality types, like to please people and see folks made happy.[19] They are disheartened when tension enters the room. They are the happy life of the party who wants everyone at the party to be happy and enjoy themselves.

16. Esth 2:19–23; 6:1–3.

17. Esth 8–9.

18. See Heb 12:14.

19. Myers, *Introduction to Type*, 28.

Queen Esther became disheartened not only when she found out her cousin Mordecai was hurting, but when she found out why he was hurting. He subsequently made a life or death request of Esther that also just so happened to have the fate of their people riding on it. Thus, she was quite conflicted. But Esther like most ESFJs put others ahead of herself, even at the potential cost of her very life, and decided to go and visit the king uninvited.[20]

Everyone benefits from the ebullient nature of a ESFJ who is well-balanced. The group benefits because the ESFJ will place the needs of the group ahead of their own needs. They will go to great lengths to make everyone happy.[21] ESFJs should remain mindful to remain in balance, because their ability to spread joy to the entire group also results in receiving blessings from God because they are peacemakers.[22]

However, they can become frustrated because things may not always go their way or according to their preconceived notions, as relative to their attempts to generate peace and harmony within a chaotic and ever-changing opinionated world. The ESFJ needs to also remember that not everyone likes or needs to stick to a rigidly constructed schedule or a strictly preconceived outcome.

Other personalities do not value traditions at the same level as the ESFJ.[23] For example, people with a Perceiving preference in reference to their organizational style love to leave things open-ended while playing many things by ear. The ESFJ may enter a situation where they create the very conflict that will later dishearten them, if they do not learn to digress and become less rigid. This will allow everyone to operate according to their individual and distinctive personality, as opposed to the ESFJ attempting to force everyone to adhere to the parameters of the ESFJ's personality type.

---

20. Esth 4.

21. Myers, *Introduction to Type*, 28.

22. See Matt 5:9.

23. Myers, *Introduction to Type*, 28.

Developing As An ESFJ

Proverbs discusses the idea that we as humans make plans.[24] However, those plans, according to Proverbs, have to be submitted to God if we want them to succeed. ESFJs can learn a valuable lesson from this.

ESFJs love their planning function. They receive information in a straightforward manner. Their Judging preference, which is the opposite of those with a Perceiving preference, can cause them to organize their world to the letter of their conceptualized law. They believe that these wonderfully constructed plans will naturally make everybody happy! After all, that's the goal of their ESFJ personality type; because of their Feeling preference they believe that it is their God-given responsibility to bring their version of peace and harmony to their little corner of the earth. So if they see their best-laid plans go awry, they turn on the Extroverted charm, and expect everybody to be happy again.

Not so fast, my ESFJ friends! Proverbs 16 implores the readers to submit those plans to God in order to allow him to make them successful. God has already given us his peace and joy.[25] However, people and situations will at times become disharmonious. It is a natural part of life. When conflict inevitably arises for our ESFJ friends, it is not their obligation to turn on the charm or correct all of the tension by slamming or even gently placing their rigidly-constructed plans down on the table and stating that, "The rules are up! We must all abide by them and then be happy!" That, my ESFJ friends, is the fastest way to make everyone unhappy.

It is not the ESFJ's responsibility to become the corporate cheerleader with your megaphone and the company logo embossed on the side. That makes people unhappy too. Take your plans and your desired outcomes to the Lord, if you hold a biblical worldview.[26] Like Mary the mother of Jesus (who I do not believe was an Extrovert but who may have been of a Sensing and Feeling and probably a Perceiving preference) said to the servants at the wedding: "Do whatever he says!"[27] Everything else will work out just fine. Water at your beloved ESFJ party will miraculously turn to wine.

---

24. Prov 16:1, 3, 9.

25. See John 14:27; Rom 14:17.

26. See Ps 63:1.

27. John 2:6–12.

PERSONALITY EXTREMES FOR ESFJS

We just described in some detail the personality extremes and potential pitfalls for the ESFJs. The ESFJs can become overly attached to their schedules, plans, and ideas. Thus, ESFJs may attempt to force others to do exactly what they have previously conceived and organized in their ESFJ minds, thereby creating the very tension that they wish to avoid.[28]

Thus, the extreme ESFJ could possibly, without realizing what they are doing, cause great harm to the group. Although I believe that they are at least subconsciously aware of the fact that what they are doing is wrong, or they may not completely understand (but I doubt it) that what they are doing is damaging to the other members of the family.

People have made so many television programs that involve the extreme nature of ESFJs. For example, the ESFJ goes on vacation with the entire family, but doesn't realize that many in the family just want to sleep in and then wander to the beach with a good book (perhaps one named *A Personality Portrait)* while listening to the sound of the waves crash against the shore. That's the whole day. There is no food, no water, other than the ocean, scheduled into that day. Just laying in bed, and then moving from laying in a bed to laying on the sand, towel optional! Meanwhile, the ESFJ has everything scheduled down to the millisecond, from the bathroom breaks, to the pig luau, to the fire-breathing dude, a mountain hike, and fishing (I think I want to go to Hawaii?).

Be careful, ESFJ. You can turn people off if you allow your personality to go to an extreme when you are actually wired to bring peace and happiness to the entire group. Remember that you are also wired to bring order with your schedules. Find balance in all things and you will be able to strengthen peace with all family members.[29]

CONNECTIONS FOR ESFJS

The Extroverted manner in which the ESFJs relate to and interact with their world is connected to the Judging preference that they employ in order to organize and make sense of their world. ESFJs like to take in information in a straightforward, no-nonsense format using their Sensing preference. That Sensing function regarding the storage and retrieval of

---

28. Myers, *Introduction to Type,* 28.

29. See Heb 12:14.

information is used to inform the ESFJ's Feeling preference and decision-making function. We can learn a lot from these connections.

Connections Between The E-J Functions

Each of these connection explorations are directly impacted by the entire personality type functioning as a whole, affecting the two connections explored within each of these expository discussions. The E-J connection relative to the ESFJ personality type brings their Extroverted nature to the forefront as their given personality type is driven to accomplish their primary goal. Their main goal is to see everyone happy. ESFJs employ their Extroverted function by engaging everyone in the joyful atmosphere that they are always attempting to create.

This Extroverted function that the ESFJ uses to engage people is directly connected to the way that they organize and make sense of their world. It only makes sense to an ESFJ to see that everyone is happy and operating in a harmonious environment. By virtue of that reality, they attempt to organize their world in a neat manner that will help them to attain their primary goal.

For example, if the ESFJ plans a party, the objective is: when everyone shows up for the party, sweep them up into a lovely ball of happiness, because the ESFJ has planned this baby out to the nth degree! As long as they are not rigid in their desire to see the plan come out the way that they had previously outlined it on paper (ESFJs love them some outlines), they will be fine.

They are invaluable to a family unit because they desire to bring peace. They will also be able to notice, if they are well balanced, everyone's tendencies,[30] and using those tendencies ESFJs can figure out how to most effectively engage each individual in order to ensure their comfort as much as possible.

Connections Between The S-F Functions

The ESFJ's S-F function allows them to gather appropriate information and make appropriate decisions that are required for them to accomplish their goals. It is a laudable desire that the ESFJs possess: making everyone happy.

30. Myers, *Introduction to Type*, 9–10.

The ESFJ can use their Sensing function to their advantage if they learn how to properly employ it. They can use that ability to gather straightforward information received both by talking to each person in the group and by remaining observant about what the person likes and dislikes. The ESFJ store that gleaned information for later use.

Since ESFJs love outlines, lists, and schedules so much, they write this stuff down as opposed to attempting to challenge themselves by storing all of it in their brains. The Feeling function can then use the gathered information to decide how to recognize individuality and construct events that will make most everyone happy, thereby helping the ESFJ achieve their goal. But remember, my ESFJ friends: some folks are just determined to be cranky.

GROWTH OPPORTUNITIES AND THREATS AS AN ESFJ

The growth opportunities relevant to ESFJs focus on the idea of not becoming rigidly attached to anything. It is very easy for a Sensing preference person to become attached to the manner in which they take in and store information. If they take in incorrect information but then become rigidly attached to the information on the paper, they will miss what the person is really trying to convey to them.

People should not make anyone guess. However, ESFJs need to remember that observation will only tell you what a person is doing. Observation, by its definition, is an information-gathering tool. On its own, it cannot tell you why a person is doing what they are doing. The ESFJ has to learn to become more iNtuitive and dig deeper, investigate, and find out what is behind the observable action. If ESFJs will keep this little lesson in mind and remember, if they are believers, to read Proverbs 16 every day until they have learned to submit all of their plans and ideas to the Lord, then they will live the happy and peaceful life that they seek for others.[31]

To state this another way: ESFJs need to visit all kinds of restaurants serving all kinds of foods. They need to go to "greasy spoons" as often as they visit a five star chef at a restaurant that has a waiting list for reservations, andd then visit every restaurant in between. Variety is the spice of life!

31. See Prov 16:1, 3, 9.

8

ISFJ: Mary of Bethany

MARY OF BETHANY

THE STORY OF MARY, the sister of Martha and Lazarus, can be found in the New Testament in Luke 10 and John 11–12. In one instance, Mary poured a day's wages' worth of perfumed oil on Jesus's feet, and then wiped his feet, including the oil, with her hair.[1] Mary engaged in many complex actions during her life, but they are explained by her preference toward the personality traits that she shares with other ISFJs.

Mary's sister Martha was a more outspoken Extrovert than Mary who was a measured and thoughtful Introvert. She sat back, observed the situation, and then decided the best course of action. She engaged in that action in a logical and organized manner.

Mary's actions were generally inwardly-directed and motivated, even though at times they appeared wasteful.[2] To other people her actions seemed too reserved. However, Mary remained true to herself and through that she showed us what truly motivates an ISFJ.

MARY'S INTROVERSION PREFERENCE

I know that some of you are very happy that I have finally chosen a New Testament biblical leader to discuss. I am, too.

1. John 12:1–3.
2. John 12:4–8.

Mary was obviously an Introvert who drew energy via engaging the world around her by sitting back and waiting, rather than jumping directly into every burning fire as was typically the case with her sister Martha. Mary, like Martha and the rest of the people in her town of Bethany, was excited about the ministry of Jesus. But Mary was not excited enough to cook for Jesus or to try to impress others with the fact that Jesus came to their house for a visit.[3]

Mary was single-minded of purpose. When Jesus arrived at their house, she sat right at his feet and did not move. She did not engage in any conversation. She did not serve Jesus a single cocktail peanut or a glass of lemonade (they had those in biblical times, I think).

She chose her seat on the floor, right at the master teacher's feet and did not move or care what Martha did to entertain and impress the guests. Mary only desired to quietly absorb and reflect on the teachings of Jesus and she chose a ringside seat for all of the proceedings. She quieted herself and just took it all in, as Introverts are prone to do.

Later, when her brother Lazarus died after battling with an illness for days, she stayed in the house and mourned her brother. She was well aware of the miracles of Jesus by that point. She knew that he had been notified of the fact that his friend Lazarus had been ill.[4] Instead of Jesus dropping everything and running to Bethany and Lazarus's house, Jesus made a pronouncement that Lazarus's sickness would not end in death but would result in glory for the Father. Jesus loved the entire family: Mary, Martha, and Lazarus. But he did not rush right over to the house to heal Lazarus. Remember that Jesus represents the perfect balance between all eight personality preferences. He knew what Mary would do and what Martha would do.

Mary did not panic just because she did not see Jesus walk through the door shortly after hearing of Lazarus's illness. She likely heard that Jesus went back to Judea, another town in a different direction, as opposed to rushing to Bethany to see how he could help his friend. Lazarus ultimately died, and Jesus came four days after Lazarus died and been placed in a tomb.[5]

3. Luke 10:38–42.

4. John 11:1–44.

5. John 11:17.

Many of Lazarus" friends went over at the house to comfort Mary and Martha.[6] This must have driven the Introvert in Mary totally insane. All of those people offered comfort that she did not want from them and couldn't receive very well from the fellow mourners at that time. Mary also knew that Jesus could have easily healed her brother. She probably would have liked to run to her room to mourn in private. However, the compassionate Feeling side of Mary compelled her to be nice to the same visitors who were likely driving her nuts. She needed to be alone with her thoughts, not entertaining all of the strange people who were there to help her. In the reality of the Introvert, these house guests were actually hindering her grieving and healing process. Introverts, you have a difficult journey.

So when Jesus finally hit town, Martha rushed right out and confronted him![7] Confronting the king of kings, huh? Extroverts out of balance can make a bad fire worse at times. But that's exactly what Mary did.Mary stayed in the house,[8] presumably waiting for Jesus to come down to the house. Interestingly enough, she and Martha made the same statement to Jesus: "If you had come sooner, my brother would not have died."[9] After Martha told Mary that Jesus was asking for her, Mary went out to meet him. Unlike his response to Martha, Jesus asked his beloved Introverted friend, Mary: "Where did you bury him?" He ultimately went out to raise Lazarus from the dead.[10] Meanwhile, Mary was doing her best to put up with the mourners while trying to understand Jesus's actions. Mary was definitely an Introvert regarding her interactions with the people in the outside world.

MARY'S SENSING PREFERENCE

Mary was definitely concerned with her present realities.[11] She processed information in a very logical, methodical, and concrete manner. She uttered one simple phrase to Jesus: "If you would have been here, my brother would not have died." It was perfectly true based on the informa-

6. John 11:18–19.

7. John 11:20–22.

8. John 11:20.

9. John 11:21, 32–33.

10. John 11:38–44.

11. Myers, *Introduction to Type*, 9.

tion that was available to her. She was keenly aware of the fact that Jesus had healed many people. She was also cognizant of the fact that he both could and would be inclined to help her brother. She did not understand why Jesus did not come to help.

In another situation that preceded the death of Lazarus, Mary chose to sit still and assimilate information. She believed that no greater teacher had ever entered the world and none greater would follow this guy.[12] So she did not busy herself with the party that could have ensued because the king of kings was coming over to the house. She wanted to take in as much information as she could glean from Jesus. She also knew that the best way for her to gather that information was for her sit right at his feet. Mary was Sensing something great happening right before her very eyes, and she refused to miss it.

MARY'S FEELING PREFERENCE

Once, Mary poured an entire jar of very expensive oil on the feet of Jesus.[13] This offended the sensibilities of Judas Iscariot, who kept (and stole from) the money bag that the disciples of Jesus contributed to during their training phase. This event occurred after Jesus provided tangible evidence of the fact that he is king of kings by raising Lazarus from the dead.[14] It also occurred after Mary sat at the feet of the master. Jesus's arrival was the only thing that could get the Introvert Mary to move on both occasions.

Mary likely absorbed the information relative to these two demonstrations, namely Jesus's profound teaching ministry as well as raising her brother from the dead, both of which occurred right before her very eyes. Mary used that information to make a sound decision. She had a bottle of spikenard, an expensive oil used to prepare someone for burial as well as other uses, during that time. It was worth a day's wages. She assuredly had to save up to buy the oil. Her brother had recently died and was raised from the dead, yet she had not used it on him. She was obviously saving it for something very special. When Jesus came back to the house for a visit, she was moved to use that oil. So she decided to pour it on Jesus's feet and then wipe the oil off with her hair. She processed the

12. Luke 10:38–42.

13. John 12:3–8.

14. John 12:9–11.

information, considered how she felt about Jesus, and made the sound decision to pour that oil on her Savior's feet and wipe it off with her hair. A humble sacrifice indeed.

Mary knew exactly what she was doing. She knew exactly who she believed that she was undertaking this action for. She decided to pour the oil based on the teachings of Jesus about his death, burial, and resurrection. These were teachings she heard while sitting at his feet instead of serving cocktail nuts to the town folk.

Only the Holy Spirit can provide someone with that kind of understanding, and only the Holy Spirit can inform the decision to prepare Christ for his burial. However, a person with a Sensing preference, who process information in a straightforward manner, would take that information and make the decision to use it to perform this action.

Mary's Feeling preference allowed her to demonstrate the required empathy that her Savior needed during that time in his life, to make the decision to prepare Him for his burial by pouring the oil on his feet, and to decide on the tender and compassionately connective act of wiping his feet with her hair. Subsequently Jesus told Judas what Mary was doing when Judas questioned her decision and apparent wasteful action. Thankfully Judas was not left in charge of deciphering Mary's decision making process. He would have placed her neither in the Thinking nor in the Feeling category, as he was not very good at thinking or feeling regarding his decision-making processes. But Mary was in charge of her actions and she demonstrated kindness as well as empathy. She was obviously guided by her personal values and by the understanding of who Jesus is. Her actions to the trained eye seemed equitable and not at all wasteful. Mary's actions were filled with tenderhearted compassion.[15] Mary was a Feeling person.

MARY'S JUDGING PREFERENCE

Mary was also a judicious person regarding the organization of her world. She saved that bottle of oil for a very special occasion. No one will know if that occasion was revealed to her to be the preparation of Jesus for his burial. I tend to think that she was saving it for her wedding, but that's just a thought.

---

15. Myers, *Introduction to Type*, 10.

No matter the reason, she likely still had to save to purchase the oil, and work hard to earn the money to save. She systematically kept the oil for just the right occasion. When motivated by her understanding of the times as well as who Jesus really is, she moved into action, reorganizing her world to fit her new plan while recognizing that this was the right time and place to use the oil. Mary was a wise and Judging person.

ISFJ

ISFJs are described as friendly, reserved, caring, and wise decision-makers. Mary demonstrated all of those qualities. She saved the oil past her brother's death, not knowing that he would be brought back to life four days later.

Mary of Bethany was also an exemplary if not an obvious leader. She was a servant leader, as demonstrated through her sacrifice of anointing Jesus's feet with expensive oil and by wiping his feet with her hair. She showed us this leadership trait by sitting at Jesus's feet, while her sister Martha scurried about making dinner preparations. Jesus confirmed this idea about Mary when he said that she had chosen better than Martha by choosing something that would never leave her, gleaning wisdom while sitting at the master's feet.[16]

Mary saved her money to purchase the Spikenard oil and conserved it with a plan to use it at just the right time. She also knew that the safest place, as well as the most peaceful and harmonious place, not just in her home, not just in her town of Bethany, but in the entire world, was sitting down at Jesus's feet. Mary was an ISFJ.

ISFJ: THE RECONCILERS

APPLICATIONS FOR ISFJS

Mary, one of my favorite ISFJs, can teach us a lot about the ISFJ personality. She appeared to be a well-balanced person of measured temperament.[17] ISFJs have excellent memories for facts, impressions, and other observations, based on their Sensing information-gathering preference.[18]

16. Luke 10:42.

17. See Gal 5:22–23.

18. Myers, *Introduction to Type*, 15.

They use their memory in an attempt to accommodate the needs, wants, and desires of family and friend alike. They can become the family glue that holds things and the team together through the tough times.

They have a healthy respect for authority and structure. That is why Mary was able to be so attuned to Jesus, and attentive to everything that he said. Mary may not have understood at all why Jesus never came to heal her brother Lazarus from his terminal illness until after he died. But Mary the ISFJ was absolutely certain of the fact that Jesus was the Son of the living God, making him the ultimate authority and completely worthy of her trust and respect. ISFJs can apply this idea about trust and respect to their daily lives, as long as they maintain balance.

Structure is good. However, it is only as good as the leader who implements and executes it within a structured environment. ISFJs seek to create their own structured environment from which, if their personality is in balance, they hope that their contribution fits perfectly into the overall construction of the organization or family and makes everything run more smoothly. They use their memory and ability to understand as well as empathize with others to their advantage in order to fix anything that may be broken or out of place with someone.[19] This broken piece or person could disrupt the orderly operation of the system.

If the leader is not good, then the ISFJ can become frustrated because things are not working according to plan.[20] This keeps them from going to their primary default, their highly attuned memory, and use that memory and knowledge of individuals to fix things and get them back on track. The ISFJ is like the loving family handyman.

Developing As An ISFJ

ISFJs have a bit of a head start on the other personality types, and specifically on those who choose to develop within the context of a biblical worldview. They have a head start because they are naturally inclined to submit to and appreciate authority. As long as they maintain their focus on the ultimate authority, namely Jesus, they will be able to help all things come together. They will also be able to hold things together because of their ability to help others via their capacity to gather and retain

19. Myers, *Introduction to Type,* 15.
20. Myers, *Introduction to Type,* 15.

knowledge about the needs and desires of all of the individuals within their purview.[21]

If you take that same highly-attuned ISFJ and stick them in a church with a less than adequate leader, they may find themselves in a bit of trouble. Their natural inclination to submit to authority guides their actions. Their abilities help the leader to not only create a positive and supportive environment but to help them to fix and maintain things, thus enabling the system to function properly. But remember, the leader is not very good at leading, nor is that leader proficient at implementing a functional structure. If you want to learn more on theories about the advantages and disadvantages of top-heavy organizations versus organizations that have spread out their leadership roles to the extent that they may have too many cooks in the kitchen, see the AFL-CIO and how they came together. The ISFJ will be at a major loss in an organization with a poor leader who has implemented a fractious structure if they are not well-balanced.

The ISFJ's job is to fit in, fix things, and rally the troops to support the vision of the leader, knowing each troop member and helping them to obtain their personalized needs and personal desires, so everyone crosses the finish line together. But the lines are blurred, the goal is unclear, and the system designed to reach it is messed up all because of our faithless leader. Thus, the ISFJ has to crawl out of their comfort zone, something that is difficult for the ISFJ because of their need for stability, structure, and effective leadership, which enables them to do their job properly. They have to find a way to take their support from the current leader and submit all of their plans, goals, and structures to God (if they are believers). They have to ask him what they should do and where they should go from here. ISFJs must remember that God is the leader.

As believers, as long as the ISFJ fits into God's kingdom system, and as long as their goal is the steady advancement of the kingdom of God, the ISTJ can keep their true goals in mind. For example, in a church setting, the current leader in that church, the structure of that organization, as well as all of their collective plans and machinations must all fall in line under the authority of the Master Teacher, Jesus. That may happen within the current church with current leadership if God is able to change the leader's heart and correct the operation of the system, or it may have to happen in another place that God is leading the ISFJ to work for the

---

21. Myers, *Introduction to Type*, 15.

kingdom. As long as the ISFJ keeps the true kingdom goal in mind and in order, the ISFJ will be able to successfully do their kingdom job, irrespective of earthly location and vocation.

PERSONALITY EXTREMES FOR ISFJS

Personality extremes for the ISFJs involve their potential intransigence, as relates to their desire to support leadership, maintain structure, and constantly repair and maintain if not improve the system. ISFJs are also seen by others as those who place a high value on structure and closure. We will discuss the ISFJ's extreme desire to support leadership and organization before we tackle closure.[22]

ISTJs must maintain their focus on the real prize, their life's true calling to remain in Jesus and to help build the kingdom of God (as stated so eloquently in Phil 3:12–14). The ISFJ must be careful not go to any extremes relating to maintaining a broken system or keeping a leader who should not be kept. If they find themselves in such an organization or family with a broken leader or structure, they should seek God for his will for their lives and leave that organization or, dare I say, that family and its leader who they so faithfully if undeservedly have supported for such a long time. It is a difficult decision but a necessary one, particularly for ISFJs to consider.

The other personality extreme that ISFJs have to learn to avoid is an outsized desire for closure.[23] I have always considered closure as an elusive concept at best. I usually call it a farce. But I can be a rather blunt ENTJ at times. The ISFJ's strong desire to obtain closure from a broken situation or from a broken leader or companion will constantly evade them. I generally say that trying to get closure from a poor mate is akin to trying to get water from a rock. Only Moses could pull that one off, and he got in trouble for it.[24]

I always tell people I am counseling with: "If that specific person could give you closure, adequately explain to you why you are breaking up and what their role as well as what their responsibilities in that breakup were, much less explain the emotional damage that they so obviously carry around inside of them, the same damage that ruined your

22. Myers, *Introduction to Type*, 15.

23. Myers, *Introduction to Type*, 15.

24. See Num 20:1–13.

relationship and put you into a horrible situation where you now have your own, brand-new emotional scars to seek God for healing for, then you two would not be breaking up in the first place."

Closure is difficult because it signals the end of a thing. It's an attempt, in this case by the ISFJ-problem fixer, to leave rather than submit to their personality proclivity. It's an attempt to stay, as well as to try to repair what is irreconcilably broken. In short, closure equals broken beyond repair. The ISFJ has to avoid extremes and just go. As I tell my students as well as my older adults who are in badly broken or abusive relationships: "run (away from that person) like your butt is on fire!"

CONNECTIONS FOR ISFJS

The Introverted manner in which ISFJs relate to and interact with their world is connected to the Judging preference that they use to organize and make sense of their world. ISFJs like to take in information in a straightforward, no nonsense format using their Sensing preference, as well as their elaborate and sophisticated memory.[25] That Sensing preference regarding the storage and retrieval of information related to the finer details about their loved ones, is used to inform the ISFJ's Feeling preference and decision-making function. We can learn a lot from these connections.

Connections Between The I-J Functions

The Introverted function within the ISFJ actually allows them to operate in a manner that informs their Sensing function as much as it connects with their Judging function. ISFJs are Introverts, thus they generally exist more comfortably by processing thoughts and ideas internally rather than to engage externally like the Extroverted cousins.[26] Processing internally allows them to develop quite a memory for facts, reactions, impressions, and responses that they gather and retain about the people who they interact with most often in a one-on-one fashion. This is why they are so readily able to help the family unit or the organization to remain together. They remember so many details about so many individual people.[27] Thus,

25. Myers, *Introduction to Type*, 9–10.

26. Myers, *Introduction to Type*, 9–10.

27. Myers, *Introduction to Type*, 9–10.

when they begin to operate within the well-organized and structured system that they not only help to create and maintain but also function so comfortably within as a result of their organized Judging preference and nature, they can use that information stored in their memory about the people who they have engaged as individuals to help them to maintain order and proper functioning of the system. It is their area of specialized gifting, their default position, and their full time job as ISFJs.

Connections Between The S-F Functions

ISFJs use their Sensing information-gathering function to inform their decisions. These decisions are usually designed to achieve a better place for everyone based on their Feeling preference. We have discussed the vast and extensive memory possessed by the ISFJ based on their Sensing preference.[28]

They use their Feeling decision-making function to not only keep them open and attuned to the needs and wants of the entire group, but also to enable them to try to fulfill the needs and wants of the group. If they are able to cohesively enact this transaction and keep everyone in the group happy and fulfilled, they can accomplish their true goal of initiating and maintaining a well-designed system or structure with a positive leader at the head who is respected, and with members who will continue to press on toward the ultimate goal of helping and benefitting others.

GROWTH OPPORTUNITIES AND THREATS AS AN ISFJ

The Opportunities are limitless for the ISFJs. They need to continue to grow along the positive path that their personality places them and function as God has designed them to operate in order to be invaluable to the system and advancement of the kingdom. Can you imagine the story of Jesus and the spreading of the gospel during Jesus's earthly ministry without Mary of Bethany . . . my favorite ISTJ?

Mary provided us and everyone in Bethany with an example of a woman with measured and temperate faith even amid the crisis of losing her brother Lazarus to a terminal illness. The worst of Lazarus's illness occurred a few days prior to Jesus coming to raise Lazarus from the dead.

28. Myers, *Introduction to Type*, 9–10.

The whole town knew how much Jesus loved that entire family, yet he never came to see about his friend.[29]

Mary did not need to run around to each person in the room and find out what they needed, as Martha did on a different occasion.[30] No, her job in this instance was to support her leader and Savior, irrespective of the fact that she found her leader, Jesus, difficult to understand. She simply asked him why he did not come? By saying that one thing to her leader, full of faith in his divine abilities and prudent judgement, she released Jesus to simply reply: "Where have you laid him?" She fixed the entire system by behaving properly, remaining in faith, and trusting her Savior to do the right thing.

According to the Bible, Lazarus was raised from the dead. The reality that Jesus was the Christ, the Son of God, was undeniably established for all to see, even if they hung him on a cross in spite of this immutable fact. Mary's place, as a beloved Introvert and ISFJ, was etched in stone, and the part that she played in spreading the good news of Jesus Christ.

ISFJs have a wonderful opportunity to grow if they can overcome their Threats and temptations that want to get them out of their innate and designed role. ISFJs: train yourselves to let go of conventional things or "the way we have always done it." Use your energies appropriately to help reconcile everyone in your world to the correct goals, ideas, and structures. You simply have to, as my pastor used to say, "stay in your lane."

29. John 11:1–44.
30. Luke 10:38–42.

9

ESTP: Jacob, Israel, The Changed One

JACOB, ISRAEL, THE CHANGED ONE

I ADMIT THAT I struggled a bit to find the most appropriate ESTP. Jacob definitely fit the bill; however, his Sensing preference, although it is his dominant information-gathering preference, is very close to his iNtuition preference. I would say that Jacob may be 51–49 percent in the area of processing information; similar to my closely related Extroversion to Introversion preference. But enough about me: this chapter is about Jacob.

God renamed Jacob as Israel.[1] He was definitely an ESTP. He demonstrated an ability to be sociable and ready to take initiative, particularly when he had to work on Laban's farm.[2] He also displayed his resourcefulness when he tricked his father Isaac regarding the receipt of Isaac's fatherly blessings.[3] Additionally, Jacob coerced his brother Esau into giving him Esau's birthright (general inheritance).[4] Jacob also appeared to have very broad interests that went beyond shepherding. Jacob was a reasonably good cook, a method actor (playing the part of Esau for his father, whose eyesight was failing, in Gen 27), a prophet as recorded in Gen 49, and a bit of a geneticist, because he could use tree bark to change the

1. Gen 32:27–28.
2. Gen 29:15–20.
3. Gen 27:1–28:5.
4. Gen 25:27–34.

94

color of the coats of unborn sheep in Gen 30:25–43. It's all documented in the book of Genesis, chapters 25–49.

Jacob was primarily a Sensing-oriented person and generally believed the facts as they were presented. He trusted his present reality, but he could also trust an inspiration as a person who demonstrated some of the qualities of an iNtuitive. He was also quite analytical. Jacob used logic to solve problems, although they were problems that often times were complications of his own making. He had to remain flexible in order to execute his frequently nefarious plans. Jacob's schemes would not execute themselves. He had to use some open-ended flexibility to achieve his goals.

JACOB'S EXTROVERSION PREFERENCE

Jacob had an Extroverted personality. After tricking his Father Isaac into giving him the blessing that belonged to his brother Esau, the older twin, Jacob had to run off to the former land of his grandfather Abraham to find a wife among his extended family members.[5] He went to northwest Mesopotamia, east of Canaan, and lived with his uncle Laban, the brother of his mother Rebekah. They were perfect strangers to him but he proved to be capable of adapting quickly, due in part to his outgoing, if also duplicitous, personality.

While he was there, away from the inheritance that he had stolen, he married two wives.[6] They were sisters and the daughters of his uncle Laban. He also hired many servants and ultimately led his new family and carted his newly-earned wealth back to Canaan, the land promised to his grandfather Abraham and to his father Isaac.[7]

Jacob, like many in his family, was a fast talker and a quick thinker. He swindled his uncle Laban out of some his best sheep after Laban tricked him into marrying both of his daughters and working for him for free for many years.[8] Jacob proved to be sociable and expressive, as well as adaptable and ready to take initiative. He took a little too much initiative at times and in many different situations. Jacob was an Extrovert.

5. Gen 27:1–28:5.
6. Gen 29:1–30:24.
7. Gen 30:25–33:20.
8. Gen 29:1–30:43.

JACOB'S SENSING PREFERENCE

Jacob had a strong Sensing preference although he demonstrated some of the traits expressed in the personalities of iNtuitives. Jacob demonstrated adaptability while in difficult situations.

Once he thought he was marrying Rachel, the woman of his dreams. Uncle Laban tricked him and gave him the oldest daughter Leah to wed instead by covering her face with what must have been a rather thick and dense veil. The fact was that Jacob had promised his uncle that he would work for seven years in order to earn the right to marry Rachel. When he realized that Jacob the trickster had been tricked into marrying the wrong woman, he could only adapt. He knew that he still wanted Rachel. So he promised to serve for seven more years for the right to also marry her.[9]

Jacob understood the present reality of the situation based on the information currently available to him. He had just been tricked into marrying Leah the older sister, while longing to be with Rachel the younger sibling. However, he also knew that the situation was tenuous at best, while working for someone was just as good of a trickster than himself, if not better. Jacob had to become even more of a quick study regarding present and future information as it unfolded while he continued to sojourn with his uncle Laban.

Jacob decided to build a shepherding empire for himself. So after his 14-year tenure as an indentured servant ended, he asked Laban if he could take the speckled, spotted, and black sheep and goats, all of lesser value, as his payment to stay on and continue to manage Laban's herds.

Jacob the trickster had started up the trick-mill again by doing this. He knew that if he asked for the sheep and goats with the best coats, Laban would not go for it, so he promised to take the sheep and goats of lesser value with blemishes on their coats. Jacob engaged his Sensing preference and used the information gleaned in the past to inform his Thinking preference when it came time to decide how to swindle Laban out of the best sheep.[10]

Jacob separated out the best goats and sheep with the pristine coats when the herds went to the watering troughs.. Then he took some poplar, almond, and plane tree branches, peeled the bark and put that bark in front of the watering troths where the animals drank and mated. The

9. Gen 29:1–30.

10. Gen 30:25–43.

lambs that were born to the sheep that mated in front of the bark at the watering trough were born speckled, streaked, and spotted because of the bark. Jacob was then able to keep the best sheep's young for himself because he made them look like they were the ones of lesser value. Jacob trusted his inspiration and imagination like an iNtuitive would. However, in reality he knew that the entire scheme would work because of his understanding of sheep genetics, based on his use of his Sensing preference to gather information. He had taken care of Laban's sheep for fourteen years, and likely he had taken care of his father's sheep before that. So he really trusted the information gathered from his experience and put a plan into action as a true Sensing person would. The plan worked to perfection. Jacob got rich and returned the duplicitous favor to Laban in the process.

JACOB'S THINKING PREFERENCE

Jacob certainly employed deductive reasoning as all those who share his Thinking preference in decision-making would. Jacob used cause-and-effect logic to solve his dilemma with Laban. He made the deal with Laban, and then put his plan to get the best sheep and goats for himself into action.

Jacob was also a stubborn and tough-minded individual. He demonstrated this by surviving many years of indentured servitude in Laban's house. He amassed great wealth for Laban before beginning to work to accumulate wealth for himself.[11] Jacob could never be accused of being a reasonable man, but he was always a man with a plan. Jacob had a strong Thinking preference.

JACOB'S PERCEIVING PREFERENCE

The same example of Jacob and the sheep can be used to demonstrate the way that he organized his world. He remained flexible and open to change. He could not box himself in to one static outcome, because as a hustler he had to leave himself room for adaptation. He was clearly spontaneous and felt energized by last-minute pressures. When he decided that he had amassed enough wealth working for Laban and the situation

11. Gen 30:43.

was no longer tolerable, he decided to leave quickly and return to the promised land with his new family and wealth.[12]

While on the way home he had to face the results of another one of his schemes: he had to travel through the land where Esau had settled. He knew their family reunion would likely not be a pleasant one. So he prepared a gift for his brother designed to ease the tensions.[13] He split his family and herds and staggered the gift presentations that he prepared for Esau. Meanwhile, Jacob brought up the rear. He hoped that when Esau saw all of the gifts, he might not kill him for stealing his birthright and tricking him out of his inheritance.

God's favor and Jacob's wrestling match with the angel of the Lord, more than Jacob's flexibility, paid off in the long run. The reunion was a great one. The brothers hugged and wept at the sight of each other.

The Lord showed Jacob that his Perceiving preference, when used by Jacob in such an extremely negative way regarding how he had organized his world up to this point by regularly running cons, could carry him no further. Jacob would keep the same Perceiving preference and remain flexible regarding the organization of his world. But Jacob needed to clean up his act and learn to trust the God of his father and grandfather for provision. Jacob understood the fact that it is the Lord who delivers his children, not their own organization, schemes, and plans.

ESTP

ESTPs like Jacob have to remain flexible when they make decisions, because the decisions may have to change at a moment's notice in order to achieve the desired goal. They learn to tolerate difficulty in the execution of the plan but keep the long range objective in mind.

Jacob was an active problem-solver. Some might call him a kinetic learner: one who learns by doing, not by brooding over theories and concepts. Jacob amassed great wealth and enjoyed the life of a rich man. He was willing to lie, cheat, and even steal at times in order to accumulate his wealth. Jacob was spontaneous, adaptable, and quick to act. Jacob was an ESTP.

---

12. Gen 31:1–55.
13. Gen 32:1–33:17.

ESTP: THE INQUISITIVE ONES

APPLICATIONS FOR ESTPS

I will admit that as I am completing the applications and development sections which I worked through following the completion of all of the personality profiles for the biblical leaders, I was forced to read the complete profiles on each personality type. This was a separate step from using the thumbnail sketches only after completing the actual profiles of the leaders. I did not realize how closely the personality profiles in this book, *A Personality Portrait*, truly align with the full profiles in *Introduction to Type*. Acknowledging again that none of the biblical characters represented in this book have taken (nor could they take) the actual MBTI Test Instrument as was discussed in the Disclaimer section of this book. Again, the free online version of the MBTI Test Instrument from CPP and MBTI is referenced at the end of this book.

I only mention this because Jacob at his best had so much potential to have a positive influence on so many people because of his ESTP personality type. Unfortunately, he spent a major portion of his life running hustles and executing his grand and nefarious schemes, until he had that run-in with the angel of the Lord.[14] But his personality still aligns very closely with the typical ESTP profile available in *Introduction to Type*. We can derive many life lessons and applications from the best as well as the less than the best attributes of the ESTPs.

ESTPs are curious and gregarious creatures. They are what educators call kinetic learners, which means that they learn by doing.[15] Jacob was definitely of that ilk. I am still impressed by the fact that he was able to learn how to change the color of a sheep's wool before they were born just by placing bark by a water trough.[16] Flesh and blood did not reveal that to him.[17] Rather he learned that trick via observation, experience, curiosity, and trial and error.

ESTPs are also quick studies and they are analytical problem solvers who like to live in the moment.[18] All of these attributes support the fact that ESTPs are important to the overarching mission of advancement.

---

14. Gen 32:22–32.

15. Myers, *Introduction to Type*, 16.

16. Gen 30:25–43.

17. Matt 16:17.

18. Myers, *Introduction to Type*, 16.

Many times I speak in reference to a particular person's importance to the team because of their specific personality type and how they will contribute to a group, organization, or to a family unit. Now, who would not want a quick study, who is also an analytical and creative problem-solver on their team, when we are choosing up sides? I tell my students all of the time to "use your powers for good and not for evil," meaning that the gifts and talents that you possess which are unique to you and can have such a dynamic impact on the lives of so many people, should be employed to accomplish the greater good. However, those gifts and talents are just as readily available to a person who uses them for their own selfish gain. I am of the biblical worldview that gifts and callings are given to you. If you believe that as well, then you also trust that God will never take them back.[19] How you use them is up to you.

This is a lesson that Jacob needed to learn as a young man. He was attuned to his present reality, which means that he took things as they were and tried to find solutions based on where he was; as opposed to what so many people very often do, which is projecting themselves in their mind where they want to be, and then try to solve the current problem from a potential future position. It cannot work!

Jacob realized that he was in a difficult position and he was "being worked," as many who run confidence games on each other would say. The man "working" him was his uncle Laban, who was just as good at hustling people and using his gifts and callings for evil and not for good as Jacob was.[20] Jacob was tricked by Laban into marrying Leah, the older and reportedly less attractive sister, rather than marrying his heart's desire, Rachel, who he had initially negotiated to marry.

He decided to do what I have often told my students on Academic Probation or Academic Suspension: "Fix it from here." I tell my academically-at-risk students that they could not dream of getting into good academic standing (a 2.0 GPA) before they started working on their desired GPA (somewhere in the 3.75+ range). They had to "fix the problem from here," working upward from the 1.00 cumulative GPA level on their transcript.

Jacob, just like my students, had to accept his present reality, live in the moment, and work from that position to find a solution to his current dilemma in order to achieve ultimate success and attain fulfillment of his

19. See Rom 11:29.
20. Gen 29:14–30.

goals and dreams. So Jacob told Laban that he will work seven more years if he is then allowed to marry Rachel too. He did not waste time trying to get out of the marriage to Leah, or argue with Laban about how he had just tricked him even though Jacob knew that Laban had. Laban tricked Jacob into marrying his oldest (and probably less attractive) daughter. Leah, who was not the true love of Jacob's life.[21] Jacob fixed it from there and moved on to find a workable solution that would allow him to marry his first choice, Rachel.

ESTPs live in the present.[22] They are very quick-thinking, analytical, and creative problem-solvers who learn by trial and error. They do this without getting frustrated. Rather they treat attempts as learning experiences. They are able to be an asset to any organization as they encounter and deal with daily problems. But they are only able to do that and help to build the organization if they use their powers, including their personality type, for good and not for evil.

Developing As An ESTP

ESTPs can develop a more fruitfully productive life by continuously dying to our flesh, our self, and our humanity.[23] There is another parable that says, proportionally speaking, the more that one receives, the more will be required of them.[24] ESTPs have been given a sharp mind, but much is required of it. They can find solutions where no one else can.

They are gregarious personalities. ESTPs love both to be around people and have as many folks around them as possible.[25] They are adaptable learners who pick things up quickly and likely work in many different fields of occupational endeavor. They are like encyclopedias: they know a little bit about a whole lot of things. If they are believers, then ESTPs need to learn to continue to submit themselves, including their thoughts, desires, plans, actions, and intellect. Specifically, they need to learn to submit their soul, spirit, and physical body to the Lord, which is our expected practice. They will then be able to use all of the gifts and callings associated with the ESTP personality for good and not for selfish

21. Gen 29:17–18.
22. Myers, *Introduction to Type*, 16.
23. 1 Cor 15:31.
24. Luke 12:48.
25. Myers, *Introduction to Type*, 16.

gain.[26] This will in turn allow them to become a benefit to others around them in their workplace, home life, and all other organizations where they are connected.

PERSONALITY EXTREMES FOR ESTPS

The personality extremes for ESTPs, using Jacob as a guide, are rather obvious. The quick-minded person who uses that analytical ability to master subjects (great and small) for their own selfish gain is the epitome of allowing their ESTP personality to go to an extreme. They can use their engaging Extroverted nature to speak to people with boldness and magnetism.[27] They are often charming, and people who do not waste time with minor decisions or conundrums; they can quickly move on toward the attainment of their goal. Their Sensing preference allows them to take in information in a straightforward manner which they also analyze for what it is and not for what they want it to be.

The best (or possibly the worst if taken to extremes) attribute of the ESTP personality type is that they are able to leave things and situations open-ended, since they are quick and adaptable kinetic learners. As a result of their Perceiving preference, they will work a situation or a scheme almost to completion before they decide how the outcome should look. When they combine this patient, open-ended approach to organizing schemes with their ability to "fix it from here," the ESTP who has allowed their personality type to go to a negative extreme works that solution to the end, without anticipating a definitive or set outcome, in order to glean maximum benefit for the ESTP. They are not disappointed if they did not get everything that they wanted going into a negotiation because they did not lock themselves into one set outcome, as would some of their Judging preference cousins. They don't decide what "should" or "must" be done in order for them to consider something a win.[28] They just wait to see the outcome, remembering what they initially desired when they entered into the negotiation. As long as they get the equivalent of their Rachel, they are willing to adjust to anything to get her. The ESTP must learn to use their powers for the benefit of all as opposed to using them to exclusively benefit themselves.

26. See Rom 12:1.

27. Myers, *Introduction to Type,* 16.

28. Myers, *Introduction to Type,* 16.

CONNECTIONS FOR ESTPS

The Extroverted manner in which the ESTPs relate to and interact with their world is connected to the Perceiving preference that they use to organize and make sense of their world. ESTPs like to take in information in a straightforward, no-nonsense format using their Sensing preference. That Sensing preference, regarding the storage and retrieval of information, is used to inform the ESTP's Thinking preference and decision-making function. We can learn a lot from these connections.

Connections Between The E-P Functions

ESTPs use their E-P connection to their advantage as relating to their overall personality type. They use their Extroverted nature regarding how they engage people in their world to help them to become the first round draft choice for all of the good teams. They are very adaptable people who can learn most processes very quickly.[29] Functioning at their best, they make everyone around them better, by ensuring that everyone is fully engaged in the process or activity. However, they can simultaneously make people feel better for having the Extroverted ESTP around.

When they figure things out and make the system or family operate more efficiently and effectively, they become invaluable members of every team. They also use their Perceiving preference to help the entire team to stay loose and not function too rigidly. They leave an open-ended conclusion to every project and task. This provides balance for the other I-J or E-J combinations who are members of the team by reminding them to also stay loose and allow things to play out to their conclusion. As long as you keep your goals in mind, the Perceiving preference ESTP would say, don't sweat the small stuff but just stay on target.

Connections Between The S-T Functions

The well-balanced ESTP personality type works seamlessly when they use their S-T connections in concert with the full ESTP personality type and use these connections for the common good. Their Sensing preference allows them to gather and store information, which they employ and apply to their natural tendency to repeat a trial and error process

29. Myers, *Introduction to Type*, 9–10.

many times without frustration. Following the repeated attempts, they store the information gleaned from each trial via their Sensing function, in order to advance their kinetic learning process.[30]

They use the infomation they gathered from the repeated attempts to inform them when they arrive at the point when they must make the best decision, via their Thinking function. This S-T connection was used by Jacob to figure out how to steal the best sheep from Laban's flock for himsel, and thereby become independently wealthy, while continuing to work for Laban by managing both his and Laban's herds of sheep.[31]

GROWTH OPPORTUNITIES AND THREATS AS AN ESTP

The Threats to growth as relative to the ESTP's personality type are focused on the idea of remembering to remain vigilant about submitting everything to God (if the ESTP is of a biblical worldview).[32]

ESTPs have immense talent and patience and can wait a situation out like no other personality type. They can be loveable, engaging, and endearing because of their Extroverted nature which helps them to display all of their other gifts and talents. They are good people to have around because they are such quick and adaptable learners.[33]

But ESTPs can easily become selfish, using these gifts to satisfy their personal wants and desires. They remain quite capable of becoming a welcomed and highly valued member of any team. That is, unless the team learns that the ESTP is not actually working toward achieving the team's goals as much as they are working toward achieving the ESTP's own. Their sentiment in these situations is: "If the team happens to benefit, great, but if not, that's fine too! Maybe even better." They presuppose that there is a little Machiavelli in all of us.

Personally, I want all of us to have a lot of Christ in us! If the ESTP is able to remain committed and submitted in all of their ways and activities, they can serve as a tremendous asset to every team, because based on their personality portrait they are usually a welcomed member.[34]

---

30. Myers, *Introduction to Type*, 9–10.

31. Gen 30:25–43.

32. See Ps 37:4; Prov 3:6.

33. Myers, *Introduction to Type*, 16.

34. See Prov 3:6.

10

ISTP: Elijah the Prophet

ELIJAH THE PROPHET

THE STORY OF ELIJAH the prophet begins in 1 Kings 17 and his journey concludes with him being taken away in a chariot of fire in 2 Kings 2. He demonstrates the traits of one with an ISTP personality.

Elijah spent a lot of time alone with God. He declared a rainless famine in Israel, and then was directed by God to hide near a brook called Kerith.[1] He stayed there until he was told by God to go to a widow's house in the town of Zarephath to stay with her and her son.[2] Elijah was generally known for living alone in the wilderness or hanging out with just one or two other people. He was an Introvert.

He was also a realist. He knew that after he performed the miracle of calling down fire from heaven to burn up an altar and sacrifice that the queen would want to kill him. He decided to go and hide himself rather than to face her wrath.[3] One can question the conclusion that he reached, because after all God had just stopped the rain from falling and sent down fire from heaven to burn up an altar, all at Elijah's behest. So what would make Elijah think that God would turn around and allow the queen to kill him?

1. 1 Kgs 17:2.

2. 1 Kgs 17:9–24.

3. 1 Kgs 18:40; 19:1–4.

Nevertheless, he used deductive reasoning to conclude that the queen would not at all be happy with him for showing up her prophets of Baal and then killing those prophets after their god did not answer. So he hid. Based on this incident and another where God had to reassure him that the soldiers sent by the same queen's son (now the king) would not be able to kill him and he could safely go with them,[4] Elijah may have allowed his Sensing preference (regarding the gathering and interpretation of straightforward information) to go to a bit of an extreme. However, throughout his life he remained flexible and adaptable.

This flexibility extended to travel. Elijah traveled from the brook Kerith to the widow's house. He also traveled following the altar experience, he traveled from hiding in the wilderness to searching for God's voice, he traveled to anoint the future kings of Syria and Israel as well as his successor Elisha, and finally he traveled to heaven in a chariot of fire in a whirlwind.[5] That's flexibility, folks! Elijah was an ISTP.

ELIJAH'S INTROVERSION PREFERENCE

Elijah appeared to be a man that drew strength from his inner world and from his alone time with God, as Introverts do. He went to hide himself from the queen after killing all of the prophets of Baal and calling down fire from heaven in order to prove that his God, who had sent the fire, was the only God in Israel.[6]

Based on all accounts, Elijah appeared to be a private man. He was sent to live with a widow and her son at the direction of the Lord, after the provisions which he received at Kerith dried up and the raven that God commanded to bring him food stopped coming.[7] Otherwise it is said of Elijah that he lived most of his life in the wilderness. Not that being alone is the only requirement of Introversion, but being alone with God or in a one-on-one setting are definitely signs. Introverts prefer interactions with fewer people.

He also spent many years in one-on-one interactions with his successor and mentee, the prophet Elisha.[8] Elijah trained him to become a

4. 2 Kgs 1:1–17.

5. 1 Kgs 19:1–21.

6. 1 Kgs 18:16–19:4.

7. 1 Kgs 17:1–24.

8. 1 Kgs 19:15–2; 2 Kgs 2:1–12.

prophet in Israel. Elijah was also the leader of all of the remaining sons of the prophets spread throughout Israel.[9] During his alone time, he drew strength from the Lord and had many one-on-one conversations with the Lord.

At one point, Elijah was quite discouraged after calling down fire from heaven. I guess he felt that he did all of that and his reward (not that he was looking for one) was that Jezebel promised to have his head on a platter by morning for killing all of her prophets. He was hungry, exhausted, and alone in the wilderness. He was ready to die.[10]

The angel of the Lord came to him and fed him. The angel gave him something to drink and then provided Elijah with additional travel instructions. By the time the journey was over, he knew he had to anoint the new kings of Syria and Israel. He also knew that there were seven thousand people in Israel who still served his God, which encouraged him. Finally, he learned that he was supposed to anoint his eventual successor, Elisha.

Elijah was encouraged and strengthened by God. After these events and revelations he was able to continue to serve as prophet in Israel. But most of his time, when he was not taunting the prophets of Baal, performing miracles in front of them, or speaking to the Israelites about repentance, was spent reflecting and interacting only with God. Elijah was an Introvert.

ELIJAH'S SENSING PREFERENCE

Elijah understood all too well the reality of his current circumstances. He had the ability to process information as a Sensing person. He asked God to shut the heavens from raining, but he also knew that God would provide for him.[11] God provided a running brook in the middle of a famine as well as food brought by a raven (I think that God could have asked a Steeler to bring him the food rather than a dirty bird Raven, but I digress).

Elijah knew that in order to demonstrate for all of Israel that they must stop worshiping idols and return their affections and allegiance to Jehovah, he would have to put on a big show. So he called 450 prophets of

9. 1 Kgs 19:18.

10. 1 Kgs 18:16–40; 19:1–21.

11. 1 Kgs 17:1–9.

the idol Baal to a mountain. After he allowed Baal's prophets to try to call down fire from their god to burn the sacrifices on the altar, it was Elijah's turn. He had the people wet the entire altar (wood, meat, and all) with gallons of water. Elijah then called down fire from heaven. He knew that the Lord would respond.[12] He used his knowledge and personal relationship with the Lord to his advantage on many occasions to perform many different and might works for the Lord in Israel. Elijah was a Sensing person.

ELIJAH'S THINKING PREFERENCE

Elijah knew, because he understood the Lord via their close interpersonal relationship, that the fire he called down from heaven would easily consume the drenched altar. He employed deductive reasoning as he was a reasonable and Thinking prophet of God. At times, his deductive logic, based on his straightforward, Sensing preference interpretation of the information available to him (which influenced his thoughts about situations) led him to the wrong conclusion. However, he always employed a causal approach in regards to decision-making.

For some reason, probably because of the toll that the great miracles he performed had taken on him, Elijah became bitterly discouraged after the incident with the altar. I would argue that he arrived at the wrong conclusion, although he made no final decisions regarding his conclusion. There was no way that God would let him get killed by Queen Jezebel after having served the Lord so faithfully. Elijah later learned that his work as a prophet in Israel was clearly not finished. But the logic and approach that he used to arrive at his conclusion were reasonable. He reasoned that because he had killed her prophets, Queen Jezebel would definitely be hunting to kill him, not to mention the fact that she said that she wanted to kill him for his act against her rule. Elijah demonstrated that Thinking and reasoning, without the additional benefit of incorporating all available information, specifically his knowledge of God, can lead to the wrong conclusion.

Thankfully, God comforted Elijah and preempted his actions, before he could make any rash decisions based on his interpretation of the information in available to him at the time. This is an example of allowing the Sensing preference to go to an extreme. He would also mix this

12. 1 Kgs 18:16–40.

information with some understandable emotional responses in order to reach his at times incorrect conclusions.

ELIJAH'S PERCEIVING PREFERENCE

In 2 Kings 1, Elijah had quite an interesting encounter with the messenger of King Ahaziah. Ahaziah was the son of King Ahab, Jezebel's husband. The Lord sent Elijah to the temple of Baal-Zebub with a message because Ahaziah had been injured. After the injury, Ahaziah sought a false idol's advice on whether or not he would recover.[13] God sent Elijah to question Ahaziah's decision to go to the false idol instead of Jehovah. When the king heard that Elijah was at the temple of Baal-Zebub, waiting on him with a message from God, the king sent his captain and fifty soldiers after Elijah. Elijah sat at the top of a hill and called down fire from heaven to burn up the soldiers. This happened a second time with a second captain and fifty new soldiers. The third captain who was sent out took a different approach. He begged Elijah not to burn him up with fire (a wise request, indeed). The Lord again comforted Elijah by telling him that it would be all right. Elijah could go and meet face-to-face with Ahaziah without burning people up this time. He would be safe.

Elijah likely considered what Jezebel, the queen mother at this time, wanted to do to him after their last encounter regarding the prophets of Baal.[14] So he did not want to go with the soldiers to meet with her son. This was how Elijah decided to organize his response to the circumstances transpiring in his world. But at the Lord's direction, he was flexible and open to change.

He went with the third captain to meet with King Ahaziah. At that meeting, Elijah told Ahaziah that he would die. Ahaziah died,[15] but Elijah allowed himself and his plans to preserve his own life to remain flexible. He allowed himself to submit to the direction of God and followed those directions each time God gave them to him. Elijah Perceived that he could organize his response to his world in a different way, according to God's plan, in order to achieve the desired outcomes.

13. 2 Kgs 1:1–17.
14. 1 Kgs 19:1–4.
15. 2 Kgs 1:17.

ISTP

Elijah was flexible and allowed the Lord to lead him in everything that he did. He was intolerant of idol worship but able to find workable solutions to every incident of idol worship and resulting conflict with the Israelite monarchy. He rectified the situations with God's help to a favorable outcome designed to guide the children of Israel back to Jehovah. Elijah identified the worship of idols as the real issue and enemy in Israel. Jezebel, Ahab, Ahaziah, and Jehoram were just symptoms of the real problem in Israel. Elijah recognized and fought against the issue of idol worship in Israel all of his life.

Finally, it can easily be stated that Elijah valued efficiency. He called down miraculous and targeted strikes that were designed to change the hearts, minds, and worship of Israel. Elijah was an ISTP.

ISTP: THE PRAGMATICS

APPLICATIONS FOR ISTPS

ISTP is my proverbial "bottle of root beer" personality type. Root beer feels like it has been around forever. The different versions taste relatively the same; it is consistent and never lets you down. It usually hits the spot. It is a reliable bottle of soda (or pop if you are from Pittsburgh). Some brands even call it "Old-Fashioned Root Beer." However, root beer comes with one warning to the wise: please do not shake it up or it will explode all over your face when you open it up.

ISTPs like Elijah are no-nonsense people relative to the expression of their personality. They take in data or information using their Sensing preference. ISTPs assimilate that information in the same straightforward manner. They prefer to deal with what is on paper or what is directly in front of them.[16] They are practical realists.

They do not want you to present them with a bunch of abstract or theoretical concepts. But if they are placed in a position within an organization or unit where they can focus on and do their job, they will "hit the spot" almost every time just like the bottle of root beer. They do not like to waste a lot of time on meaningless chatter.

They are probably the ones who bring the meeting to a swift conclusion, generally by summarizing the discussion. ISTPs usually summarize

16. Myers, *Introduction to Type*, 22.

and close the meeting in an annoyed (highly-carbonated) fashion. After the meeting is over, they go off to their Introverted corner and complete the work that they were assigned to complete during the meeting.

They are the company's computer troubleshooter and quick-fix problem solver.[17] If you need someone to dig into the BIOS (basic input/output system) of your computer and try to fix a more abstract issue, they are not your person. But if the "little pointer thingy" keeps disappearing, they are your person. "When in doubt, pull the plug out," is well within their arena of mastery.

However, if they are placed in an uncomfortable arena for their personality type for extended periods of time, they start hiding and putting off the issues and concerns that they face.[18] ISFPs do this because they just love to stay on task and on message.

ISFPs generally like to avoid their emotional side as often as possible. However, when someone comes by and "shakes them up," watch out! They will spray out all of the things that they stored up inside in one rather large explosion.[19] It is an explosion that they will typically regret because they do not like their emotional side, which is why the bubbles and pressure started to build inside of them in the first place.

One of my favorite counseling examples is one that I made up about washing dishes. I originally used it with a friend back when I was in undergrad (I wonder if she was an ISTP?). She was under a lot of pressure which was mounting and building on the inside. She discussed the problems with me when I noticed that she was looking troubled. She had some family issues occurring with her parents back at home, as I remember. She was likely facing issues relating to school as well. She sang on the university choir, which also doubled as the church choir, and was our fearless section leader in the tenor section (I called her the "whole" tenor section). She probably had some other things occurring that I cannot remember.

Speaking metaphorically, I told her that her problems were piling up as if she had been stacking dishes in a sink and not washing them for a few weeks. I said, if you ate off of a plate every night for dinner and stacked that plate in the sink but did not wash it, and the next day you did the same thing, and repeated this for approximately two weeks, then if I

17. Myers, *Introduction to Type,* 22.

18. Myers, *Introduction to Type,* 22.

19. Myers, *Introduction to Type,* 22.

asked you what you ate for dinner last Wednesday; would you be able to go back to last Wednesday's plate and tell me by looking at that plate what you ate for dinner that night?

She of course said no. She could not tell because everything in the sink had run together. She had turned the faucet on at least once or twice during the two-week period (maybe she ran out of silverware). The water would have caused much of the food on the plates to run together and she would never know what she ate a week and a half ago.

Hopefully you are not so extreme that even if you are an open-ended Perceiving type, you will wash the dishes before the two-week period has ended. Hey, don't question my counseling examples, they may seem strange but they work.

My advice to her was that she must wash each dish as they came in, thus temporarily taking her from a Perceiving preference person to a Judging preference person by habit in this area of her life. However, I would never try to get her or anyone to permanently leave their personality preference, not even back then. The reason that I asked her to engage this exercise was related to her memory and current dilemma. She had to begin to unlayer each issue while she could still recognize it.

However, at this point the dishes are already dirty; she needed to start at the top and begin to work her way down to the bottom. By doing this she would clear up each issue, at least as well as she could remember it, by taking those issues one by one and leaving them with God. She would be able to remember the stuff on top much better than she would remember what she had eaten and then shoved to the side in her memory or psyche two weeks ago. She would more easily be able to get the top plates really clean. But she would have to work a little harder at the ones near the bottom, because they had been sitting there for a while and the food would be caked-on and crusty. Finally, I told her to slide over to visit the other preference, relative to how you organize and make sense of your world. I told her to begin to adopt the habits of a Judging preference person, although she may not have been of that specific personality preference zone.

I was a marketing major back then, but I believed that I had (and still have) a gift! I told her to wash the plates (or take care of her concerns) from then on as they came in each day. She could do this by taking care of all of her concerns in the order that they occurred.[20] If she did this, she

20. See Ps 55:22.

would not get this build-up of pressure that needed to explode, similar to my ISTP bottle of root beer.

Developing As An ISTP

I am going to pick up that little lesson on the ISTPs here this section. My point to my student in the previous section was that she needed to face each issue as it presented itself in order to continue to grow. But more immediately, this would help her to relieve her current backlog of mounting pressure and help her to avoid an accumulation of such deeply troubling concerns in the future by dealing with one as they presented themselves in need of attention. In other words, she needed to wash each of the dishes as they were used.

ISTPs are quite proficient and capable people as long as they are able to "keep it simple, smart-person." I prefer the acronym be expressed in this way as opposed to how it is typically expressed. However, when ISTPs allow things to build up inside they end up having to face uncertainty in present situations. Ambiguity requires a heightened amount of iNtuitive thought in regards to the abstract concepts, which creates tension in the ISTP who isn't experienced in the use of iNtuitive thought. This causes in turn an emotional build-up on the inside of the ISTP.[21] When this build-up occurs as a result of what they shoved in to the drawer because they did not want to deal with it immediately, they may explode.

I believe that God is there for all of us, whether or not you choose to embrace that belief system. Many believe that Jesus is seated next to the Father on his right-hand side, constantly praying and interceding for us.[22] But we have to take our cares and concerns to him because he is concerned about our well-being.[23] However, I also believe that God will not move in our situations unless we ask. My little dish-washing example is not exclusively able to be used with ISTPs, but their particular personality type needs to be mindful of this conundrum because they could easily fall into this trap.

Other points for ISTPs that will help them to grow and develop, relate to becoming overly focused on receiving information in one set

21. Myers, *Introduction to Type*, 22.

22. Rom 8:34.

23. 1 Pet 5:7.

format.[24] There are times and circumstances where God tests our limits. He wants to stretch us such that we become a better, more well-rounded, and more useful person to the kingdom. Therefore, if you do not like abstract theoretical concepts like most ISTPs do not, then he will likely present you with a situation where you have to use your ability to understand what cannot be easily discerned for the ISTP.

ISTPs may have to go and ask an iNtuitive for assistance instead of being able to get into their routine, go directly to their corner, and troubleshoot. They are comfortable helping others if they are well-balanced. But they are not as comfortable when they have to ask for help with things that do not fit their program. They are also uncomfortable with things that do not readily make sense to them because they are more concrete by nature.[25] If they have a biblical worldview and choose to keep walking with God like Enoch, they will continue to grow closer to God, remain more stress-free, and become more comfortable with multiple sensory inputs.[26]

PERSONALITY EXTREMES FOR ISTPS

We have spent some time discussing the potential negative impacts for ISTPs when they allow their personality to go to an extremely negative place. But if we explore those extremes by individual preference zone we can understand that when the four come together, the ISTP can end up in a place where they are under pressure and ready to explode.

The ISTP's Introverted nature means they are an internal processor of information; that is, information is received via their Sensing or information-gathering preference, enabling them to function as good problem-solvers. They are quite adept at fixing things when the information is presented to them in a straightforward manner so that they understand and can digest that information.

But if they are asked to look for "the thing behind the thing" as their iNtuitive cousins do, they enter an uncomfortable place. Their decisions will not be crafted as they are accustomed to rendering them using their Thinking function. They prefer: "see problem, fix problem." They

---

24. Myers, *Introduction to Type*, 22.

25. Myers, *Introduction to Type*, 22.

26. See Gen 5:21–24; Heb 11:5–6.

operate in a logical and progressive fashion similar to a computer.[27] Good information comes in and good information goes out. However, if bad, mysterious, or incomplete information comes in, the ISFPs can become uncomfortable, and then something not so good comes out.

Their Perceiving function allows them to work through a problem to undetermined conclusion. But their Perceiving function is their least dominant preference zone when combined with the others. As all four preference zones combine to make up one ISFP, and they are presented with a challenge or scenario where things are not input or presented in a clear manner, they may not allow themselves the room to continue to function as the team troubleshooter. Everyone on the team usually becomes accustomed to the ISTP serving in their role as the helpful troubleshooter. They are accustomed to going to them for help with general concerns. It is difficult on the team when the ISTP allows themselves to go to an extreme end of their personality profile because that means a valued member is temporarily out of position.

CONNECTIONS FOR ISTPS

The Introverted manner in which the ISTPs relate to and interact with their world is connected to the Perceiving preference that they use to organize and make sense of their world. ISTPs like to take in information in a straightforward, no-nonsense format using their Sensing preference. That Sensing preference, regarding the storage and retrieval of information within the ISTP, is used to inform the ISTP's Thinking preference and decision-making function. We can learn a lot from these connections.

Connections Between The I-P Functions

The connection between the Introverted function and the Perceiving function has not been discussed in enough detail. The Introverted function causes ISTPs to be more comfortable in engaging people in a one-on-one format. Of course, similar to other Introverts, they are comfortable being alone and enjoying their internal thought processes. This makes them easy for one person to approach for the ISTP's help. Their ability to appear as a calming and steady hand when handling concerns also makes them the go-to person for assistance. When that Introverted

27. Myers, *Introduction to Type*, 22.

nature is combined with the Perceiving function that is used to organize and make sense of their world, this is an easy connection to describe. They troubleshoot so well because they have not predetermined the outcome, using their open-ended Perceiving preference.

Connections Between The S-T Functions

ISTPs make sense of their world based on the information that they have stored inside using their Sensing preference. They do not like to travel outside of their preferred comfort zones very often, but they are extremely competent when they are allowed to remain inside of their arena of expertise. This connection and the ISTP's comfort level depends greatly on the connections formed between their S-T preferences.

I do not want to present a negative picture of the ISTPs. They are the family troubleshooting expert.[28] Everyone needs someone who is reliable and steady. Hur in the Bible could have been an ISTP. He and Aaron gave Moses a rock to sit on and held his arms up so that Israel could win a battle with the Amalekites.[29]

ISTPs make the complex become simple. This is particularly useful to the other personality types when they face a problem that they simply cannot solve, yet they can feel inside that it must have a simple solution. ISTPs are always there to help in those instances. They can be most helpful in those cases because they process information in a straightforward manner using their Sensing preference. When the information seems complicated to others, it likely does not seem so complex to the ISTP because they can look at the information and process it through their analytical mind so that it becomes simple for them. They can also interpret that information for others and help them make a quality and sound decision because their Thinking preference, working in concert with their Sensing preference, allows the ISTP to present solutions in a very rational and logical format.

GROWTH OPPORTUNITIES AND THREATS AS AN ISTP

ISTPs can grow by being willing to steadily develop. They have a tendency to enjoy their routines and comfort zones (they function so very

---

28. Myers, *Introduction to Type*, 9–10.

29. Exod 17:8–16.

well within those comfort zones).[30] They do not like things that are not clearly presented to them, nor do they like being required to look into data that requires abstract thinking or is based on intricate theory. They can even begin to shut down when they are required to engage in a theoretical discussion. Remember when I told you who ends the meetings? This ISTP guy!

The Bible says that God walked with Adam in the garden in the cool of the day prior to the fall of man.[31] They had fellowship and communion as God designed. This could not occur again until after Jesus died for us, was resurrected, and ascended to heaven. Then the Holy Spirit, the comforter, was sent.[32]

ISTPs with a biblical worldview need to remember to take their long walks with Jesus and tell Him all about . . . everything. This will ensure that all of their plates remain clean. Thus they remain readily available to be of assistance when they are called upon by those who need their help and clear-minded input.

---

30. Myers, *Introduction to Type,* 22.

31. Gen 3:8.

32. Acts 2:1–41.

11

ENFJ: Habakkuk the Prophet

HABAKKUK THE PROPHET

THERE EXISTS LITTLE WRITTEN evidence that Habakkuk the prophet interacted with anyone other than God. This is true if you only use the book of Habakkuk as reference material. Since that is the modus operandi of this endeavor, I will not include additional materials as I prepare the analysis of Habakkuk's MBTI personality portrait. However, a closer examination of his concerns leads me to know that Habakkuk was an Extrovert and an ENFJ.

Habakkuk was deeply troubled over not only the plight of his Judean people but also the inequities that he perceived as existing in the world. Habakkuk was similar to Peter in the New Testament in that he spoke his mind.

He had no problem telling God how he felt about issues facing his people. He had no problem telling God that he was deeply disturbed about the fact that the evil Babylonians prospered while the Judeans suffered.[1] He revered the Lord, but he did not allow that to cause him to dismiss his inner turmoil about the things occurring in the world which he believed to be wrong. As an Extrovert he talked to God about the injustices that bothered him as often as they bothered him. He experienced no moment of pause while continuously taking his concerns to God until he received a satisfactory response.

1. Hab 1:2–4; 1:12–17; 2:1.

Habakkuk liked to gain a clear understanding before he went to serve the people as prophet. Although there is no written evidence that he spoke directly with the people as mentioned in his eponymous book, he constantly mentioned the plight of the people and his interactions with them in the form of service to them as a prophet in Judah.[2] Thus, he must have had no problem speaking to the people once he found out from God how the Lord was leading them.

He definitely looked to the future as an iNtuitive.[3] Habakkuk was also very compassionate and made decisions based in that compassion. He was very orderly, particularly when it came to positioning himself to hear from the Lord.[4] Habakkuk was an ENFJ.

HABAKKUK'S EXTROVERSION PREFERENCE

Habakkuk was an Extrovert. He was a prophet and a songwriter.[5] He often went to God with boldness on behalf of the people. He definitely preferred talking to God rather than writing out his thoughts.[6] However, he wrote at the direction of God, such as when he was told to write down the vision.[7]

He talked (the preferred method of communication common to most Extroverts) through all of his ideas with God. Many of his thoughts were really complaints about the treatment of the people of Judah, while his perception was that the Babylonians who would enslave them seemed to prosper.[8] He appeared to have an understanding of both local and world politics. He also learned by doing, as he climbed the tower to see the Lord's response, and specifically to see how the Lord would respond to his complaint (recorded in the previous chapter).[9]

Habakkuk took the initiative by presenting the issues of his heart and his concerns for his people's plight to the Lord.[10] He was quite expres-

2. Hab 1:3–4; 1:13–17.

3. Hab 1:17.

4. Hab 2:1.

5. Hab 3:19.

6. Hab 1:2, 4; 1:12–17; 2:1–2.

7. Hab 2:2.

8. Hab 1:2–4; 1:12–17.

9. Hab 2:1.

10. Hab 1:2–4; 1:12–17.

sive as he described metaphorically and literally the fact that, although there was no fruit growing on the vines in Judah and there were no cattle or livestock in the stalls in Judah, he would continue to rejoice in the Lord amid the poverty because God was his strength.[11] The rest of his prayer-song is quite eloquently written as well.[12] Habakkuk was an Extrovert.

HABAKKUK'S INTUITIVE PREFERENCE

Habakkuk was also an iNtuitive processor of information. He knew that the children of Judah were impoverished. He also knew that the Babylonians were thriving. He saw the connection as well as the inequality between the state of his nation in contrast with state of the Babylonian nation.[13] He believed that this was neither an adequate existence for the Judeans nor was it an acceptable circumstance for his people to endure without a clarifying explanation from God.

He did not see the situation getting any better, so he sought the Lord with diligence until he received answers that he could take to his people. He was inspired, as iNtuitive people are regarding information-gathering, to call to call on the Lord for help and continue to do so, trusting and believing that God would eventually supply him with the insight that he was requesting. God answered Habakkuk on a couple of occasions.[14] This diligence as well as a learned patience paid off: he received the answers that he sought.

On the second occasion when he discussed his concerns with God, Habakkuk climbed on a tower and said that he desired to "see" what God would say to him.[15] We all know that a person cannot "see" spoken words. However, Habakkuk used his iNtuitive preference as he attempted to gain some insight from God about the plight of his people. This was a creative way to describe his method of seeking the Lord for answers. He was inspired to gain clarity about the disparate states that existed between these two connected nations.

The lessons that he learned through his time spent seeking God helped Habakkuk to obtain the foundation that he needed to do his job

11. Hab 3:16–19.
12. Hab 3:1–15.
13. Hab 1:2–4; 1:12–17; 3:2.
14. Hab 1:5–11; 2:2–20.
15. Hab 1:12–17.

as prophet to the Judeans. Specifically, his time spent seeking God for information and revelation produced patience and diligence in his life. He had a need to receive clear instruction from God and he was determined to get answers.

He ultimately learned that the people who are justified by God must live by faith and not always by observable facts.[16] These were lessons that would help him as he took the vision of God to the people of Judah. Habakkuk was an INtuitive and insightful learner.

HABAKKUK'S FEELING PREFERENCE

Habakkuk was very empathetic. Modern-day vernacular might describe Habakkuk as a man who led with his heart. He was guided in his decisions to seek God as well as to discover the best way to serve his people as prophet. He served them through the use of compassion, empathy, and a desire for equitable justice.

He could not stand to see the wicked Babylonians prosper while his people suffered through poverty and lack.[17] The poverty and lack were a part of the chastening of the Lord toward the Judeans, but Habakkuk was determined to gain a clear understanding of the situation before deciding what he was going to say and do about the situation.[18] His conclusion was simple: I and the people have to trust the Lord, whether we are in poverty or during times when we have all that we need;[19] we Judeans will live by faith and trust in the Lord.[20] Habakkuk had a Feeling preference.

HABAKKUK'S JUDGING PREFERENCE

Habakkuk is the eponymous biblical book that he authored, thus the organization of the book, the circumstances that are described in his world, and the layout of the book are all of Habakkuk's conception. The design structure is demonstrative of how Habakkuk made sense of his world as prophet to the Judeans.

16. Hab 2:4.
17. Hab 1:2–4; 1:12–17; 3:2.
18. Hab 2:2.
19. Hab 3:16–19.
20. Hab 2:4; 17–19.

Habakkuk's second recorded time of complaining to the Lord about the plight of his people and then seeking the Lord's direction is described in Habakkuk 2:2–20. This passage describes how Habakkuk positioned himself to hear the voice of God. He said that he would climb up on his guard post and station himself on the lookout tower. He said that he would stay there and watch in order to "see" what God would say to him. He wanted to find out how God would respond to his complaints. He would then know how to organize the message that he would convey to his people.

God told him to write the vision down and make the writing clear,[21] place it on tablets so that anyone can read it, even someone running past the tablets or reading them on the run. God told Habakkuk that he and his people would have to be patient while waiting for the Lord to help them, but that in the end, if they were patient and systematic like Habakkuk, the vision would speak for itself and not lie.[22] However, they had to wait for the vision to manifest.

The processes that Habakkuk had to endure in order to find out what was in the Lord's heart regarding the Judeans were parallel to the processes that the Judeans would go through in order to discover the vision that God had for them in the future. God was using Habakkuk's Judging preference as an example in order to teach patient endurance to the Judeans as they desired to see God deliver them from their impoverished state. Both Habakkuk and the Judeans had to be organized and methodical regarding the way that they would have to live in order to achieve the desired results. Habakkuk had to use an iNtuitive preference approach to obtain information from God. Then, both he and the Judeans would have to use a Judging preference approach in order to achieve their desired outcome, which was to see the manifested vision of the Lord for the Judeans.

Habakkuk had to learn to be patient while he was waiting to understand the Lord. The people of Judah had to learn to be patient while waiting for God's vision and provision for them as a people to manifest. Habakkuk was of a Judging preference and God was encouraging the Judeans to employ some of the same Judging preference personality traits.

21. Hab 2:2.

22. Hab 2:3.

ENFJ

Habakkuk was a determined leader and a compassionate advocate for his Judean people. Habakkuk also demonstrated a tremendous empathy for them. He was very responsible; he responded to their needs and plight by going to the only one that he knew had the information that they needed: the Lord. He believed that the Judean people, although they were in the situation because of their own disobedience, did not deserve to be abandoned by God or treated as a people who were inferior to the Babylonians.[23]

He was definitely open to whatever answers God gave him. But he was determined to receive those answers. Habakkuk was a revolutionary thinker; he climbed up on that guard tower and positioned himself to see and hear from God. His diligence was a catalyst for the growth and development of his people. He demonstrated inspiring leadership in the execution of his quest to seek God for his vision for Judah. Habakkuk was an ENFJ.

ENFJ: THE EMPATHIZERS

APPLICATIONS FOR ENFJS

My former pastor once asked a room full of us college students, "What business are we in?" This was primarily a ministry made up of college students and recent graduates, with some campus faculty members as well as community members also a part of the church. I may have been a deacon at that point as well as a graduate student who had returned after finishing my undergraduate degree. I do not remember exactly when he asked. We all gave the deepest answer that we could think of. He then told us that "we are in the people business."

ENFJs are also in the people business. They like to encourage and aid others in their effort to reach their personal goals. They are warm and engaging people who have an internal determination to ensure that the people who they are assisting reach their full potential.[24] ENFJs are equally as adept at identifying what a person is capable of accomplishing as they are at figuring out the best path for them to take in order for

23. Hab 1:12–17.

24. Myers, *Introduction to Type*, 14–29.

them to reach their desired destination, via their iNtuitive, information-gathering preference. They epitomize the slogan, "People first."

Very few personality types enable a person to be equally adept at leading and following, but ENFJs fit this description because they are so attuned to the feelings of the people. They use their Extroverted nature to engage lots of people. Then their Feeling preference helps them to empathize with all of the people in the organization. They function as people who can rally the troops and build a nexus of consensus among the group. This ability allows the group to achieve a commonly agreed upon goal. ENFJs do not force their teammates to accept their point of view because that would emotionally damage "their people." They enjoy group brainstorming sessions and make sure that everyone is heard, so that everyone feels affirmed when they leave that meeting.

I mentioned earlier in this book that there is a noteworthy difference between leaders and managers. Both are necessary if the group or organization desires to fulfill their mission. Leaders, in short, pay a lot of attention to the people. However, if not in balance, leaders can pay too much attention to how people feel. They can err on the side of attempting to ensure that everyone feels happy when the truth is that many people enter an organization or a marriage being unhappy about a great many things, things that have nothing to do with the organization or union. Then, their personality extremes further complicate their ability to successfully function with emotional balance within an organization.

ENFJs, when they are not in balance, can become this type of leader, even if they are not the primary leader in that organization. They can begin to approach life like Absalom, King David's son.[25] At some point, because he was already an appointed leader as one of the princes in Israel, likely an Extrovert, and a very handsome young man, Absalom used his people skills to subvert King David's rule and usurp the leadership of Israel by telling the people what they wanted to hear. He could have been an out of balance ENFJ.

The point is that ENFJs and all poorly-balanced leaders can use their ability to relate to people and forget all about the systems and purpose of the organization. Leaders lead people, and managers manage things, as the saying goes. However, those who are good at being managing-leaders will learn to attune themselves to the needs of the people, and they will

25. See 2 Sam 15.

keep in mind that the organization has goals. They will also keep in mind that people are there to help the organization achieve those stated goals.

Thus, a good and well-balanced managing-leader will not focus too much attention on either the people or the organization. Rather they will remain in balance relative to the people, as well as to the mission of the organization. Similarly, ENFJs need to attend to ensuring that they do not allow themselves to pay so much attention to the people that they forget that the people, including the ENFJ, are there to bring everyone together as one in order to achieve the overarching mission and goals of the organization.

Developing As An ENFJ

ENFJs should learn to visit their Thinking preference from time to time in order to continue to properly develop. ENFJs can be used in a capacity that is sorely missing in many organizations. For example, people walk around church organizations presenting their best face to each other. But very few people, including the author of this book, like to allow people to truly see the real person behind the mask. ENFJs have an ability to see the "thing behind the thing," using their iNtuitive, information-gathering preference. ENFJs are also naturally empathetic people because they make many decisions based out of their Feeling preference.

Physical healing is much easier to achieve than healing that needs to occur in a person's emotions. People carry a lot of damage, scars, and old wounds inside that most others cannot see. I have a given ability to feel the hurts of some specific people, those who, I believe, God chooses to allow me to connect to with in this way. Therefore, I can help those people, if they allow me to and want my help, by using that empathy. I am able to do this even though I am of a Thinking decision-making preference. I guess I visit the "Feeling restaurant," by gifting and grace, quite often.

Similarly, the ENFJs need to walk over to their Thinking preference with some regularity in order to ensure that their Feeling preference does not get them out of balance. If they are imbalanced in their personality type because they are not using logic, detached reason, and objective analytics regarding their decision-making function even as it relates to hurting and broken people, they will not be as effective as they need to be when they attempt to help those people.

As I have seen on far too many occasions, they may get swept up in the emotion of the story that they are being told by the person who they are attempting to help. This will cause them to lose sight of the fact that they are only hearing one side of this story from one hurting person's perspective and point of view. Extreme ENFJs could become overly empathetic, as opposed to remaining objective when helping people.

ENFJs need to remember to gather all required information. Then they can use their iNtuitive preference to look into the information and try to discover some hidden concepts that may be present behind the information. But when the time comes to help the person in front of them make critical life decisions, it is better to be detached and objective.

Empathy helps us to make connections with people. It drives the ENFJ's passion to ensure that people who are willing to achieve emotional healing (or go through "a corrective emotional experience") complete their desired journey. But only through objective analysis applied to detached decision-making, as their Thinking preference cousins employ, can they truly present the person that they are helping with every opportunity to receive transformational emotional healing.

As a final thought in this section: most people do not press toward the mark and uncover all of their emotionally-damaged roots, certainly not to the extent required in order to reach complete emotional healing.[26] Complete healing is difficult to attain. But all things are possible.[27]

We who help others hope and pray that everyone will stay with the process long enough and allow the Lord to dig deeply enough into their emotional reservoir in order to heal everything that is hurting inside. The healing is already available for you.[28] You just have to be willing and choose to walk with God until you reach the goal.[29]

PERSONALITY EXTREMES FOR ENFJS

Personality extremes relevant to the ENFJs derive from the concept that the ENFJ needs to remain in balance. Habakkuk was quite driven to hear from God on behalf of his people.[30] He needed answers and he was deter-

26. See Mark 9:23.
27. Phil 3:14.
28. See Isa 53:5; Matt 15:26.
29. See Gen 5:24.
30. Hab 1–2.

mined to get them. However, if Habakkuk had ignored the larger point that God was trying to communicate through Habakkuk to the people of Israel, then he would never have received the answers that he sought. God was telling the children of Israel that they were going through their present struggles because of their disobedience. Habakkuk knew that they had been disobedient and that was the reason for their issues. However, Habakkuk also knew that they were God's children. Thus, he wondered if they truly deserved to be treated as second-class citizens while the Babylonians prospered.[31]

Habakkuk had a balanced perspective. He did not allow his empathy for his people to cause him to lose sight of the fact that they were being punished as a result of their disobedience. Similarly, ENFJs have to avoid personality extremes that may take them to a place where they lose sight of the big picture, as a result of allowing themselves to become overly attentive to their empathy and compassion for the hurting.

CONNECTIONS FOR ENFJS

The Extroverted manner in which the ENFJs relate to and interact with their world is connected to the Judging preference that they use to organize and make sense of their world. ENFJs like to take in information and interpret that information using their iNtuitive function in order to find abstract concepts behind the information. That iNtuitive preference, regarding the storage, interpretation, and retrieval of information within the ENFJ, is used to inform the ENFJ's Feeling preference and decision-making function. We can learn a lot from these connections.

Connections Between The E-J Functions

The connections between the E-J preferences for the ENFJ allows them to successfully engage those people who they would like to help. The connection also allows them to organize that presumptive assistance in a fashion that will enable the person who they are helping to reach their goal.

ENFJs could be attempting to gain consensus within a whole room full of people who they want or need to decide upon a specific list of objectives that the company needs to agree to pursue, or they could be

31. Ps 2:1–4; Hab 1:1–4, 12–17.

helping people with more personal concerns. But the ENFJ is excellent at engaging people and then helping them to make sense of their world as they move toward their desired outcomes.

Connections Between The N-F Functions

The N-F connected functions relative to the ENFJs personality are the nerve center and driving force behind how ENFJs operate. ENFJs are "people-people," meaning they enjoy engaging and helping people.

They perform this vital function using their iNtuition to look behind the clearly presented information in order to discover the real problems as well as the as-yet-undiscovered solutions. Because the ENFJ is so good at relating to people, they create a natural bond with many people without looking like they are being a phony. That is how true empathy works.

Empathy helps to make people comfortable around ENFJs. Compassion also helps the ENFJ appear as sincerely interested in the person as possible. Once the connection is successfully established and trust is gained by the well balanced ENFJ, they can work with people using their Feeling preference to help them to make appropriate and at times life-altering decisions.

GROWTH OPPORTUNITIES AND THREATS AS AN ENFJ

Threats to the growth opportunities relate to the ENFJ's focus and their attention. ENFJs have to press toward the ultimate goal.[32] While doing this, they must also remain vigilant regarding their ability to remain balanced. They must also refrain from becoming too emotionally connected to a person or to a situation.

Broadening this discussion on how ENFJs can properly help organizations rather than exclusively focusing on aiding specific individuals, ENFJs are required to employ the same focus, as related to avoiding the pitfall of becoming imbalanced. I have worked in organizations where the people focused too much attention on the emotional well-being of the employees.

This was particularly problematic while working at a university as an administrative faculty member, because we were all supposed to be objectively implementing policies and procedures that would benefit

32. See Phil 3:12.

the educational outcomes of our students. Many of the people I worked with were far more concerned about helping to improve the national or international ranking of the specific college within the overarching university structure in order to later impress their peers at the next conference. Others wanted to keep the exclusively teaching and research faculty members happy. This was generally and blithely done to the detriment of the procedures required to ensure that the students under our care were learning what they needed to learn, and that we were equipping and enabling them to graduate as well as to ultimately become productive citizens. That was our goal, as well as the stated mission of almost all Colleges and Universities: to educate and develop students.

However, we were not all working toward that end. Some people wanted to make sure that all of the faculty members in the room from our department, or from other departments around campus who we worked with, felt good. Even if the decisions would negatively impact the students, here comes that feelings bus! Watching this occur quite often, I have learned that I got into this business because my first priority has always been, and always will be, the proper education and healthy development of my students.

I am fine with ensuring that my colleagues are also happy. But we all needed to function in a manner which also employs our Thinking preference. Thereby, we will all make decisions that will help us to reach our goal, which is always supposed to be student achievement and student success.

ENFJs need to remember to remain in balance by visiting their Thinking preference as often as possible. They also need to keep in check their empathetic heart associated with their Feeling preference. Please remember that your heart does not have a brain, and therefore you cannot use your heart or your "I feel . . ." statement, to guide your decisions. Finally, ENFJs, please always remember to move toward the true goal while also ensuring that everyone arrives at the destination safely, healthy and happy, as only ENFJs can.

12

INFJ: John, The Beloved Apostle

JOHN, THE BELOVED APOSTLE

IF THE APOSTLE PAUL, who we will discuss later, receives credit for writing the most books in the New Testament, John the beloved apostle has second place firmly in his grasp. John is mentioned in all four Gospels, the Acts of the apostles, and his eponymous books of 1, 2, and 3 John, as well as being the author of the book of the Revelation of Jesus Christ. Through the writings of and about John the beloved apostle, he demonstrates many of the traits often ascribed to the INFJ personality type.

John is one of my beloved Introverts as I described them earlier in this book. He demonstrates his Introvert preference by the sheer volume of his preferred method of communication, his completed writings. The book of Acts also records many instances where Peter and John were together, spreading the good news of Jesus Christ as they were commissioned by him to do.

The majority of the time, whether in front of the citizens of Jerusalem or in front of the high priests, Peter generally did most of the talking.[1] John however was the closest interpersonal friend and apostle of Jesus.[2] John referred to himself throughout his writings as the beloved apostle or as the disciple who Jesus loved. He was also an extraordinary leader as he demonstrated in later writings.

1. Acts 3:11; 4:5–7.
2. John 13:23–25.

John was allowed to lay his head on Jesus and ask questions such as who Jesus's betrayer was.[3] No other apostle appeared to share this same level of intimacy and special bond with Jesus. Jesus answers his question by identifying Judas Iscariot, the one who dipped his hand into the bowl at the same time as Jesus.[4] The obsessively clean and orderly perfectionist ENTJ in me is screaming inside as I write this: "Yuck, they dipped their hands into the bowl at the same time? For what, to wash them? What about germs?"

John was also given the responsibility of caring for Mary, Jesus's mother, by Jesus while he was hanging on the cross. Jesus was Mary's oldest son, as well as the Savior of the world. Jesus said: "Woman, here is your son." And to John, he said, "here is your mother."[5] In other words, Jesus was telling John and Mary that he was leaving and the nature of their relationship would soon drastically change. Jesus was further intimating to John and Mary that John his dear friend, and that not his brothers James and Jude, but John the beloved apostle would be placed by Jesus in the position of serving as the eldest son and caretaker of Mary. John had a tender heart.[6]

John focused on the future as he wrote the book of the Revelation of Jesus Christ, in which he was prophetically shown impending events. John and his biological older brother James, also an apostle, once asked Jesus if they could sit in the places of honor on each side of Jesus in the future when he came into his kingdom.[7] Jesus said that the seat of honor which they sought was not his to give away. When the other apostles heard about their request, they were angry with James and John. But John had a sense of future events. Through this incident and many others, he demonstrated the ability to focus on short-range and long-range plans. He had a desire to have things settled in order to avoid last-minute stress. He also had a clear sense of personal values, which dictated his acts as an apostle and his writings about Christ the king. John the beloved Introvert apostle was an INFJ.

3. John 13:22–26.

4. Matt 26:23.

5. John 19:25–27 (NIV).

6. 1 John 3:1–24; 4:7–19; 5:1–5.

7. Matt 10:2; Mark 10:35–41.

JOHN'S INTROVERSION PREFERENCE

Clearly John's preferred method of communication was writing as is the case with most of my beloved Introverts. John saw many visions which he described in the book of Revelation. He had a clear sense of the future. Jesus knew this was true of John because in Revelation 4, he told John to "Come up here and I will show you what take place after this."[8]

John drew strength from one-on-one encounters with Jesus. I am sure he honored Jesus's dying request to care for his mother and to be a son to her as Jesus himself had been. It is very significant to me that Jesus, as the oldest son of Mary and Joseph, selected John to fill this special role.[9]

John appeared to be a largely private person, preferring individual interpersonal encounters to speaking in front of crowds as Peter seemed to favor. John was also a humble man. In the Gospel of John, John never referred to himself as anything other than "The apostle (follower) who Jesus loved."[10] The reader is left to figure out who he was talking about.[11] In 2 and 3 John he refers to himself as "The Elder." The only time that I can find where John referred to himself by name was in the book of Revelation where he called himself Jesus's slave.[12] He was a humble and excellent leader, elder, pastor, and teacher as demonstrated in the books of 1, 2, and 3 John, but he performed these roles primarily through writing. John was a beloved Introvert and a slave of Jesus Christ.

JOHN'S INTUITIVE PREFERENCE

We have discussed John's inclination toward future possibilities as a personality trait shared with other iNtuitive preference persons. John was quite expressive and creative in writing. Read 1 John chapter 3; one of my favorite passages is where he describes real love as: that which occurs via true caring and genuine actions or deeds, not through spoken or written words nor via verbal expressions.[13] So many people need to learn what

8. Rev 4:1 (NIV).

9. John 19:25–27.

10. John 13:23; 13:25; 18:15; 19:26; 20:2; 21:7; 21:20.

11. John 21:24.

12. Rev 1:1.

13. 1 John 3:18.

real love is, in my experience. John understood real love. John taught his followers the true meaning of love.

The entire book of Revelation is an example of the fact that John trusted inspiration. Other examples are his work as an apostle (both in writing and via his acts), the miracles that he was used to perform, and his strength and inherent inspiration to endure the persecutions that he personally suffered. He suffered exile to the isle of Patmos, which is where it is recorded that he wrote the book of Revelation. Through John's interpersonal interactions with Christ on earth and as the risen Savior, John gathered his information directly from the source, Jesus. John was an iNtuitive information gatherer.

JOHN'S FEELING PREFERENCE

John was the epitome of an empathetic person, and I do not use that description lightly. I enjoy reading his writings and he is probably my favorite author in the Bible. He was compassionate and the way he employed that empathy enabled him to become the closest apostle and friend to Jesus.

Peter, James, and John were the three disciples who were closest to Jesus.[14] They were the ones who Jesus took on all of the big prayer missions. But of those three, John was interpersonally the closest to Jesus.[15] Jesus knew that he could trust John's heart. Thus, he could trust John's decision-making process and knew he would be the best one to care for Jesus's mother after he was gone.[16]

I believe that Jesus uses our personality traits to his advantage regarding callings and revelations. I believe that he uniquely made us and created us to be in the best position to receive what he would show us. At his leading we are to go out, make appropriate decisions, and perform the tasks associated with those God-inspired revelations.

This is exemplified in John. John was oriented toward future possibilities. He also demonstrated his imagination and his creativity primarily through his writings. John received many revelations directly from Jesus.

From caring for Jesus's earthly mother to serving as a slave to Jesus Christ, John epitomized the creation plan of God via personality traits.

14. See Matt 17:1; 26:37; Mark 5:37; 9:2; 13:3; 14:33; Luke 6:14; 8:51; 9:28; Gal 2:9.

15. John 13:23–25.

16. John 19:25–27.

John demonstrated that through his Feeling preference as well as through his INFJ personality, he was the man that God created to be the beloved apostle.

JOHN'S JUDGING PREFERENCE

Another example regarding how our personality works to allow us to become a part of the plan of Christ is shown through John's Judging preference. Read the book of Revelation: the first time that John heard the voice that sounded like a trumpet and saw the person who looked "like a Son of Man (Messiah)" speaking with that voice, he says that he, ". . . fell down at his feet like a dead man."[17] Then John repeats some combination of phrases, in this vain: "After this I saw, . . . I heard, and . . ." more than thirty times in the book of Revelation. He is quite expressive and descriptive in his responses to the "voice that spoke to me like a trumpet, saying . . ."[18]

Jesus, knowing that John was a methodical man, revealed things to him in a logical and progressive manner. John wrote them down as they were revealed. At the end of the book of Revelation, Jesus triumphed in victory. This was an example of John's method for organizing his world. I believe that Jesus knew that John organized and made sense of his world in this fashion. Therefore Jesus revealed things to John in the format that he could understand and relate to them. John conveys these revelations to his readers. John had a clearly expressed Judging preference.

INFJ

INFJs seek meaning, such as when John sought and then revealed what real love is to his readers. John sought interpersonally-connected relationships with Jesus and then with Mary his adopted mother who was also Jesus's mother.[19]

John spent much of 1 John, especially in chapters 2–5, discussing the motivations of others and why love was difficult for them to attain, achieve, and demonstrate. John was firmly committed to being an apostle and slave of Jesus Christ. He knew how he could best serve the kingdom

17. Rev 1:13, 17 (NASB).
18. Rev 4:1 (NRSV).
19. John 19:26–27.

of heaven as Jesus taught the kingdom to him and the other apostles during his time on earth. John received instruction in a logical and orderly fashion. Then he conveyed that information via his writings, as well as the potentially positive outcomes if the people learned to trust and employ Jesus's instructions. John was an INFJ.

INFJ: THE INSIGHTFUL ONES

APPLICATIONS FOR INFJS

I began the thought process regarding INFJs, who I greatly admire and with whom I identify very closely, by thinking that there really was not one word, descriptor, or metaphor that could be chosen to represent them as I have chosen with some of the other personality types. I use those words to help us to discover practical applications relative to the referenced personality type.

INFJs are a rare group. They are insightfully iNtuitive as they operate within their relationships. They can iNtuitively discern what people are saying, thinking, or feeling just by watching them. On top of that, they trust their gut instincts and insights fairly easily.[20] King David's seldom-discussed uncle could also exemplify this personality type.[21]

I prefer to think and say that they trust the God inside of them, who reveals those things to them, about other people, more readily than the other personality types. They are insightful, metaphorical, global thinkers, all wrapped up into one personality type.[22]

Another reason that I find them difficult to describe using simple metaphors is that you rarely find a group of people who can read people as well as the INFJs simply by placing them in a room. As Introverts, they are quite capable of reading people and do it all of the time, as I described about myself earlier in this book. INFJs are also simultaneously capable of taking what they have discovered about those people and converting that knowledge into a usable format. This allows them to decide how those gifts and talents may be used in order to most effectively advance the mission of an entire group, organization, or cause.

20. Myers, *Introduction to Type*, 19.

21. See 1 Chron 27:32.

22. Myers, *Introduction to Type*, 19.

INFJs are long-term planners.[23] All good organizations make short, medium, and long-term plans. The long-term plans are the plans that the group uses to project where the company is headed after at least five years of growth. INFJs can readily describe those long-term projections to others if they effectively employ all four aspects of their personality type.

It is no wonder that Jesus was so close to John the apostle and made him one of the true heads of the church at such a young age. John would be invaluable in that leadership role as the church, following the ascension of Christ, began to take shape as described in the book of Acts.[24]

We all need leaders, such as the 200 leaders of Issachar who understand with equal proficiency the organization as well as where it is mandated to advance in order to accomplish its mission.[25] We also need people who iNtuitively understand the people in the organization and how to put the people in the best positions to be used to their maximum capability. INFJs are just such people and they should employ all of those gifts and talents as often as possible, and employ them wherever God has placed the INFJs to help. People need to know what INFJs see and think.

Developing As An INFJ

When I was advising and teaching in the college of business at one of my university career stops, I used to describe some specific groups of my students as people who "work with their hearts." Some business majors want to become the typical Wall Street corporate titan. They appeared to my students in other majors as very coldhearted people. I had one student in my marketing class for non-business majors say that "I get a tension headache every time I walk into the business building." That is not to say that all or even most business majors are coldhearted. However, I would describe them as focused, driven, and quite goal-oriented. This often results in them not remembering to add enough warmth to their interactions while they are working toward the attainment of their larger goals.

INFJs can make excellent business majors because they are insightful and global thinkers. But I also believe that they fit the profile of people who like to "work with their hearts." You can place them in a large organization, but it should be a large nonprofit organization or they will not be

23. Myers, *Introduction to Type*, 19.

24. See Acts 1:13; 2:7–8; 3:1–10; 4:1–3, 23; 8:14; Gal 2:9.

25. See 1 Chron 12:32.

fully satisfied with their work life. Working for nonprofit organizations will allow the INFJ, business major or otherwise, to satisfy their need to find purpose and meaning in their work. This environment will also place lots of people around them who they can read and give them a larger company vision that they can advance via their ability to think globally.[26]

INFJs who also have a biblical worldview likely do not have a difficult time submitting themselves or their thoughts to God in some areas, due to their ability to iNtuitively read and interpret the unobservable actions, secret desires, and indiscernible needs of people. This ability can only come from God. Some people summarily call it discernment. When INFJs use this ability to discover and interpret the unseen concepts present in the room, they simply need to realize and connect those insights to the progenerative source of those insights.[27] Once they find out where they and their abilities came from, they will desire to remain more connected to the source so they can use their insightful gift in very purposeful, meaningful, and helpful ways. This in turn will allow the INFJ to benefit those individual people who they may desire to help, people who are likely outside of their workplace. However, the INFJ will be capable of supplying more effective help to those people within the nonprofit organizations where they will often find themselves working.

PERSONALITY EXTREMES FOR INFJS

On the surface, INFJs do not seem like very extreme people. I believe that they are not prone to extremities regarding their disposition and demeanor. However, we are all humans who are conceived into a fallen world. Thus, we are all equally susceptible to falling into the traps that allow us to take our personality to extreme places.[28]

INFJs need to remain aware that they receive a lot of insightful revelation. For example, John the apostle wrote the biblical book of the Revelation of Jesus Christ. INFJs should also remain cognizant about their many perceptions regarding people and global progress which I believe come from God. They should consider these ideas in order to help themselves ensure that their entire personality does not go to an extreme.

26. Myers, *Introduction to Type*, 19.

27. See John 15:5–8.

28. See Ps 51:5.

To further explore these points, my biblical worldview leads me to believe that INFJs should first understand that they need to remain connected to the true Vine, and should remain humble enough to realize where their gifts come from.[29]

Second, because INFJs quickly trust what they see, they may not always effectively interpret the information that they have just received in the correct, or dare I say, iNtuitive manner that it was presented.[30] They can also become very frustrated with people or with a general lack of progress. If this occurs, they will shut down and choose not to help by refusing to share their insights with the group which they consider to be broken.

INFJs can read a room like none other. They gain useful insights about individuals, using their Introverted as well as iNtuitive preference zones. They also possess the ability to view an organization and its mission as one single entity, thus fitting with their Introversion preference to engage their world in a one-on-one fashion. However, when the INFJ does not feel that they are going to be well-received and they do not remember that their heart does not have a brain, they are basing their pending withdrawal on a potentially incorrect, short-term, and emotional response or false assumption. This is opposed to basing their decision on a well-thought-out plan of action. The INFJ will soon withdraw all of their useful insights from people or from an organization where they are needed.

I have both done this and seen it happen with INFJs at various meetings or encounters. In these scenarios, everyone at the meeting understands that the INFJ knows more than they are telling us. However, they are not willing to share their insights and information for reasons that they also will not disclose.

This shutdown can also operate as a part of the INFJ's personality, because they are capable of astutely using their insight to discern the fact that this person who they are speaking with will never understand, nor will they receive what the INFJ are about to share with them. So the INFJ will not share it, thereby avoiding the subsequent feeling of rejection that accompanies the misunderstanding. Sometimes INFJs simply need to develop a thicker skin, get out of their feelings, and share what they have

29. See John 15:5–8.

30. Myers, *Introduction to Type,* 19.

inside. Because their contribution is generally vital, no matter how others respond or react to what INFJs are led to say.

In short, INFJs need to be careful of becoming too isolated, particularly when they are walling themselves off from the rest of the group for the wrong reasons. They should also stop themselves from going to the extreme place where they begin to think more highly of themselves than they should.[31] Rare, but it happens.

Truly INFJs have many gifts and talents, as do we all.[32] However, I believe that they need to realize that God made all of us, and their gifts, while useful and necessary, come from God. Therefore, as Job learned: God can provide me with anything as he sees fit, and he can take it away at any time as he sees fit.[33]

CONNECTIONS FOR INFJS

The Introverted manner in which the INFJs relate to and interact with their world is connected to the orderly Judging preference that they use to organize and make sense of their world. Also, INFJs like to take in information in an extremely insightful and discerning format using their iNtuitive preference. The iNtuitive preference regarding the storage and retrieval of information within the INFJ is used to inform the INFJ's Feeling preference and decision-making function. We can learn a lot from these connections.

Connections Between The I-J Functions

The connections between the Introverted and Judging (I-J) preferences as they operate within the INFJ's personality allows them to see organizations as one entity, which can dramatically impact the world. They can do this just as well as they can see how the gifts that individual people possess can positively impact the world. The Introverted preference encourages the INFJ to seek out meaningful one-on-one interactions with others. INFJs also like to engage in deep thought.

The highly-organized Judging preference allows them to make sense of the world in a way similar to the manner that allows them to use their

31. See Rom 12:3.

32. See 1 Cor 12:4–11.

33. Job 1:21.

Introverted preference to see an organization or family as one functioning unit, as opposed to viewing it as a bunch of disparate parts. They can
then look at that organization as one person that they must learn about.
Then they can use that information in order to organize it, allowing it to
have the maximum impact on the environment where it functions.

Connections Between The N-F Functions

The iNtuitive function for the INFJ does not function independently,
rather it informs and impacts the overall personality of the INFJ more
than the other three preferences. The iNtuitive function for the INFJ
works in concert with the Feeling preference in regards to the type of and
reasons for the decisions that they make.

INFJs are insightful thinkers who can see the big picture and what is
going on behind the eyes of people, things, and organizations with equal
alacrity. They use these highly attuned insights in concert with their capacity to Feel what others are experiencing in order to help them decide
the best course of action in a situation. They can decide that the person
is in need of help via the sharing of these perceptions, or they can listen
to God as believers and decide not to share those insights because the
person may be in emotional pain. This same person may not be ready to
receive what God has just shown the INFJ. In those instances, the INFJ
should pray or do whatever else God has told them to do or not do with
that revealed insight.

GROWTH OPPORTUNITIES AND THREATS AS AN INFJ

At times I believe that God will reveal some very specific information to
me regarding a person or situation. Of course, I will not tell them what
God has revealed to me without gaining his corresponding permission to
speak. I also realize and am humble enough to understand that I have no
right to know the revealed information. I only know it because God has
chosen and trained me to be able to handle that revelation exactly as he
would have me handle it.

Others often ask me, "Why didn't you share it with the person? The
insight would have most likely helped them to see that the painfully difficult situation which they are currently facing or the circumstance that
they may be about to enter is not a healthy one for them if they continue

along the pathway that they are currently pursuing." I tell them that God revealed the information to me, but he alone gets to decide what I am supposed to do with what he has revealed to me.[34]

INFJs likely face this same scenario on a daily basis. The Threats occur when they do not realize who has revealed their insights to them, or when they don't recognize that they are being disobedient or full of hubris by sharing things that they are not supposed to share. Both come with devastating consequences.

I always offer this disclaimer which acknowledges the fact that "God will only show me what he needs or wants me to know." In other words, I and my INFJ cousins do not have carte blanche insight into every detail or reaction which is generally imperceptible to the naked eye. Nor do we have carte blanche insight into all of the pain and facial responses relative to a person's life

I support this concept by telling them to read 2 Kings 4:8–36. This is where the Shunemite woman whom Elisha told would have a baby one year from that point in their conversation, came back to Elisha because her son, that same predicted baby, had died some years later. She ran up to Elisha, grabbed his feet, and would not let go. Gehazi, his attendant, walked over to her in order to remove her from the feet of the prophet. Elisha told him to leave her there on the ground. She was grieving and obviously in great emotional distress. However, the Lord had not yet shown Elisha what was troubling her so deeply.[35]

Elisha went on to raise her son from the dead. But the point of the story provides my insightfully gifted INFJ friends with an opportunity to grow. Elisha knew that all of his revelation came from God. However, if God does not show the INFJ something, or if he tells the INFJ not to discuss the possibly partial insight, then they must wait to speak until he clearly shows them exactly what they saw as well as what they did not see, and what to do with the revelation.[36] They also need to remember to obediently share exactly what God tells them to share, irrespective of how they may already know via God-given insight how others will react, feel, or respond after they are finished talking.

---

34. 2 Kgs 4:27.

35. 2 Kgs 4:27.

36. See 1 Cor 13:9.

13

ENTP: Peter, The Lionhearted Apostle

PETER, THE LIONHEARTED APOSTLE

IF THERE WAS EVER a brother who was willing to jump right into the fire, as extreme Extroverts can have a tendency to do, it was Peter the lionhearted apostle. There was that one time that he had to convince the Lord, or really himself, that he genuinely loved the Lord and would feed the Savior's sheep and lambs after the ascension.[1] That incident notwithstanding, Peter was always ready for action.

The story of Peter is written throughout much of the New Testament. He appears in the Gospels, the Acts of the Apostles, and in the two eponymous books that he is given credit for writing. Many Bible scholars also agree that the Gospel of Mark is really the Gospel of Peter, who dictated his account through the use of Mark's pen.

In addition to Peter's Extroverted tendency to jump right into the fray, he demonstrates an iNtuitive propensity for seeing "the thing behind the thing" as I have previously mentioned in reference to myself. He made a Thinking preference decision and stepped out onto water following a hunch.[2] He did not know for certain that the water would support his weight, but at the word of Jesus, he stepped out there by faith and walked on water. He walked for only a few steps, but could you do any better?

1. John 21:15–19.
2. Matt 14:27–31.

Peter definitely had a fair-minded orientation to justice. Peter did not consider many of the things that could appear to be fair to all parties concerned, as a person with a Feeling preference would have done. In one instance, he cut a soldier's ear off because of his perception regarding the lack of equity surrounding Jesus's arrest.[3]

One would think that with such a strong sense of justice, Peter's way of organizing his outer world would lean toward a Judging Preference, but an examination of the attributes demonstrates that Peter had an ability to adapt to various situations and he definitely felt energized by last-minute pressures. Therefore he certainly had a Perceiving preference regarding the way he organized things in his outer world. I will remind us again that the terms used within Myers-Briggs Type Indicator (MBTI) research do not mean exactly the same things that they do when we use those same words in everyday conversation.

PETER'S EXTROVERSION PREFERENCE

I make light of Peter's apparent extreme bent toward Extroversion, particularly as a younger disciple of Jesus, but it reminds us to strive for balance in all of our preferences, whether MBTI or otherwise. Peter was a fisherman by trade and was called by Jesus to become a disciple while fishing. Jesus promised that he would teach Simon Peter and his brother Andrew to bring men into his kingdom, instead of fishing for sea bass or some such. The brothers immediately left their fishing nets behind and followed Jesus.[4] This flexible change of course, based on his Perceiving preference, was unlike that of Elisha, who was an Introvert with a Judging preference and had to think about his calling before accepting it. Peter (as well as his brother Andrew) jumped right in to the fray from the outset.

The next time that we see Peter in earnest was when Jesus came across the twelve disciples' path, walking on water.[5] The Bible reports that Jesus had no intention of stopping and helping his followers with the storm that they were facing. The apostles thought that they had seen a ghost walking on the seas.[6] Jesus called to them and told them not to be afraid because it was him and not a ghost. Peter stepped up and said, "If

3. John 18:10.
4. Matt 4:19.
5. Matt 14:22–31.
6. Matt 14:26.

it is you, command me to come to you on the water."[7] This demonstrates many of Peter's attributes not only as an Extrovert but as a fully-caffeinated ENTP.

PETER'S INTUITIVE PREFERENCE

Peter was an Extrovert and ever ready for a challenge, stepping to the front of the line made up of his other eleven friends and painting in bold colors. He also demonstrated an ability to imagine the future possibilities. After Peter absorbed the peculiar information presented to him regarding the fact that it was really Jesus walking on water,[8] Peter jumped to the conclusion that if it is Jesus and he can walk on water, then I must be able to walk on water too if he says that I can. Dare I say that most would not have interpreted the same information in quite this manner?

Jesus called, and Peter walked on water. He may have only taken a few steps, but he concluded that he too could walk on water based on the current information available to him. Cephas (another of Peter's names which means "rock") did not ponder the thought for a long time. He jumped right out of the boat onto the water. And it held him! Peter definitely trusted his gut, demonstrating the true personality trait of an iNtuitive person and a leader by example. In this instance, no one else followed him out onto the water.

PETER'S THINKING PREFERENCE

Peter was one of Jesus's very close followers. He was one of the three closest disciples during the three and a half years of the earthly ministry of Jesus.[9] Thus, when Peter saw that Jesus could walk on water, using deductive reasoning (a Thinking preference trait), he concluded that he too could walk on water. Simon Peter used a cause-and-effect decision-making model and then sprang to action.

Peter took in information and used similar objective reasoning techniques during his time with Jesus to arrive at an undeniable truth. Jesus asked the disciples: "Who do people say I am?" The followers told him that people have said that he was the reincarnated version of John

7. Matt 14:28 (NSRV).

8. Matt 14:22–31.

9. See Matt 17:1; 26:37; Mark 5:37; 9:2; 13:3; 14:33; Luke 6:14; 8:51; 9:28; Gal 2:9.

the Baptist (who had been beheaded), Elijah, or one of the other prophets of old. Then Jesus asked them, "but who do you, my followers, say that I am?" Peter jumped right in once again, demonstrating his Thinking preference as well as all four aspects of the ENTP at work, and said, "You are the Christ, the Son of the living God."[10]

Peter probably said to himself, "Did I really just say that?" But he said it, and in typical Peter fashion without thinking, just proceeding on gut instinct as iNtuitive Thinkers tend to do. Jesus went on to tell him that flesh and blood could not have allowed him to arrive at that conclusion, but that only the Holy Spirit could have revealed it to him.[11] Peter had to trust the information inside and allow the Holy Spirit to help him to arrive at only one logical decision: Jesus is the Christ, the Son of the living God. Peter had a Thinking preference.

PETER'S PERCEIVING PREFERENCE

As I have previously mentioned, at times we can allow our personality traits to take us to extremes and get us into some trouble. This happened to our boy Peter. Jesus told Peter that he was going to be tested, but that Jesus had prayed that his faith would not fail him during the test, and when he overcame the challenge he should use that testimony to strengthen his brothers.[12] Jesus was likely telling Peter to use the entire humbling experience for growth, just as he would at a later time when Jesus had to restore Peter by having Peter convince Jesus, or really convince himself, that he genuinely loved Jesus by professing his love for Jesus three times. Jesus followed this by telling Peter, after each confession of love, to feed and shepherd his sheep.[13]

Jesus telling Peter that he was about to encounter a trial did not elicit concern or worry from Peter. No, Peter the lionhearted apostle piped right up and told Jesus that he was ready to go to jail with him or even die for Jesus right then and there. Jesus tried to keep Peter from jumping into the fray again so quickly, and told him that before the sun came up and

10. Mark 8:27–30 (NASB).

11. Matt 16:17.

12. Luke 22:31–34.

13. John 21:15–19.

the rooster crowed that very day, Peter would deny that he knew Jesus three times.[14]

They moved on and Jesus was subsequently arrested in the olive grove by Judas Iscariot and the guards.[15] Peter and John followed Jesus to the temple where Jesus would stand before the high priest and discuss the reasons that they had arrested him. After John got Peter into the courtyard, the people in the courtyard began to accuse Peter, who they knew was from Galilee, of being one of the disciples of Jesus. Peter, not quite as full of courage and bombast at this point, denied that he knew Jesus to the first person.

A person with a Judging preference, who had just told Jesus that he was ready to "go to the mattresses" with and for him, should have stuck to his previous statement and said to the first accuser, "Yes, I know Jesus. I follow him as one of his twelve disciples, and he is the Son of the living God." Peter had said that on earlier occasions; why not now? Peter swings for the fences. Alas, Peter's Perceiving preference kicked in with a vengeance, and he decided that he needed to leave his options open in this unfolding situation. He denied that he knew Jesus, much less had followed him as a disciple. At that very moment of the first denial, the rooster started crowing. The same servant of the high priest came again and accused Peter of knowing Jesus, while they were all out in the courtyard of the High Priest, looking at Jesus, who was facing an interrogation of his own. Peter once again vehemently denied knowing Jesus, for a second time. According to Peter's own account in Mark 18:66–72, the heat in the kitchen got really hot for our boy Peter! Some of the others standing around turned that heat up by not only accusing Peter of being a disciple of Jesus, but also that he had to be a follower of Jesus because Peter was a Galilean.

I mentioned earlier in this book that people with an iNtuitive preference were linguistically creative and imaginative. When you combine those traits with a Perceiving preference within a man who is determined to leave his options open in case he needs to get out of a jam, you might have a personality-extreme recipe for disaster on your hands!

Peter started cussing. He said that "I told y'all that I don't know that man!" Then he swore an oath to them that he was not lying, restating that he did not know Jesus. Peter (the so-called lionhearted apostle) just so

14. Luke 22:31–34.
15. John 18:1–27.

happened to be hanging around the courtyard where this other Galilean named Jesus was being interrogated by the high priest? Okay, if you say so, Peter. Sadly, just then the rooster crowed again, the sun came up, and Peter ran out of the courtyard and wept bitterly, as Jesus turned around and looked directly at him.[16] People with a Perceiving preference can get into trouble if they get too attached to leaving all of their options open in an unfolding situation instead of allowing themselves to take a position come what may. Some might say to Peter that his mouth will write checks that the rest of him cannot cash.

The final illustration that I will use (among the scores of references to Simon Peter in the Bible) is the olive grove experience. Judas Iscariot, the betrayer, and some Roman soldiers approached Jesus and the other eleven disciples in the grove. They were obviously there to arrest Jesus. Jesus asked the soldiers who they were looking for, according to the account in John 18:1–11. They said that they were looking for Jesus. Jesus told them that he was Jesus the Nazarene that they were looking for. Then they fell down to the ground because the Holy Spirit was going to show them exactly who they were attempting to arrest and give them enough information to rethink their ill-conceived notion. They decided to continue to try to arrest Jesus. He told them to let the disciples go since they were determined to pursue this ill-fated course of action.

Peter, my favorite extreme Extrovert, cried havoc and sprang into action once again. I can hear a trumpet fanfare playing in the background (every hero needs some good theme music). Peter unsheathed his sword—why he had one in the first place was another question. Dude was a fisherman-turned-itinerate disciple, apostle, and preacher. Why did he need a sword? But he had it, he drew it, and with great alacrity in one fell swoop, he swiped off the ear of one of the soldiers (named Malchus). He probably went right past that guy's helmet. Nice! Well . . . maybe not so nice? Jesus put the ear back on for the unwise servant of the high priest and told Peter to put his weapon away.[17]

Peter astutely decided that arresting Jesus was totally unfair and he needed to show them exactly what he thought of them. Peter was always ready for action. He was spontaneous and ready to change courses of action at a moment's notice. He was definitely energized by the pressure-filled interaction with Judas Iscariot and the Roman soldiers. Peter had

16. Luke 22:60–62.

17. John 18:10–11; Luke 22:51.

a Perceiving preference regarding how he organized and made sense of
things in the world that were transpiring around him.

ENTP

Peter is so much fun to describe. ENTPs like Peter are described as:
quick-thinkers, alert, ingenious, and outspoken (very much so in Peter's
case). Peter also became a tremendous and dynamic leader in the early
church in Jerusalem during his later, apostolic days.

ENTPs like Peter are quick to take action while also being great
conceptualizers. They assimilate and process information quickly. They
do not waste time making decisions, even if those decisions are highly
questionable at best. They abhor a mundane existence doing the same
things day after day. That's why Peter so readily left the daily grind of his
fishing job behind at a moment's notice in order to become a disciple and
later an apostle of Jesus Christ. ENTPs need a little *joi de vivre* (joy of life)
in their daily activities. Peter was the epitome of an ENTP.

ENTP: THE MERCURIAL ONES

APPLICATIONS FOR ENTPS

I'm sorry to say it, but I doubt that the ENTPs will mind my description
one bit: ENTPs are a wild bunch if I have ever seen one. This appearance of
unpredictability is a part of their charm. ENTPs are very quick-thinkers.
They find possibilities, options, and opportunities where others would
consider them unavailable.[18] They have the ability to look at information
using their iNtuitive preference and then quickly as well as insightfully
find all of the possible avenues of pursuit within that data. This process
occurs because of the ENTP's need to remain mentally stimulated. They
bore easily.

ENTPs may start discussions which some may consider arguments,
simply to encounter some stimulation,[19] and to see if they can uncover
any information that they had not previously discovered which they can
analyze for future possibilities. This conversational style can be good or
bad depending on who they are engaging in conversation. If the other

18. Myers, *Introduction to Type*, 20.
19. Myers, *Introduction to Type*, 20.

party does not know or understand what is going on, or if they are not familiar with the ENTP with whom they are speaking, they might find themselves quite put off by the ENTP. ENTPs can either be the life of the party or the party crasher, depending upon the circumstance or situation.

ENTPs may need to learn the appropriate times and places to unleash the full revelation of their personality, out of concern of offending someone when they are simply being themselves. However, they are also invaluable people to have around. They can figure out complex processes and not only fix a problem but improve the overall functioning of the system. If they can focus their attention span (which at times is rather short), they will help you fix anything from your used Chrysler to your broken political campaign.

They are also enthusiastic, particularly when engaged by a great leader, movement, or exciting challenge. They have to be careful to fully understand the nature of their attention span, as well as remain mindful of being too blunt or glib when speaking.[20] But they are a lot of fun to be around. They are very creative and insightful. When someone in the organization says, that it's time to bring in the big guns, I will bet that one of those big guns is an ENTP.

Developing As An ENTP

I would be doing the ENTPs a disservice by simply calling them a problem-fixer, because their skills are more complicated than that. They will create a problem in a system that they have already analyzed, and repair that problem in their mind. In other words, they will break the system just so they can put it back together bigger, better, stronger, and faster than it was when they first came to encounter the issue.

When it comes time for these wildly gifted people to learn to harness themselves, they may also have a leg up on the rest of us. They like to analyze large problems.[21] The Bible teaches that God's thoughts and ways are eminently beyond whatever we can conceive.[22] Thus, they have likely already started their search for hidden mysteries and to find the places where they fit in best.[23]

20. Myers, *Introduction to Type*, 20.

21. Myers, *Introduction to Type*, 20.

22. Isa 55:9

23. See Mark 4:11.

Their concerns may focus on perception. They are good at reading the room, but they can present themselves poorly at times because of their need to remain mentally stimulated. Some tasks take a long time. For example, Enoch walked with God and he and God grew closer by the day. This happened until he could get no closer to God and still remain here on earth. So God took him.[24] But I always tell people that it took Enoch 300 years before he got close enough to God that Enoch was taken to be with him. Enoch could have been an ENTP, although there is not enough information about him presented in the Bible to tell. The ENTPs can grow and continue to develop in their chosen faith by not only continuing to walk with God but also by applying patience in all that they do.[25]

This will allow them to successfully engage any and every challenge that God presents to them. They are not always looking for the correct solution, but rather they are looking to resolve the issue quickly because they want to move on to the next stimuli as soon as possible.

PERSONALITY EXTREMES FOR ENTPS

Because the ENTPs are such movers and shakers and many times have such outsized personalities, many people vary in how they receive ENTPs. This is not the ENTP's issue, per se. However, it becomes a problem if God is telling the ENTP to rein in their personality in a certain situation, or to not fix that situation because God broke it for a reason.

Peter the apostle can illustrate these extremes. Peter was always ready for action. He was ready when the soldiers, led by their informant Judas Iscariot, wanted to arrest Jesus. Peter became so emboldened that he applied one of his quick-witted ENTP solutions. He did so to such an extent that he sliced Malchus's ear off.[26] Jesus had been telling all of his followers and listeners that he would have to die and be raised again on the third day.[27] Thus, when the soldiers came to take Jesus to the next stage of his destiny, he knew they were coming and that he would have to go with them. He had warned Peter that they were coming.

24. Gen 5:21–24; Heb 11:5–6.

25. See Ecc 7:8; Heb 10:36.

26. John 18:10–11.

27. Luke 9:22.

Another time, Jesus told Peter: "Get behind me, Satan."[28] This occurred when Peter intimated that Jesus should stop saying that he would die, though that was the very purpose for which the Christ came in to the earth.[29] Peter needed to realize that this particular situation did not require his clever curiosity, nor did it require one of his innovative solutions.[30] It simply required his faithful concern for his leader as well as his patience. He would have to wait three days and nights before he would learn the full outcome of the events that were unfolding.[31]

Peter's Perceiving preference, which prefers open-ended outcomes, did not recognize that this outcome had been preordained prior to God creating the heavens and the earth in Genesis 1:1. At times, ENTPs need to look into their information, and then take a step back, be patient, wait, and listen, before acting. There is a time and an appropriate place for every action, my ENTP friends.[32] They may also benefit from a Newtonian physics refresher so that they can appropriately anticipate the equal and opposite reaction.

CONNECTIONS FOR ENTPS

The Extroverted manner in which the ENTPs relate to and interact with their world is connected to the Perceiving preference that they use to organize and make sense of their world. ENTPs also like to take in information and immediately search that information for hidden possibilities using their iNtuitive preference. That iNtuitive preference, regarding the storage and retrieval of information within the ENTP, is used to inform the ENTP's Thinking preference and decision-making function. We can learn a lot from these connections.

Connections Between The E-P Functions

The connection between the Extroverted preference and the Perceiving preference makes the ENTP exciting to be around. They are Extroverted and engaging people.

28. Matt 4:10 (NIV).
29. Matt 16:13–23.
30. Myers, *Introduction to Type*, 20.
31. Matt 12:40; 27:45–28:15.
32. Ecc 3:1.

I did a workshop based on personality types once at a community college. There was one person in the workshop who most likely would have been described as an ENTP, if I had not been using different personality typology material to conduct this workshop. They were the life of the party. My friend, a dean at that college who brought me in to conduct the workshop, told me that in the days following the workshop, everyone in attendance finally understood their colleague. They would say good morning to him with a completely new understanding regarding why he behaved as he did. If they knew that he was also an ENTP, they would have greeted him by saying "HI ENTP!" They no longer took the ENTP-type's outsized and engaging personality the wrong way. This person was now just a really big personality and likely an ENTP.

The Extroverted nature in all ENTPs interacts with their Perceiving function, which always leaves the back door open in case they need to make a quick escape. They do not like to box themselves in. Thus, when they are in conversation with you, wildly spinning their ideas as they often do, and telling their plethora of jokes and stories, they will always have another way out of the situation that they have gotten themselves into (the very situation that they are describing or discussing), even if it involves an *ex post facto* fish tale.

Everything remains lighthearted and fun when you have the ENTPs around. However, they can also be like coffee if they are out of balance and allow their personality to go to extreme places. As occurs with caffeinated drinks, one must be careful to not drink in too much of our ENTP friends or your legs will start to cramp, your muscles will tense up, your heart will race, you will get nervous and get sick in the stomach.

Connections Between The N-T Functions

The connection between the iNtuitive preference and the Thinking preference advances the ENTP's value to most people and organizations that they will encounter. They are able to take in information using their iNtuitive function and see endless possibilities. But their orderly and comprehensively attuned Thinking preference allows them to create a plan based on their quick analysis of any system. This enables them to improve it as well as fix what is broken.

GROWTH OPPORTUNITIES AND THREATS AS AN ENTP

Using Peter as an example, I would say that ENTPs grow best as they move forward from falling down. Peter, at an early stage, was able to hear and receive revelation from God. Jesus told him so when he said to Peter that no human could have revealed to him that Jesus was the Messiah.[33]

Peter could, like all ENTPs, analyze information and situations quickly and then move to unprecedented action based on their analysis. Peter asked Jesus if he too could walk on water, based exclusively on the fact that he saw Jesus doing it.[34] This was in addition to the fact that, when all of the disciples saw someone walking toward them on the water, they thought that they were seeing a ghost.

Peter was a full-fledged ENTP, but he was also a callow, growing, and developing ENTP. After Jesus told Peter that he would deny knowing Christ, his leader who he loved and supported, three times, Peter took an ENTP-like fall.[35] But Jesus put old Peter back together again. Jesus did this by asking him multiple times if Peter loved Jesus. If he did, Jesus had an assignment for Peter (as wekk as for all of the others) in the upcoming days and years.[36] Metaphorically speaking, Jesus trusted Peter with the football even after he had just thrown a horrible interception during the preceding series.

Peter was confused and hurting in the moment. But after Pentecost occurred and he was filled with the Holy Spirit, who could reveal things to Peter now on a full-time basis. Peter became the bold leader of the early church and performed many great miracles.[37] The concept of denying that he knew Jesus was so far from Peter at this point because Peter had grown up and matured into a man that God could use. All of his ENTP gifts and talents were now ready to be used to benefit many generations to come. We all fall down from time to time. However, for ENTPs, falling down and getting back up again is all a part of the growth process that they must endure.

33. Matt 16:13–20.

34. Matt 14:22–33.

35. John 18:1–27.

36. John 21:15–19.

37. Acts 2.

14

INTP: Paul the Apostle

PAUL THE APOSTLE

PAUL IS THE AUTHOR of thirteen books in the New Testament of the Bible. He is possibly the author of the book of Hebrews, though some dispute that fact. It doesn't matter; he is still the most prolific writer in the New Testament and an INTP. Interestingly enough to me, unlike John the beloved apostle, Paul always announced himself by using his name when writing an epistle to one of the churches that he apostolically planted.[1] This fact casts further doubt on the book of Hebrews, but I will leave that for the Bible scholars to debate.

People may raise an eyebrow or two at the idea that Paul was an Introvert, but I believe that he definitely was, although he spoke with boldness. Introverts are more than capable of being bold and impactful leaders as well as public speakers. The prolific writing serves as a clue to his true Introverted personality preference.

Paul was an imaginative and creative communicator. Paul also had many terse discussions with Peter and the other apostles in Jerusalem over the direction of the early church in regards to spreading the good news.[2] He clarified the ideas related to the kingdom before going out

---

1. Rom 1:1; 1 Cor 1:1; 2 Cor 1:1; Gal 1:1; Eph 1:1; Phil 1:1; Col 1:1; 1 Thess 1:1; 2 Thess 1:1; 1 Tim 1:1; 2 Tim 1:1; Titus 1:1; Phlm 1:1.
2. Acts 15:1–35; Gal 2:11–14.

to spread the gospel. He studied for about a year prior to leaving on his missionary journeys.[3]

Paul was a Pharisee prior to following Jesus and an expert on Jewish law.[4] However, immediately after his conversion experience occurred on the road to Damascus, he was not an expert on the good news of Jesus Christ. He had to learn a new revelation which required additional study time.

Paul had an analytical mind and used deductive reasoning quite extensively. He discussed his Hebrew clerical credentials in Philippians 3, but went on via deductive reasoning to explain why he no longer esteemed those Pharisaical credentials highly.[5] He stated that it was because he believed that he now had the highest esteem for his newly-found revelation of Jesus the Christ.

The apostle Paul also provided an eloquent written display of deductive reasoning in an impassioned yet foolish defense or establishment of his apostolic authority in 2 Corinthians 11:16–12:19. Paul's true nature was to be flexible, although simultaneously very deliberate. He was adaptable to many situations that occurred as a result of his calling. Paul was an INTP.

PAUL'S INTROVERSION PREFERENCE

Paul was a bold man when the situation was required. Prior to being converted to Christianity after his experience on the road to Damascus, he persecuted Christians with zeal. His apparent primary method of communication was definitely via writing, not talking.[6] He was a prolific writer, although his calling as an apostle and missionary required him to speak to many crowds and individuals alike.[7] Paul went so far as to call himself an untrained public speaker, yet quite well-steeped in the acquisition and retention of knowledge, in 2 Corinthians 11:6.

He wrote very intimately to Timothy, whom he regarded as a son, in his letters to him. The type of genuine bond that Paul shared with

---

3. Acts 9:19, 23, 26–30; 11:22–26; Gals 2:1.

4. Acts 23:6; Phil3:4–6.

5. Phil 3:4–11.

6. Rom 1:1; 1 Cor 1:1; 2 Cor 1:1; Gal 1:1; Eph 1:1; Phil 1:1; Col 1:1; 1 Thess 1:1; 2 Thess 1:1; 1 Tim 1:1; 2 Tim 1:1; Titus 1:1; Phlm 1:1.

7. Acts 9:1- 31; 11:19- 30; 21:37–22:40; 23:1–28:31.

Timothy, "a dear child to me,"[8] as well as Titus, "his true child,"[9] indicates his Introversion preference. Paul had a select few close friends and spoke of them often in his writings, which also included Silvanus and Philemon.[10] He appeared to prefer one-on-one or written communication over public speaking, although he was a persuasive public speaker and an exemplary leader, as are many Introverts. Paul was an Introvert.

PAUL'S INTUITIVE PREFERENCE

Paul gave many of the churches that he established (while functioning as an apostle) guidance, as well as order for their operation. He supplied detailed instructions in writing regarding the ordination of elders and deacons in many of his epistles, including the one written to Titus.[11] He also gave instructions on church order, sin in the church, and provided a detailed description of love.[12]

When he was inspired by the blinding light of Christ, it changed his life, his perspective, the way he organized his world, and his insight into who God is. Paul quickly trusted the inspiration and revelation that he received based on that experience and quickly followed that light.[13] He also executed his callings with great zeal, trusting by faith that his Inspirer would take care of him and supply all of his needs, as he stated in Philippians 4:19. Paul also spoke of future events and the Lord's coming in 1 Thessalonians 5. Paul was iNtuitive regarding the gathering and dissemination of information to his followers and readers.

PAUL'S THINKING PREFERENCE

Paul stood toe-to-toe with Peter the apostle who trained under Jesus.[14] Paul knew that he had a revelation of and from Jesus as well. Paul knew that he had a calling to spread the good news to the gentiles. He would not allow the original eleven remaining apostles or the other Hebrew dis-

8. 2 Tim 1:2.

9. Titus 1:4.

10. 1 Thess 1:1; 2 Thess 1:1; Phlm 1:1.

11. Act 14:23; 1 Tim 3:1–13; Titus 1:5–9.

12. 1 Cor 13.

13. Acts 9:1–9.

14. Acts 15:1–35; Gal 2:11–14.

ciples in Jerusalem to stop him from going to the uttermost parts of the world to spread the gospel and establish churches.[15] He proceeded along a logical but flexible course when executing his two missionary journeys.

Paul (also known as Saul before his conversion experience) of Tarsus maintained a standard as well as a high regard for the truth. He was a zealot regarding his persecution of Christians before his conversion.[16] When he received a new revelation, Paul approached the process of imparting the word of God with the same zeal as he did before his conversion, but this time in regards to sharing the truth of Jesus Christ with the gentiles.

Paul also took a very logical and analytical approach as he defended himself after being imprisoned. He appealed to the correct authorities as a man who was a Roman citizen as well as a Hebrew. He presented a logical case in his own defense to all officials he was brought in front of. If you enjoy the law and the logical, determined, and progressive way that a Thinking preference lawyer decides to lay out his case, you should read Paul's defenses in Acts.[17] He was an expert in Hebrew law but he also understood his rights as a Roman citizen very well. He used that knowledge to his advantage in his own defense against the laws of the land that caused his imprisonment. Paul was a Thinking and logical decision-maker.

PAUL'S PERCEIVING PREFERENCE

The area in which Paul seems to be closest to having a borderline personality trait is in regard to how he organized his world. He seems like he can be methodical in some of his actions, similar to one with a Judging preference. He exemplified this in his actions leading others to persecute the followers of Jesus. When Saul was on the road to Damascus, he met the reincarnated Jesus, who blinded him and spoke directly with Saul. He was there because he had asked the high priest and Jewish church leaders for permission to find and persecute more Christians.[18]

But I believe and can find evidence to support the idea that those methodically-inclined incidents all transpired prior to his experience on

15. Acts 9:19–25; 11:19–26; 13:2–28:31.

16. Acts 9:4; 7:58; 1 Cor 15:9; Gal 1:13; Phil 3:6; 1 Tim 1:12–13.

17. Acts 21–28.

18. Acts 9:1–19.

the road to Damascus. He was changed following that experience. He then displayed the spontaneous and flexible nature that was always inside of him as a part of his Perceiving personality. The converted Paul would organize his world in a totally different and more flexible fashion.

He would engage in many missionary trips.[19] He lived through snake bites and ships torn apart by storms, having to float to shore. Begged by his followers not to go to Jerusalem, Paul felt compelled to go and if necessary to die for the sake of the gospel.[20] He would also be imprisoned for years, all because of his faith. He also endured many other trials. He faced them with an open-ended flexibility because he had faith and confidence in Jesus. Paul's true organizational preference was Perceiving.

Additional evidence exists of the apostle Paul's Perceiving preference as well as of his iNtuitive preference, as it relates to understanding what God was showing him via visions and revelations, all spoken of in 2 Corinthians 12:1–10. Paul said that he was caught up into the "third heaven" fourteen years prior to writing the Corinthians for a second time. He spoke of hearing words that he was not allowed to repeat. In order to ensure that Paul was not able to become self-absorbed or begin to think too highly of himself, but rather that he remain humble enough to encounter all of these experiences as well as relay the appropriate meaning to his readers and other audiences, he was given a "thorn in his flesh" accompanied by a messenger from Satan sent to torment him. He asked the Lord to remove these obstacles, but the Lord taught him instead to rely on the grace of God to get him through each experience. Thus, Paul said that "he only derives pleasure from his weaknesses, insults, catastrophes, persecutions, and in pressures, because of Christ. Because only when he is weak, can he consider himself strong."[21]

Paul had to remain quite flexible, demonstrating his Perceiving preference, in order to survive and prosper through all of his challenges regarding spreading the good news. He also had to remain open to not only visions and revelations but to seeing iNtuitively the revelation behind the visions and behind hearing those "unspeakable words."

19. Acts 13:1–28:31.

20. Acts 27:27–28:31; 2 Cor 11:22–33.

21. 2 Cor 12:10.

INTP

Paul definitely developed logical explanations and processes to defend himself and to spread the gospel of Jesus Christ. He could cite Hebrew law as an authority as he did in the book of Romans in order to explain to the Romans that gentiles were grafted into the plan of salvation through Jesus Christ.[22] He explained that the plan was first presented to the Hebrew people.

He also used a similar abstract and metaphorical process to describe in his letter to Timothy.[23] He compares his work to that of a soldier, an athlete, and a farmer, all working to spread the gospel with joy and diligence. Paul was an incredibly analytical man.

He was also very flexible. He assuredly considered the many, many, many trials he faced as well as the heavy weight of the leadership mantle that he carried in service to Jesus Christ and the work of spreading the good news. Paul was an INTP.

INTP: THE EXPERTS

APPLICATIONS FOR INTPS

INTPs are fiercely independent. They value games like Jenga, where they can take something apart and put it back together again while attempting to find new and creative ways to ensure that the whole thing remains operational. Personally, I cannot stand Jenga; I consider it a slow trip to nowhere.

INTPs also have inquisitive and investigative minds.[24] They would much rather work on a problem than they would work on implementing the solution. Particularly if the solution means that they also have to organize and motivate the people to accomplish the task.

INTPs can best be put to use by a group or organization at the beginning stages of a process. If someone has to discover a solution to a complex problem, then the INTP is your person to put on the case. Many times churches and other organizations seek to find and move into larger facilities due to growth. They have simply outgrown their current facility.

22. Rom 11:11–24.

23. 2 Tim 2:2–7.

24. Myers, *Introduction to Type*, 23.

I worked for an organization that faced a problem like this, although it was not a church.

My organization was facing an issue regarding what we called being "land-locked." What that meant was that most of the buildings in the area that we wanted to use as a new facility were already occupied, and we could not find an opened space nearby to build upon. When you couple that with the idea that we could not move our organization to a completely different location, like a suburban or rural area, in order to find enough land to build on, we faced a complex problem to solve.

This is where the INTP is at their best. They will engage an issue like this by presenting themselves with many different alternatives. They will go through their list in creative ways, after learning as much about the issue as possible. They find ways for their solution to fail, calculate the possibility of success versus failure, and then start all over again. If you leave them alone to work on the problem, when they come back to you and the team they will produce a list with multiple contingencies that will enable everyone to decide the best course of action for the organization. They need to be left alone to fully investigate the issue, but they will discover amazing potential solutions.

Developing As An INTP

In the previously discussed scenario, it may not be the best option for the church or organization to change locations, or for the family to move to a new home. However, have no concern, the INTP has also taken a look at the options related to remaining in your current facility, and they have discussed the maximum capacity regarding expanding the current facility if the team decides to stay.

One important fact for the INTP to remember as they are working out their solutions is for them as believers to remain prayerful through their entire process.[25] Prayer, more than any of their wonderfully attuned investigative abilities or their individual personality preferences, will inform their ability to arrive at the most salient and useful list of alternatives for the group.

INTPs like to investigate possibilities. They also like to view data in creative ways.[26] Therefore, they will come up with an impressive list of

25. 1 Thess 5:16–18.

26. Myers, *Introduction to Type*, 23.

alternatives. However, if they subscribe to a specific biblical worldview and learn to add prayer and an intimate as well as dependent relationship with God to their work, they will be able to see why certain things will not work before they finalize the list; they will also be able to understand why alternatives that look appealing are actually not very useful as solutions for this particular problem.

INTPs are, as I have mentioned, very independent.[27] They like to be turned loose, left to do their work, and allowed to come back with their list of solutions. They will even discuss in great detail all that they have learned.[28] Nevertheless, some INTPs who are believers will face an issue at first because they like to work alone. They also do not like to depend on anyone. These INTPs should develop a consistent prayer life.

PERSONALITY EXTREMES FOR INTPS

The extremes for INTPs involve defending the wrong land or defending an idea that should no longer be defended. INTPs are creative and investigative problem-solvers. Give them a problem, give them some time, and they will return with a solution. They are diligent and serious problem-solvers.[29]

But they, like all of us, are fallible. They can make mistakes in analyzing data even though they are adept at looking at information in insightful ways. If they are imbalanced and allow their personality to go off to extremes, they may enter a place where they are applying their INTP personality type to defending an incorrectly constructed list of alternatives, simply because they made some minor or major miscalculation in one of their attempts to deconstruct and reconstruct scenarios. Think: *A Beautiful Mind*.

INTPs need to learn to open themselves up to feedback and input. This may be difficult for them due to their Introverted preference, but it is important for people who enjoy the deconstruction and reconstruction process. Also, those who are fiercely independent should learn to remain open to the possibility that someone else may have an idea that will work.

INTPs must in many instances force themselves to open up and allow room for assistance as well as admit that they might miss the mark

27. Myers, *Introduction to Type*, 23.

28. Myers, *Introduction to Type*, 23.

29. Myers, *Introduction to Type*, 23.

from time to time. I believe that God created all of us to look to and depend upon him for everything.[30] At times, God will put the answers that the INTP needs inside of someone else in order to get INTPs more accustomed to the process of seeking so they can find.[31]

CONNECTIONS FOR INTPS

The Introverted manner in which the INTPs relate to and interact with their world is connected to the Perceiving preference which they use to organize and make sense of their world. INTPs like to take in information, and filter it though their creative, diligent, process-oriented, and investigative mind using their iNtuitive preference. That iNtuition function, regarding the storage and retrieval of information within the INTP is used to inform the INTP's Thinking preference and decision-making function. We can learn a lot from these connections.

Connections Between The I-P Functions

The Introverted function for the INTP informs their Perceiving function, allowing for their ability to repeat a trial many times before they exact a list of reasonable alternatives. Most people do not have the patience to employ a strategy of repeating a trial many times in order to decide upon the best alternatives. Many may look at a scenario and become worried after a few trials. They're immediately ready to move on to present their findings.

This is not the modus operandi for the INTPs. They enjoy working alone due to their Introverted nature. Their Perceiving preference ensures that they do not predetermine the outcome even after repeated trials. This ensures that their research is not biased or skewed. Thus, you can be sure that when a INTP comes to your group with a list of alternatives that list has been tested many times and vetted for all possible outcomes.

30. See Prov 3:6.

31. Matt 7:7–8.

Connections Between The N-T Functions

The iNtuitive preference is the personality trait from which the INTP draws on in order to help them to generate so many creative alternative solutions to a problem. INTPs do not move directly to a solution. They must thoroughly and comprehensively vet the data through their creative and beautiful mind's eye. This before they can even begin to generate a list of alternatives.

Notice that I did not say that they make decisions based on their assiduous vetting of the data. The Thinking preference, the decision-making function for the INTPs, involves deciding upon which alternatives are useful and which ones are not as beneficial. Then they bring only the most useful alternatives to the group. This is how INTPs make their contribution to the final decision of the group. INTPs will present their findings to the group and then leave the group to make the final decision as well as decide on the implementation strategies. INTPs have already moved on to the next problem to solve.

GROWTH OPPORTUNITIES AND THREATS AS AN INTP

Paul the INTP was a great example of all that makes the INTPs so special yet also all that can present challenges for them. When Paul thought he was doing the right thing, he was willing to hold the coats of those who stoned Stephen to death.[32] Then he went to the high priest to find new and inventive ways to persecute more Christians in Damascus. He wanted to take his show on the road . . . to Damascus (insert rimshot here).

However, he was introduced to a show of a different kind when he was on that road to Damascus. Jesus knocked him off of his high horse and changed Saul's course forever.[33] Paul then followed the INTP program of learning as much as one can regarding this newly-presented issue to work through by remaining for a year where he was after his eyesight was restored. He realized that he had a new calling and needed to approach this calling as only an INTP can. Once again Paul functioned at a very high level in the role of a burgeoning leader in the early church.

Paul was also the perfect person to send out as a missionary apostle to the gentiles. Something that was comfortable for Paul the Introvert

---

32. Acts 7:58.
33. Acts 8:1–3; 9:1–31.

was that he was usually only accompanied by one or two other people. He began his missionary work by serving with Barnabas.[34]

He was not required to hang around in one place for a long enough period of time that he would be obligated to implement the plan or organize the people to work through the plan.[35] Paul was an apostle and a church planter, one who employed similar INTP personality traits to those that he expressed when he was a Pharisee and tent-builder in his previous life.[36] He did not have to live in the tents, which were temporary dwelling places in any case. He was simply required to construct them and then move on to the next challenge.

He faced Peter and met his challenge when the rules and organization that presently governed the fledgling Christian church were about to change.[37] God wanted to spread the good news to the uttermost ends of the earth.[38] Previously it had been contained to throughout Jerusalem and Judea, just as the believers were told that they would do. But they were also told to take the gospel to Samaria and then to the outermost parts of the world. Paul embraced the idea of taking the gospel far and wide, but the members of the early church, the Christians in Jerusalem, as well as the original apostles including Peter, James, and John, were somewhat resistant to taking the gospel to the gentiles.[39] Paul persuaded them to believe that he had heard from the Lord just as the other apostles who directly trained under Jesus had. Paul also convinced them that he was the one to take the gospel far and wide in order to continue to spread the message of faith. INFPs embrace a challenge. They will fiercely defend an idea if they know that they are right.[40]

Paul was met with an opportunity to grow in Jesus in a way that was very different from the teachings that he had followed as a Pharisee of Pharisees. During that time as a Pharisee, Paul was known as a person who was blameless in the standards of the law.[41] However, Paul was now able to embrace a new life, and he ran with that new life, overcoming all

34. Acts 9:27–31.

35. Myers, *Introduction to Type*, 23.

36. Acts 18:3; Phil 3:5.

37. Gal 2:11–21.

38. Acts 1:8.

39. Matt 24:14; Matt 28:19; John 4:42; Acts 13:47.

40. Myers, *Introduction to Type*, 23.

41. Phil 3:4–7.

threats and applying his same zeal as well as creative problem-solving abilities to this new problem of spreading the gospel among the gentiles.[42]

42. Acts 23:6.

15

ESFP: Job, God's Faithful
and Enduring Servant

JOB, GOD'S FAITHFUL AND ENDURING SERVANT

AFTER AN ASSIDUOUS SEARCH, I found just the right leader to serve as representative for the ESFP personality. "Have you considered my servant Job?" This was the question that the Lord asked Satan in Job 2:3. I guess I had not considered him either until I had previously tried many other characters. Job was the right choice to represent the ESFP personality, and Job was the right choice to face extremely difficult trials.

Job was an Extrovert. He had many friends and family members until great tragedy struck his life by permission from God.[1] Job was God's recommended choice because he was oriented toward being able to live in his present reality and maintain his faith and trust in God, irrespective of the circumstances. Job was always guided by his deep faith in the Lord his God as well as by his flawless integrity.[2]

Job also strove for positive interactions with his friends. Just before God told Job to pray for his three friends who constantly accused Job of wrongdoing that he never committed, God told the friends to ask Job, the humble and faithful servant leader, to pray for them.[3] God told the friends that he would only forgive them if Job was the one who prayed.

1. Job 1:1–5, 1:6–2:10; 42:11.
2. Job 1:1.
3. Job 2:11; 42:7–10.

Job prayed for them and they were forgiven for leveling their false accusations about hidden sin at Job as he sat in inexplicable misery.

Finally, Job was probably the most flexible man that lived and not named Jesus. Job went through many trials not understanding why they came upon his life. But he uttered the famous words spoken in Job 13:15 (NIRV): "even if God kills me, I have hope in him." What a guy! Job was an ESFP and anything else he wanted to be. He earned it!

JOB'S EXTROVERSION PREFERENCE

The Bible shows us throughout the book of Job that Job had many friends and family members both before and after the tragedies that impacted his life.[4] He spent many hours talking to his three friends Eliphaz, Bildad, and Zophar about his plight.[5] They held many discussions about the current and tragic state of affairs that had become a part of his life.

It is believed by some that Job was the third son of Issachar, Jacob's grandson, who is mentioned in Genesis 46:13. No one knows for sure.

What we do know is that God recommended Job to Satan as a man who would never curse God's name no matter what Satan did to him. Satan twice asked for permission to take everything away from Job and do everything imaginable to him, short of taking his life.[6] God permitted this because Job demonstrated godly character and integrity.[7] God created Job with a personality that could enable him to endure unspeakable hardships. Job faithfully endured each and every one.

He also never broke fellowship with the few accusatory friends he had left.[8] He and his wife also remained connected, although at one point she asked him why he was trying to maintain his innocence. "Just curse God and die!" she tells him.[9] But he simply replied that she spoke as one of the foolish women, and he remained faithful to God.

4. Job 1:1–5; 2:11–37:24; 42:10–17.

5. Job 2:11.

6. Job 1:6–12; 2:1–7.

7. Job 1:1.

8. Job 2:11–37:24; 42:10–17.

9. Job 2:9.

Most importantly, Job never broke communion with God.[10] Job was consistent in his affection and humility toward God throughout his ordeal.[11] Job loved God and trusted him as completely as possible.[12]

Job often searched for answers.[13] As with most Extroverts, he had no problem expressing his feelings to God in front of his friends.[14] He wondered if he had committed a sin that he did not know about and that was the reason that God was punishing him.[15] He was in so much pain that he cursed the day that he was born. But Job never cursed God, as God knew he would not.[16]

Job overcame every trial.[17] Consequently, God restored everything that Satan took from him many, many times over. Job was an Extrovert and an inspirational man. He was also a leader to his family, his accusatory buddies, and especially to his wife.

JOB'S SENSING PREFERENCE

Job was highly attuned to endure his present reality. When Job had accumulated great material wealth and God had protected everything Job possessed, Job enjoyed that life.[18] When God allowed Satan to take everything away from Job, he declared that he will have his say, even if God kills him for saying it, and will continue to trust him.[19]

Job did not believe that he had consciously done anything wrong. He did not live in the land of make-believe. I believe the fact that Job knew he did nothing wrong to deserve anything that happened to him was his saving grace. He would not do as his wife requested and admit to a sin that he did not commit. He would also incessantly contend to his three friends that he had never committed a sin that he was trying to hide. Quite the contrary, he said that he would defend his integrity

10. Job 38:1–42:9.
11. Job 1:20–22.
12. Job 6:10.
13. Job 6:24.
14. Job 13:15–16.
15. Job 31:5–6.
16. Job 2:10.
17. Job 42:10–17.
18. Job 1:1–5.
19. Job 13:15.

to "God's face."[20] Job 15 recounts his boldness regarding his defense. He said that no guilty person would ever dare to challenge God face-to-face as he had done, expressing the confrontational Extrovert in himself once again.

Job remained faithful to the trust that he had in God's character. He trusted his information which was based on his experience and previous relationship with God. Thus, when things in his life had changed for the worse and he lost all of his material wealth as well as his health, he relied on the Sensing preference traits to help him to remain consistent.[21]

He knew that God was a just God. He also knew that he had not knowingly done anything wrong. Thus, he concluded that he would ultimately be proven innocent and recover from this tragedy. In the end, Job got through the trial and had everything restored.

JOB'S FEELING PREFERENCE

Job ultimately showed empathy for his three critical friends.[22] He was a compassionate man, so much so that, despite everything he had endured as well as the fact that these three guys did nothing but accuse him of unconfessed sin and not being man enough to admit his sin, he still prayed for them.

Job's friends reasoned that no blameless man would have to endure losing his family, his land, his home, and having painful skin boils grow on himself unless he had sinned against God. Job had to scrap the boils off with a piece of a broken pot.[23] Yuck!

Yet the ever-vigilant Job stayed true to his conviction that he had done nothing wrong and would not curse God because of what happened to him. He was fair-minded enough to empathize with his indicting friends, such that he prayed for God to forgive and restore them. Job made sound decisions throughout the trial because he operated out of his Feeling preference.

20. Job 13:15.
21. Job 2:10.
22. Job 42:7–10.
23. Job 2:8.

JOB'S PERCEIVING PREFERENCE

Job remained flexible and adaptable in his approach to his life. Things changed in an instant in Job's life. One moment, Job was known as the richest man who lived in the eastern region of the land identified as Uz.[24] The next moment (literally), Job lost everything: his houses fell down on top of his family. He lost his sons, daughters, and all of his livestock. Talk about a disorganized world!

Then Satan sought permission to attack Job's health. He did so and Job still did not accuse God of any wrongdoing. On the contrary, after God confronted Job, Job demonstrated the ability to change the way that he understood the world and who God was.[25] Job proved that he could adapt to any painful change that Satan could throw at him. Job had a Perceiving preference that allowed him to maintain this adaptable approach to dealing with his world and his present circumstances whatever they were at the time.

ESFP

Job was welcoming and accepting to his friends, his children, and to his wife who had told him to "curse God and die." Job's sons prior to the tragedy were great partiers and lovers of life.[26] I believe that they got that zest from Job. They certainly did not get it from their mother.

Job's realistic approach allowed him to become the richest man in the land. He was flexible through all of his trials and tribulations. When God showed Job that God was in charge of everything that transpired in the universe, including what transpired in Job's life, Job responded as the humble man that he was. However, even Job could stand to be humbled just a little more.[27]

Job admitted the error of his ways in making all of those complaints about his circumstance to God. However, he never cursed God. Job endured the hard situations that were presented to him, and pressed

24. Job 1:1–20.
25. Job 42:1–6.
26. Job 1:4–5.
27. Job 38–42.

through each one like a soldier in battle.[28] Job was an ESFP as well as a man who faithfully trusted his God.

ESFP: THE OPTIMISTS

APPLICATIONS FOR ESFPS

ESFPs are zest-filled lovers of life and all things fun.[29] Why I chose the man with one of the most difficult lives (or at least a portion of his life) to represent this personality type was a matter of comparable typology analysis. But Job's personality remained consistent through the good times and the bad.

Job's ESFP personality type demonstrated why he was able to remain consistent through every trial. I have mentioned that Job's sons were great partiers, and I believe that they got that penchant for amusement from dear old dad.[30] Job was also referred to as the greatest man in his town of Uz, as well as throughout the entire region of northern Arabia, during his time.

When times became difficult for Job, he responded in the same ESFP manner that he would have when everything was going well. ESFPs love life and they despise the constraint of convention, which they generally find a way to avoid.[31] They are loyal friends who quickly notice concerns with their friends. They will swiftly move to help their friends get to a better place, whether it's emotional, monetary, or physical.

Job behaved in the same consistent way toward God as he did toward his friends and family, whether he was enjoying great prosperity or if he was covered in skin boils while being accused of hiding some sin.[32] Like all ESFPs, he was known to his friends (even the accusatory ones) as a great encourager who was always willing to help.[33]

His personal value system and his dedication to his God guided his every action and made him a fun person for everyone to be around.[34] So

---

28. See 2 Tim 2:3.

29. Myers, *Introduction to Type*, 17.

30. Job 1:1–5.

31. Myers, *Introduction to Type*, 17.

32. Job 4:1–5:27.

33. Myers, *Introduction to Type*, 17.

34. Job 42:7–17.

when the Lord expressed his anger toward Job's friends and told them to go to Job to have him pray for their restoration to God, Job was the same consistent and helpful ESFP that he had always been, despite their constant accusations throughout his trial period.

ESFPs have a balance and optimism that should be infectious. Others, of any personality type, can learn from the ESFPs better ways to: pay attention to your friends, help them when they are in need, enjoy themselves, and enjoy life. ESFPs are optimistic and engaging.[35] We can all learn from that.

What we do not want our ESFP friends to do is to go around shining their little light in everyone's faces. This will likely turn many people off, as I will explain in detail, later. We also want ESFPs to avoid blithely sharing their happiness when a situation requires a serious-minded decision or a decision that requires constraint. Their behavior may make people uncomfortable. Otherwise, ESFPs simply have to be themselves and allow their light and behavior to shine before men.[36] I believe that God can use the ESFPs as great examples for all of us.

Developing As An ESFP

If they desire to do so, ESFPs can learn to grow in their biblical worldview in some significant ways. They can be greatly used by God as an example if their personality remains in balance. However, they have a genuine disdain for mundane or conventional rules, and they will find ways to avoid that convention because they want the party to resume as soon as possible, or they want that party to never stop in the first place.[37]

ESFPs seldom plan ahead because they love to live in the moment. They enjoy life as it comes. ESFPs generally do not anticipate problems very well, nor do they typically plan contingencies for life's unexpected eventualities. As previously mentioned, there is also that little concern regarding their tendency to shine their little ESFP light of unquenchable happiness in people's eyes.

ESFPs like Job need to realize that even though they are exemplary members of society, they also have to follow the same rules as everyone else. Additionally, ESFPs need to remember that there will inevitably

35. Myers, *Introduction to Type,* 17.

36. Matt 5:16.

37. Myers, *Introduction to Type,* 17.

come a time when all people must plan ahead. Finally, ESFPs should keep in mind that avoiding the rules can get you into big trouble. If they remain mindful of these concepts, they will be able to be used exactly as God created them to be used in his kingdom.

Considering the case of Job, I believe that he should have stuck to his guns. I do not believe that there was a man of more exemplary faith as Job. However, he had three friends left, following the unspeakable tragedies that had befallen his life. Those three constantly accused him of a crime or sin that he did not commit throughout the book of Job.

Job knew that he had done nothing wrong, including having committed a sin that he had forgotten. He, like all ESFPs, was a consistent person.[38] Knowing and being confident in this fact, he should have relied on his faith. Job should have told his friends that there are some things about God that we simply cannot know until he decides to tell us. Easy for me to say, I know. But this will help the ESFPs as they learn to walk by faith in a more consistent manner (if they choose to do so).

None of us will begin by being able to say: "I know that I have done nothing wrong that would cause God to punish me.[39] So, if times are difficult, they cannot be so as a result of my error." None of us except for Job, that is.[40] This sounds like a simple declaration. However, it is an important one for all other ESFPs not to mention the rest of us to make because it is the truth. We have to have confidence in our position if we stand in faith and if we have asked God to show us what, if anything, we are missing.

We may not start there, however. Those of us who choose to continue to walk with God should reach the point where we are able to just stand.[41] ESFPs like Job may struggle with the above declaration a bit because they are so open to their friends. They have to learn to balance that openness with their knowledge of their relationship with God.

We may not start out as a great person of faith. However, if we who have chosen to continue to walk with God arrive at that point, one that Job had long ago reached, we have to have confidence that God has a

38. Myers, *Introduction to Type*, 17.

39. See Rom 3:23.

40. Job 1:1.

41. Eph 6:13–14.

plan, and that we actually did nothing to incur the issues that we face in our lives. In short, to just stand.[42]

PERSONALITY EXTREMES FOR ESFPS

ESFPs have some potentially dangerous personality extremes, particularly considering how otherwise exemplary they can be when they are in balance relative to their personality type. ESFPs, as mentioned, do not like to plan ahead: they love to live in the moment.[43]

When an ESFP lives with their spouse and family, the desire to just "party, party, party" all of the time can cause major issues and concerns. Remember, everyone has different personalities. Even if they have the same personality type as you, they are likely to express each of their four preference zones in combination at different places along the continuum, thus making the whole personality type appear different from one person to the next. When a confluence of circumstances occurs where the ESFP has not prepared for future events and meets with some unforeseen disaster, conflict will inevitably result. The extreme ESFP will find themselves unprepared to go forward through the pending disaster, which now includes conflict within the family.

CONNECTIONS FOR ESFPS

The Extroverted manner in which the ESFPs relate to and interact with their world is connected to the Perceiving preference that they use to organize and make sense of their world. Also, ESFPs like to take in information in a straightforward, no-nonsense format using their Sensing preference. That Sensing preference, regarding the storage and retrieval of information within the ESFP, is used to inform the ESFP's Feeling preference and decision-making function. We can learn a lot from these connections.

42. Eph 6:13.
43. Myers, *Introduction to Type*, 17.

Connections Between The E-P Functions

The connection between the Extroverted preference and the Perceiving preference for the ESFP can get them into trouble, or it can be of a tremendous benefit to many. ESFPs are Extroverts so they are naturally engaging and most likely fun for everyone to be around.[44] Their Perceiving function allows them to keep the party going without planned conclusion. The Extrovert in them keeps bringing in guests.

ESFPs avoid the constraint of closure as a result of their Perceiving preference. If all is well, keeping everyone uplifted is a great thing. But if the moment requires a definitive decision, that will cause some tense feelings. For example, if a company has to lay off some employees and the ESFP attempts to influence the decision to move forward, based on their desire to "see what happens if we play this out a little longer," their ESFP personality expression guided by their Perceiving preference may result in bankruptcy for the company.

Connections Between The S-F Functions

The connections between the ESFP's Sensing preference and Feeling preference work in concert to make them into the joyful people that they appear to be around others. Their personality type is infectious and not faked. Using their Sensing preference to gather information about their friends makes ESFPs loyalists; they remain consistently attuned to the needs of their friends. They can remain reliable in any situations that may arise. They like to leave things open-ended. However, they are empathetic friends based on their Feeling preference.

I just think that it is great that an ESFP host always has the best A-list parties in town and at the same time the host is a gracious person who will remain loyal, faithful, and dedicated to the welfare of all of their guests and friends. You go, ESFPs!

GROWTH OPPORTUNITIES AND THREATS AS AN ESFP

I have discussed three potential threats related to the ESFP personality. ESFPs do not like rules or convention, they do not like to plan ahead, and they may have a tendency to spread their joy where the situation requires

44. Myers, *Introduction to Type*, 9–10.

a different demeanor. I have discussed some opportunities for growth relative to the first two threats. I likened the third one to going around shining their little light in everyone's eye like a flashlight.

Actually, a former pastor of mine came up with that last example. I once constructed a panel of speakers for my job as a graduate assistant during my master's program. It was a panel of people who represented various religions. The panel caused concern for some of the people in my church at the time. Personally speaking, I had no problem with it because I had confidence in who I was in God. It did not matter to me what the participants believed or said during the panel discussion. I was just checking boxes.

Remember, I can be very detached. I am certain that I did not listen carefully to a word that the speakers on the panel had uttered. I do not even remember if I put myself on the panel to represent Christianity. However, I think I was the moderator. I believe that people can believe whatever they want! It was my attitude then and it remains my guiding philosophy to this day. I am interested in the development and overall health of "the humans" far more than I am interested in the development of their faith and belief system as it relates or does not relate to the one that I have chosen to believe in and ascribe to. It is a choice. Free will, people! But I digress.

The pastor discussed the issue in church. Although I had never discussed it with him, some other people with concerns must have talked to him about their issues. He addressed it by speaking about a job that he once had in a mall. A woman who worked in a different store at this indoor mall would stand outside and say something like "Praise the Lord" every morning when she saw him because she knew that they were both Christians. I believe he said that it made him so uncomfortable that he started entering the mall a different way so he could avoid contact with her. I have done the same in grocery stores that I frequent.

I am all for praising the God that we believe in. However, we also have to be led by the Holy Spirit in everything that we do if we are of a particular faith. If the situation does not call for making that expression of praise to the other Christian friend of yours on a daily basis, then I believe it to be perfectly acceptable for two believers to just say, "Good morning."[45] In effect, you are simply using an expression of gratitude to supplant a customary greeting. We of that specific faith are to be all

45. See Eph 5:14–16.

things to all people so that we might convince some people to come to Christ. We can do this by letting our light just shine, but not by shining our light in people's faces.[46] That may completely turn off Christians and non-believers alike.

My ESFP friends can continue to grow in their areas of potential threats while realizing that no one starts at the end, or in other words, no one of that particular faith enters their relationship with God in the same place that they will finish. ESFPs should learn to overcome those inherent obstacles. Thus, they can grow into well-rounded people who are also great examples of remaining prudently but consistently uplifting.

46. 1 Cor 9:19–23.

16

ISFP: Ruth the Moabite

RUTH THE MOABITE

RUTH WAS ONE OF the great-grandmothers of Jesus.[1] Ruth married the son of a woman named Naomi who was from Judah, but Ruth herself was from a land called Moab. A famine drove the family from Judah to the land of Moab, where the two sons of Naomi found wives, one of whom was Ruth.[2]

While in Moab, all of the men in Naomi's family died. Thus, Naomi, Orpah (one of the daughters-in-law), and Ruth (the other daughter-in-law) were all left without husbands in Moab. The famine finally subsided in Judah and the three women headed back to Judah.[3]

Naomi told her daughters-in-law to go back to Moab and live with their families because their husbands were dead and they no longer owed anything to Naomi. Orpah went back to Moab, but Ruth remained dedicated to her mother-in-law.[4] After they moved back to Bethlehem in Judah, we are permitted to see a portrait of all of the personality traits of Ruth the ISFP.

1. Ruth 4:14–22; Matt 1:5.
2. Ruth 1:1–4.
3. Ruth 1:5–7.
4. Ruth 1:8–18.

Ruth had a quiet inner strength.[5] She was imputed with a fierce dedication to her mother-in-law Naomi.[6] Ruth showed great initiative, both to stay with Naomi and to ensure that she and Naomi had enough resources to sustain themselves for the rest of their lives.[7] These attributes are associated with those of an Introvert leader.

Ruth was also a realist, expressing the Sensing part of her personality. Ruth understood the ramifications associated with leaving her homeland without a husband. However, she still moved to a foreign land with her widowed mother-in-law. She had a much better chance of finding a husband in her homeland of Moab than she did in the foreign land of Judah. After all, her first husband found Ruth in Moab, not Judah.[8]

Ruth was guided by her personal set of ethics and values as all great leaders are directed.[9] She assessed the impact of her decision to move from Moab to Judah, as Naomi had requested that both daughters-in-law do, and her decision to stay true to her conviction that she stay with Naomi no matter what life situations presented her and Naomi in Judah. Ruth also did this regardless of whether or not she would remarry. She told Naomi that "your people will be my people, and your God will be my God."[10]

Ruth was flexible and adaptable enough to go where she needed to go while remaining true to her convictions. Ruth was malleable enough to do what was required to survive. When she finally met Boaz, a relative of Naomi's family, and he told her how and where to collect food, as well as who to stay with, she did exactly as instructed. This exemplifies her Sensing preference.[11] She kept the larger goal in mind of caring for her mother-in-law.[12] Ruth was an ISFP and a dedicated leader by example.

5. Ruth 3:10–11.
6. Ruth 1:16–18.
7. Ruth 2:1–3.
8. Ruth 1:8–18.
9. Ruth 1:16–18.
10. Ruth 1:16 (NIV).
11. Ruth 2:4–18.
12. Ruth 2:19–23.

RUTH'S INTROVERSION PREFERENCE

Ruth was an Introvert and an excellent example of an MBTI Introvert leader. You may be asking why I refer to Ruth as a leader. After all, she followed her mother-in-law back to Judah, leaving her homeland of Moab behind.

Ruth knew where she belonged. Using her Sensing preference, she believed it to be an immutable fact that she had to take care of Naomi. Ruth understood her job and calling. She was flexible, dedicated, and willing to do whatever it took to accomplish the task that had been placed upon her heart. She followed her heart and led by example.

Ruth provided a picture of a dedicated servant leader. Leaders are only as good as those whom they serve and lead. Ruth was called upon to lead her family, which for a time consisted of only herself and her mother-in-law. She felt compelled to ensure that her family, albeit a small one, was well-supported and taken care of. Naomi had no one else, and Ruth had been given an assignment in her heart by God. She took her charge and led herself as well as her mother-in-law past all obstacles to victory.

No, that victory was not achieved by finding Boaz;[13] that was a bonus for her obedience. The burden of leadership fell on Ruth's shoulders and she was up to the job of providing for her family.

Ruth drew inner strength while working alone in the fields collecting grain.[14] Ruth was generally found in conversation with only Naomi or Boaz. Otherwise she was by herself, thereby expressing her Introverted preference.

After the two widows settled in Bethlehem, Ruth took the initiative to tell Naomi that she thought she should go to the field and collect grain for them to eat. Ruth mused that maybe she would find someone kind who would help them by allowing her to collect grain in their field. But as the leader, Ruth submitted to authority and asked her mother for permission, which she received. Ruth was an Introverted servant leader who demonstrated quiet power.

---

13. Ruth 3:1–18; 4:9–17.
14. Ruth 3:1–9.

RUTH'S SENSING PREFERENCE

Ruth had a clear understanding of the consequences to following her heart and the internal call of God to go to Judea with Naomi. She realized that they were two women and she was the only one of working age; therefore she would have to be the primary bread-winner in a foreign land. However, I believe that there was a greater reality for Ruth to follow; this greater reality involved the conviction inside her which told her to go and care for her mother-in-law and dedicate herself to service and provision for Naomi.

When Ruth got home from the grain fields of Boaz that day, she had quite a story to tell. Her mother-in-law asked her where she got all of that grain.[15] Ruth conveyed the information to Naomi in a straightforward and detailed manner and related what happened to her that day. Ruth told Naomi that she met a man named Boaz, and that Boaz was going to act as the protector or kinsman-redeemer for their little family, because he was related to them through Naomi and her deceased husband. Naomi told Ruth that she was safe under the care and protection of Boaz.

Ruth demonstrated the attributes associated with her Sensing preference. She understood their present circumstance. She was also very detail-oriented and she trusted in her innate knowledge of God. She understood that as long as she did the right thing, God would provide for them.

RUTH'S FEELING PREFERENCE

Ruth was definitely empathetic toward her mother-in-law and allowed herself to be guided by her personal values and morals. She would not abandon her mother-in-law who she knew had nothing and was too old to take care of herself or marry someone who could take care of her. Naomi had lost her sons and the only person that she really had left as family was Ruth. Ruth was compassionate and, as I say about some people, Ruth worked with her heart. Ruth served with a whole-hearted dedication to the purpose, calling, and vision placed inside of that heart. Ruth led and served via her Feeling preference.

15. Ruth 2:19–23.

RUTH'S PERCEIVING PREFERENCE

When Ruth felt led to go out to the fields and collect some grain, she knew that she was doing so at great personal risk.[16] She was a foreigner in a strange land. But she had a family to feed. Her mother-in-law was too old to take her around introducing her to their kinsmen. So, Ruth was on her own.

Ruth went to the field just hoping to collect some grain that was left behind by the field hands. She did not know what field she was going to, much less that it belonged to Naomi's relatives. She ended up in a field owned by Boaz, who was a relative of Naomi's deceased husband, Elimelech.

When she was directed by Boaz to follow behind his workers and collect the best grains, not just what was left behind, she humbly thanked him and changed her plans. She was able to collect what she wanted, rest where she wanted, drink as much water as she wanted, and eat with the others from Boaz's food supply set aside for his field workers. Ruth was immensely blessed because of her obedience and flexibility. Ruth demonstrated the organizational skills and flexibility of a Perceiving-oriented person.

ISFP

Ruth appeared to be friendly, although also quiet, and definitely sensitive to the needs of others as are many ISFPs. Ruth was very loyal, even one of the most loyal leaders in the Bible. Ruth was also quite committed and dedicated to her values. She greatly esteemed the traits of loyalty and commitment.

Ruth exemplified those values with empathy, grace, trust, and perseverance. She probably did not like conflict and disagreements. Her mother-in-law noticed that about her, so she stopped arguing with Ruth about Ruth's plan to stay with Naomi instead of returning to the land of Moab.[17] Yet Ruth did not force her opinion on Naomi. Rather, she humbly insisted. She was a dedicated leader and remained true to helping her family. Ruth was blessed for her faithfulness.

16. Ruth 2:1–18.
17. Ruth 1:18.

She found a husband in the foreign land of Judah after all. The man Boaz, her protector, became Ruth's husband and helped her care for Naomi. The women of Bethlehem told Naomi that "Ruth is better to you than seven sons."[18] Ruth was the great-grandmother of King David, an exemplary servant leader, and an ISFP.

ISFP: THE CARETAKERS

APPLICATIONS FOR ISFPS

ISFPs are probably the greatest support personnel in the world. They are wonderful people to have around. They are warm and caring. As I tell one of my friends about herself, ISFPs are eminently positive!

ISFPs like Ruth are loyal almost to a fault. However, they demonstrate very little desire to force themselves into leadership positions. They prefer to observe, evaluate, and help where they are supposed to.[19] This brings us to another point: ISFPs have an innate ability to identify need areas and fill them. My mentor tells me to always help. ISFPs always help.

I seem to be working all of my counseling and advising axioms and idioms into this book, so why stop now? I tell people that men and women make one huge communication mistake apiece in their interactions with each other. I will discuss the one that I accuse women of making, as a part of this discussion. They make this communication mistake principally in their interpersonal relationships. Women often (I actually mean, always) say that "he should just know." I respond by saying, "He doesn't know. As a matter of fact, he has no idea" in regards to whatever the conflicting situation that we are discussing is. My point is that we all have to stop using these little "love tests" if we indeed use them. People who fit my example say to themselves that if he "just knows," then he loves me! For now, anyway, until the next test! Conversely, if he does not pick up exactly what I wanted him to discern through my veiled actions, then . . . he still loves you. Maybe he was just watching the game, paying you no attention, and he completely missed it. Just kidding; maybe he just missed it . . . sorry, guys!

In other words, the ISFP and all people need to learn not assume that a person who does not easily discern your actions, or one who does

---

18. Ruth 4:15 (NASB).

19. Myers, *Introduction to Type*, 26.

not remember each detail, or one who understand things in the same way that you do, is trying to hurt or slight you. They simply have a different personality type as well as different behavior patterns.

ISFPs are Introverts so they are comfortable being alone with their thoughts. They demonstrate care and affection in ways that may not be discernable to others. These demonstrations may be particularly imperceptible to those who do not know them well enough to pick up on what they are trying to communicate, or by those who do not know how to properly translate the actions of an ISFP.[20]

ISFPs have to remember that no one can read their minds. Some people are sensitive enough to feel it when ISFPs or others are hurting. But that is a gift or an inherently iNtuitive ability and ISFPs cannot assume that everyone has it, nor can the ISFP assume this specific feeling or musing was revealed to or sensed by the person in question.[21] It takes a long time to get to know another person and ISFPs are a special breed. To further confound their adjustment, their ISFP personality type makes them very observant. They can discern, via their personality type, when some people are hurting; it is their job. However, this is not typically the case for many other personality types. Thus, ISFPs, for some people, may be difficult to understand. However, this is no knock on the ISFP. ISFPs do things differently, and others, particularly if they are extreme, see things in only one way.

ISFPs: do not give up on anyone who you are not supposed to give up on. Always remember to continue to be yourselves. Do this while also allowing people to get to know you. If you are comfortable and desirous then do for others all that you believe that you should do for them.[22] If you are not comfortable, then do not become discouraged and take yourself away from those who you wish to support. Your ISFP personality is essential to the interconnected growth and development of the people whose lives you touch.

Developing As An ISFP

Everyone wants to be understood. However, the ISFP does not let people know what they are doing, some people may miss it. As a result, an ISFP

20. Myers, *Introduction to Type*, 26.

21. See 2 Kgs 4:27.

22. See Luke 6:31.

may leave the situation feeling misunderstood. This can result in hurt feelings for the ISFP.

ISFPs are characteristically sensitive people. This can be good or bad depending on the situation. I learned this lesson a long time ago: if I detach to a great extent, I will not be able to use my inherently sensitive and tender heart to enable me to feel what certain others are going through or to try to help them as I sense their hurts through the use of a sensitive and tender heart.

ISFPs naturally tend to protect themselves. Anyone who has a personality type that guides them toward being sensitive and supportive helpers try to protect themselves. However, remember that you may not be able to use the self-protecting and damaged idea that "I will not ever let that happen to me ever again, so I will just withdraw" if you want to become the ISFP that you are inherently designed to be.

If this is the case, please seek healing and move forward in order to live out the true nature of your ISFP personality. I call this "getting out of position" as relative to your intended purpose. If ISFPs become isolationists, they will take themselves out of play. As a result, so many people will miss out on all that they have to offer.

PERSONALITY EXTREMES FOR ISFPS

Can you imagine if Ruth the ISFP allowed herself to get out of position? What would have happened to Naomi, her mother-in-law? As a result of remaining open to God's leading, Ruth took it upon herself to stay with her mother-in-law through thick and thin regardless of the circumstances. Ruth also knew that there was a chance that she would never remarry.[23]

Ruth from Moab was going to a different land, so she knew she might have a more difficult time encountering a future mate, one with whom she could be the complete ISFP person and support him while doing all that she was called to do. After making the decision to follow Naomi, Ruth decided that she must take the lead and go to the fields in order to collect food for herself and her mother-in-law. She did this after she humbly asked her mother-in-law for permission to go.[24] ISFPs

23. Ruth 1.
24. Ruth 2.

will take the lead but they do not seek out the spotlight like many other personality types.

If Ruth had gotten stuck in her feelings at any point and allowed her naturally sensitive heart to take her out of position, imagine how things would have turned out for Naomi, not to mention for her great-grandson King David, who might not have been born. The little family of Ruth and Naomi would not have been able to eat, nor would she have met Boaz, whom she eventually married.[25]

Sensitivity is an important trait. ISFPs are naturally sensitive; I would even say that they are "giftedly-sensitive." It allows their ISFP personality to impact many people in positive ways. But if ISFPs of a biblical worldview allow this area to go to an extreme and withdraw because of a misunderstanding, then they are withdrawing from God and his ability to use them to their maximum impact. They are also withdrawing themselves from people who absolutely need them, as well as hindering them from using all that my beloved ISFPs bring to the table.

By the way, being supportive is not a weakness. It is a strength. I figured I would throw that one in for my ISFPs and for everyone else, free of charge!

CONNECTIONS FOR ISFPS

The Introverted manner in which the ISFPs relate to and interact with their world is connected to the Perceiving preference that they use to organize and make sense of their world. Also, ISFPs like to take in information in a straightforward, no-nonsense format using their Sensing preference. That Sensing preference, regarding the storage and retrieval of information in the mind of the ISFP, is used to inform the ISFP's Perceiving preference and decision-making function. We can learn a lot from these connections.

Connections Between The I-P Functions

ISFPs are Introverts. They are quite happy talking with one other person. They are equally as happy spending time in the world of their own thoughts. As a result, the ISFP may act out of something that they are thinking about without realizing that others cannot read their thoughts.

25. Ruth 4:13.

Their actions, relative to their Perceiving function, will likely be an open-ended action that does not force a person to draw a definite conclusion.

ISFPs would prefer to communicate and connect via this idea: "I would rather you notice than require that I have to tell you." The connection can potentially result in hurt feelings if the other person does not realize what the ISFP is attempting to show them through their actions. At times the Introverted ISFP may have to tell someone what they are thinking, feeling, or doing, instead of hoping that they notice. This can be quite affirming to the sensibilities of many ISFPs. However, it can also set unrealistic expectations for other people and their inherent abilities.

Connections Between The S-F Functions

The ISFP's Sensing function allows them to take in information in a direct manner. They use this preference to help and to support many people. They can interpret how people are feeling as well as issues where they need to involve themselves in order to bring about a quick resolution to a challenging problem. ISFPs naturally use this Sensing function to inform their Feeling preference. They use their Feeling preference to decide upon the best course of action in order to help those in need.

GROWTH OPPORTUNITIES AND THREATS AS AN ISFP

One threat to growth that is relevant to ISFPs is related to the idea that they can be too hard on themselves at times.[26] ISFPs may set an unrealistically high standard for themselves. ISFPs may also have an outsized expectation of themselves to make everything all better.

Obviously, everyone needs to be led in regards to the help that they provide for other people. But ISFPs by personality type will put themselves in positions to help others. I always say, "Never allow your passion to precede your prejudice." In other words, at times you have to review a situation or the issue that a friend is facing and allow yourself to be honest with yourself. At times you have to objectively know that you are not the best one to provide assistance in this circumstance for whatever reason.

---

26. Myers, *Introduction to Type*, 26.

Jesus said, "my sheep know my voice."[27] This means that the people who are open to receiving his love are his sheep. He can help them. The others are not his sheep, yhus, when He called to them they would not answer, because they could not recognize the voice of the one calling.

ISFPs also need to learn to live their lives from the inside-out. They need to understand that people may not always know what they are thinking, feeling, or trying to communicate unless they actually tell and show them. I hate it when college professors play what I call "Guess what is in my head," instead of fully explaining the concepts being instructed to the students who do not know what the professor is thinking.

Remembering how beneficial you are to the world as an ISFP allows you to present yourselves with an opportunity to grow in this area. ISFPs have a lot to offer. However, no one can receive a letter that does not have a stamp on it or one that is never mailed.

27. John 10:27 (NIV).

17

ENFP: King David

KING DAVID

KING DAVID RULED IN Judah and Israel after King Saul died.[1] David was considered an obedient man after God's own heart.[2] He demonstrated the traits of an ENFP.

David was a pronounced Extrovert. He was a king, a general, a fierce warrior, a husband and father, a shepherd, and a prophet (as demonstrated throughout the prophetic psalms that David wrote and through his use of the priestly prayer garment, the ephod, to seek the guidance of the Lord).[3] David was also a prolific and passionate writer of the Psalms, and an expressive dancer who had many, broad-ranging interests.

David was oriented toward future possibilities, even if some of them were in error. David wanted to build a temple as a permanent resting place for the ark of the covenant. He recognized that the ark of the covenant needed a permanent home, but God told David that building the temple would not be his role as king. That duty would fall to his son Solomon when he became king, because David was a man of war.[4] David was

---

1. 2 Sam 1:1; 2:4.

2. 1 Sam 13:14.

3. 1 Sam 16; 17–18; 25:42–44; 2 Sam 5; 23:1–2.

4. 2 Sam 7:1–17; 1 Kgs 5:1–5.

also a great general who followed his INtuition when it came to gathering information and used his godly insight about the coming battles.[5]

David was a man who went through many trials. Some trials David faced because of others, such as King Saul's jealousy.[6] David also faced some trials because he was disobedient to God. He took Uriah the Hittite's wife, named Bathsheba, for his own, even though Uriah was one of his most faithful followers and chief lieutenants.[7] He ordered his general, Joab, to send Uriah to the front line of a fierce battle to be killed, in order to cover up his adultery with Bathsheba. This act was committed while King David remained in the palace, far from this particular battle. As a result, David lost his kingdom for a time to one of his sons, Absalom.[8] But when he had to make decisions regarding sparing the life of that son, David displayed empathy, compassion, and a desire to spare the life of Absalom who had betrayed and stolen the kingdom from his father David.[9]

David was very flexible in battle, although he was vigilantly dedicated to his values.[10] He would not harm Saul, even though Saul sought to end his life because he was jealous of David.[11] David was adaptable to the many changes that occurred in his life. David was an ENFP.

DAVID'S EXTROVERSION PREFERENCE

Once David danced with joy in the streets, much to the chagrin and dismay of his first wife, Michal. She was also King Saul's daughter. When she balked at his demonstration, he told her that he would dance even harder because of all that the Lord had done for him.[12] David was an Extrovert.

David had to flee the kingdom of Israel because Saul was jealous of David's fame and acclaim as a warrior. Saul wanted to kill him. This occurred in spite of the fact that David became one of Saul's mightiest

---

5. 1 Sam 18:5–7; 30:7–25.

6. 1 Sam 18:5–17.

7. 2 Sam 11:1–12:23.

8. 2 Sam 15:1–18:33.

9. 2 Sam 18:5.

10. 1 Sam 23:2, 4, 10–14; 30:7–25; 2 Sam 2:1–2; 5:19, 23–25; 21:1.

11. 1 Sam 24:1–22; 26:1–25.

12. 2 Sam 6:14–22.

generals.[13] David had the courage of a lion. He even killed a lion and a bear with his bare hands.[14]

When David fled Saul's wrath, he went to hide in the forest inside of some caves.[15] Hundreds of men followed him out there. David led these men as their general and anointed king while on the run from Saul. These men would ultimately serve David in his kingdom following the death of Saul, when David would finally be able to ascend to the throne in Judah and Israel.[16] David was a singer and songwriter, writing many songs listed throughout 1 and 2 Samuel, in addition to being a great leader, general, and warrior.

David ultimately became the king of Judah and Israel. David also wrote many of the psalms in that book in the Bible. David was sociable and expressive. He took the initiative when no one else would to face a giant from the land of the Philistines with a slingshot and five smooth stones. David was an Extrovert, though he shared some qualities with Introverts.

DAVID'S INTUITIVE PREFERENCE

David was an iNtuitive warrior and general. He quickly formed battle plans after assessing the available information. Whether it involved grabbing a lion or bear by the fur before beating it to death with his staff and thereby saving his sheep, or formulating an attack plan for facing the giant Goliath, attacking the Philistines, or attacking the Jebusites in Jerusalem, all while remaining elusive and never being captured by Saul.[17] His information-gathering and assimilation may have involved seeking the Lord in regards to how to attack many different enemies in battle as king.

David followed his iNtuitive nature. He would gather the appropriate information by seeking the Lord's guidance in prayer.[18] David would then quickly move to conclusions and follow his gut instincts as well as the leading of the Lord. David was an iNtuitive and insightful leader.

---

13. 1 Sam 24:1–22; 26:1–25.

14. 1 Sam 17:34–36.

15. 1 Sam 22:1–2.

16. 2 Sam 2:1–11; 5:1–5.

17. 1 Sam 17:38–54; 18:5–27:4; 2 Sam 5:17–19; 5:6–10.

18. 1 Sam 18:30; 23:9; 30:7; 2 Sam 6:14; 1 Chron 15:27.

DAVID'S FEELING PREFERENCE

David was always guided by his relationship with and profound love for the Lord. Even when he did what was wrong in the sight of the Lord, he said that he preferred to be in the hands of the Lord for punishment rather than to leave his fate in the hands of man.[19]

David displayed empathy for his son Absalom, even after Absalom betrayed him and stole his kingdom, setting himself up as *de facto* king of Israel. David knew that the whole thing occurred because of his disobedience in deference to God's laws. David pleaded with Joab to be kind to the young man Absalom, as they would face off in battle.[20]

David took into full consideration the ramifications of his decisions. On one occasion when the Amalekites raided David's camp at Ziklag, kidnapping all of the men's wives and children, David sought the Lord for answers and emotional strength.[21] David once again demonstrated the qualities of a Feeling Introvert, although his stronger preference was clearly toward Extroversion. David was told by the Lord to pursue the Amalekites and that he and his men would recover everything that was stolen from them. On the journey to find the Amalekites, some of his men were too tired to continue pursuing their enemies, as they were just returning from battle when they arrived at Ziklag. So these men sat out the remainder of the pursuit while David and the rest of his men continued the chase. They ended up being victorious. David and his men recovered everything that the Amalekites had stolen, including their wives and children. They also took valuable items from the defeated Amalekites.

When they returned to the men who could not continue the quest to find the Amalekites, the soldiers who had won the battle did not want to share the new bounty with those who stayed and rested. David expressed his empathetic Feeling preference and told those men that they should not be so mean to their brothers. They were a team and they would always share everything taken in battle. David was a fair-minded man. He demonstrated his Feeling preference in decision-making.

---

19. 2 Sam 12:1–15; 24:1–25.

20. 2 Sam 18:5.

21. 1 Sam 30:1–31.

DAVID'S PERCEIVING PREFERENCE

David was quite an organized leader, both as general and as king. David would begin by seeking direction from the Lord. There were times that the Lord told David to lead his men in a head-on attack pattern and that they would be victorious.[22] There were other times that the Lord changed the plans and had the army pursue an alternative flanking strategy. David had to remain adaptable to the battle plans presented to him by the Lord and go with the flow.

Another example of David's flexibility came regarding the impending battle between those that remained loyal to King David and those who switched their allegiance to side with Absalom, David's estranged son. David wanted to participate in the pending battle between his men and those of Absalom. His high general (Joab) and the other two commanders that he appointed, Abishai and Ittai, told him that no matter what happens in that battle, Absalom's men would go after David as their sole target. They told him that he was worth ten thousand of his loyal subjects and none of them could afford to have him perish in this battle. He agreed to their request, and after laying out the battle plan and pleading for them to be generous with Absalom, he decided to remain in Mahanaim, sitting the battle out.[23]

Each time he was faced with a challenge, David would go through the appropriate process and seek the guidance of the Lord. Then he and the army would follow the plan to the final detail. David was obedient and usually victorious because of his flexible yet deliberately expressed Perceiving preference. This made him successful as a general and as a king.

ENFP

David was quite imaginative. He wrote beautiful psalms. Once, he became so enthusiastic about his God that his passion compelled him to face a giant who dared to "speak against the armies of the Living God."[24] He also wanted to face that giant because Saul promised that the one who faced Goliath would get to marry his daughter, Michal (Well, the one

---

22. 1 Sam 18:30; 23:9; 30:7; 2 Sam 6:14; 1 Chron 15:27.

23. 2 Sam 18:1–5.

24. 1 Sam 17.

who faced Goliath would marry her provided he survived the conflict). The prospect of dying did not dampen David's eagerness. He rushed right out there because he knew that he had the Lord on his side.

He remembered and made connections to the events from his past, specifically his conflicts with the lion and the bear. He drew on the wisdom derived from those connections as he faced his future. He said he was confident in the fact that the same God who saved him from the lion and the same God who delivered him from the bear, would deliver him from the uncircumcised Philistine giant and give him victory in the battle. So he packed up his smooth little rocks and his sling and walked down into the valley to whip a giant. David was spontaneous and flexible, but always well-prepared because he sought the Lord. They asked David to wear some armor to face that giant, but he did not need it. He was able to improvise and beat the giant with the help of the Lord.

Finally, David was quite a creative writer. He was very expressive. Many of the passages that he wrote in the Psalms are commonly cited by people of all backgrounds thousands of years later. David was an ENFP.

ENFP: THE INTREPID ONES

APPLICATIONS FOR ENFPS

David can serve as an easy frame of reference for the ENFPs. ENFPs can learn many positive life applications associated with their personality type through gaining a better understanding of the many examples that were present in David's life. David demonstrated the best and the worst attributes associated with the ENFP personality type. ENFPs can easily address people and crowds, even if required to do so without much notice.[25] ENFPs make engaging leaders who people are willing to follow due to their Extroverted nature.

They can also be creative problem-solvers, as exemplified by David when he slayed Goliath and by his ability to kill lions and bears while herding sheep.[26] ENFPs use their insight to spur an ability to quickly trust God, although his messages to us are not always easily translated. However, David knew how to trust what he saw and iNtuitively knew.

25. Myers, *Introduction to Type*, 21.

26. 1 Sam 17.

ENFPs gather and interpret information using their iNtuitive preference. Thus, when David faced a situation where his sheep were being
attacked by a lion or a bear, he knew that he could defeat it because he
trusted God.[27] He trusted his insight into his profound relationship with
God when he spontaneously went out to fight with Goliath, the giant
from Gath, whom no one else in the army of Israel wanted to fight.

ENFPs can apply the good and the bad lessons from David's life to
their own. On the good side David was willing to trust what he knew
about God. He said that this giant had no right to defy the armies of
God.[28] He knew that he would defeat Goliath because he had previously
learned to trust his godly insight when deciding to fight lions and bears
in order to save his father's sheep. Thus, he knew that his God was worthy
of honor and respect no matter how great the opposition. David knew
that if he was on the Lord's side, he would come out victorious.

However, David the ENFP also allowed situations to go on too
long. He did not always face reality or problems as his Judging preference counterparts would. He allowed his son Absalom, who had killed
his half-brother for raping his sister, to just go away.[29] Absalom had to
set fire to the field belonging to Joab, David's four-star general, in order
to gain audience with the king. But this occurred some two years after
David brought his son back from exile for his crime.

The situation resulted in a huge mess. But the real and underlying
problem was that Absalom, due to David's avoidance of problems, was
left feeling rejected. David did not need to frustrate his son. Rather, he
needed to make a decision as father and king.[30] It was a difficult decision
to be certain, but so was the decision to fight a giant, and he did not
hesitate on that one.

27. 1 Sam 17:34–37.
28. 1 Sam 17:31–47.
29. 2 Sam 13–19.
30. See Eph 6:4.

Developing As An ENFP

ENFPs have dynamic and curious personalities.[31] They are able to get people to follow them due to their natural charisma and their way with words.[32] But they need to attend to their decision-making function.

I mentioned early in this book that people who have a Feeling preference like to make decisions with their heart. They are almost offended if someone tells them that they have to take the feelings (not compassion, but feelings) out of their decision-making process. This would force them to use their innate compassion while balancing that mindset by thinking objectively and rationally, as the Thinking preference folks do.

The ENFP David allowed this recurring issue to present a problem for him on a few occasions. At times he did not make a decision quickly enough, nor did he consult the Lord as he had done so many times as a younger man when leading his men into battle.[33] When Absalom killed his half-brother Amnon, David did not step in or make a decision as king or father.[34] Finally, when Absalom was permitted to come back home after fleeing because of the murder, David ignored him rather than dispensing justice, neither restoring his son nor punishing him for his crimes.[35]

The Absalom and Amnon issue's result was that David did not continue to consult the Lord in all of his ways.[36] Prior to the Absalom and Amnon incident, David also allowed himself to fall prey to his emotions by taking Bathsheba for himself at any cost.[37]

Additionally, David esteemed anyone that the Lord had anointed, irrespective of how that person (for example, King Saul or General Abner) walked under their mantle of that anointing from the Lord. David, too, walked with the Lord.

I am not sure what happened to David the ENFP to cause him to divert from his values. We know that ENFPs have a very deeply-rooted values system which they adhere to closely.[38] But at some point, whatever

---

31. Myers, *Introduction to Type*, 21.

32. 2 Sam 3:35–37.

33. 1 Sam 18:30; 23:9; 30:7; 2 Sam 6:14; 1 Chron 15:27.

34. 2 Sam 13.

35. 2 Sam 14.

36. Prov 3:6.

37. 2 Sam 11–12.

38. Myers, *Introduction to Type*, 21.

the specific cause, David's walk with the Lord took a poor turn or two which resulted in him veering off course later in life.

I pray that everyone chooses to begin to walk with the Lord. If they do, when they start they should remember that it is just as important to continue the good habits and practices that once accompanied them when they first chose to walk with the Lord.[39] Then, it is equally as important to allow him to add to theircharacter as they continue your walk. This prevents them from becoming so frustrated to the point that they stop walking. I encourage them to press on and continue in their old practices but allowing God to add new ones.

PERSONALITY EXTREMES FOR ENFPS

David's personality was extreme later in life, and it occurred for some reasons that are difficult to explain. King David saw Bathsheba on the roof and decided to take her for his own. Sure, she was beautiful. However, she was also the wife of one of David's thirty most valued warriors, Uriah.[40]

The reason that I call his behavior inexplicable is because up to that point David demonstrated a desire to follow the Lord in all of his ways.[41] It appears that as David became older and more settled as king, he took an apparent turn for the worse. However, I have never fully understood what led to some of his issues later in life.

It was possible that as a young general, David had to constantly seek the Lord in order to receive the detailed battle plans from the Lord of heaven's armies.[42] As king, his regular participation in the war against Philistia gradually diminished, as that duty now fell to his general and nephew, Joab.[43] David may have no longer continuously engaged the Lord regarding receiving daily guidance and direction like he did as a young general.

This is unconfirmed speculation. Yet it may have an element of truth in it. David also took a census much later in life, and he had to repent once again as the Lord passed judgement against him.[44]

---

39. See Luke 9:62; 14:25–34.

40. 2 Sam 11; 23:8–39.

41. Prov 3:6.

42. See Isa 47:4.

43. 2 Sam 8:16, 11:1, 12:26–29, 18:1–4, 20:23, 21:15–17.

44. 2 Sam 24.

I can only explain these decisions by basing them on a flawed decision-making process related to David's Feeling preference. It is important that we who choose to walk with the Lord fully and continuously submit ourselves to him and in turn allow him to direct us as well as the steps that we take in life. Feelings are really a function of our soul, or our ego as Freud would call it. But emotions should not guide us or our actions. David allowed his feelings, which were temporary and like passing busses, to rule the day. As a result, he allowed his entire personality to go to an extreme place.

CONNECTIONS FOR ENFPS

The Extroverted manner in which the ENFPs relate to and interact with their world is connected to the Perceiving preference that they use to organize and make sense of their world. Also, ENFPs like to take in information and insightfully interpret that data using their iNtuition preference. That iNtuition preference, regarding the storage and retrieval of information relative to the ENFP, is used to inform the ENFP's Feeling preference and decision-making function. We can learn a lot from these connections.

Connections Between The E-P Functions

David was willing to allow things to play out. This was both good and bad. David never lacked for friends and company because of his Extroverted preference. Even when he was on the run from Saul, many of his family members and friends who were frustrated with King Saul's rule came to stay with the rightfully anointed king, David,[45] even if that meant that they had to live in the wilderness with him while he was fleeing from Saul.

David's son Absalom killed his half-brother Amnon for raping Tamar, Absalom's sister.[46] David did not respond appropriately to the entire situation, preferring to leave the matter open-ended using his Perceiving preference. David continued to serve as king, holding banquets and other regal events for years, while he allowed his son to live in exile.

---

45. 1 Sam 22:1–2; 1 Chron 12:1–22.

46. 2 Sam 13.

David's son Absalom was an outcast and was not allowed to see his father for years, even after David allowed Absalom to return to the kingdom.[47] The open-ended manner in which his Perceiving preference allowed him to organize his world resulted in him losing his kingdom to Absalom for a period of time.[48] David needed to learn to deal with issues by confronting them and making a decision. This was his job as king and his responsibility as a father.[49]

Connections Between The N-F Functions

David's iNtuitive preference was remarkable regarding the manner in which he could look behind information to see how the Lord was leading. Then he would act without hesitation. He did this when it came to facing Goliath. As David stated, he took action against Goliath because he felt that Goliath had no business insulting, much less opposing, the army of Israel. David interpreted the information in front of him and decided, based on his Feeling preference, to take swift and decisive action.[50] He was not afraid to fight the much larger Goliath. He prevailed in his battle with Goliath as well as in so many other battles because he confidently trusted his interpretation of information and he trusted the Lord to fight all of his battles.[51]

GROWTH OPPORTUNITIES AND THREATS AS AN ENFP

As a young man, David always sought the Lord for direction and strategy.[52] He provided Israel with a great example of leadership, beginning with the time that he was anointed by Samuel through the time that he assumed the thrones of Judah and Israel.[53]

King David did not dispense his own brand of justice when it came to the slight that he received from Nabal the fool.[54] Of course, Abigail

47. 2 Sam 14.

48. 1 Sam 15–19.

49. Eph 6:4.

50. 1 Sam 17.

51. See Exod 14:14

52. 1 Sam 18:30; 23:9; 30:7; 2 Sam 6:14; 1 Chron 15:27.

53. 1 Sam 16–2 Sam 5.

54. 1 Sam 25.

helped a lot. But he still decided to stay on the Lord's side because of his decision-making preference.

David also did not take advantage of the situation and kill Saul on the two occasions when he easily, and justifiably some may say, could have done so.[55] He set this example for Joab, but Joab chose a different path.

Joab was David's lead general. Once he took revenge into his own hands in spite of the fact that he had an excellent example in David.[56] Joab, killed Abner, who was King Saul's ranking general. He engaged in this act of vengeance because Abner killed Joab's baby brother, Asahel. Abner could have possibly avoided killing Asahel.[57] Joab and Abner knew each other well because they served as colleagues in the army of Israel before Saul turned on David.[58] Joab saw David consult the Lord countless times. Joab also saw King David avoid touching God's anointed ones, no matter the situation.[59] Joab chose not to follow David's example.

Later in life after he became king, David would not follow his own earlier example of seeking the Lord prior to rendering any and all decisions. David was also challenged by virtue of allowing his son Absalom to effectively go rogue and in an act of treason to usurp David's crown, taking it for himself and becoming king.[60]

ENFPs can allow themselves to become overextended.[61] David organized his world via an open-ended and emotion-based, organizational strategy; when this was coupled with the fact that David did not continue to seek the Lord for direction regarding all of his affairs, he lost the kingdom. He also took another man's wife; I would even say that David married too many wives, acting out of an ENFP personality extreme.

King David was an extremely confident warrior, man, and king. This was demonstrated through almost all of his early actions and decisions. ENFPs have an inherent and radiant quality of self-assurance. However, King David seemed to forget to always "dance with who brung him" (the Lord). He continued to act out of that same confident nature

55. 1 Sam 24:1–7; 26:1–12.

56. 1 Sam 23–24; 2 Sam 2.

57. 2 Sam 2:18–31; 3:22–30.

58. 1 Sam 17; 1 Chron 11:6.

59. 1 Sam 23–24; 2 Sam 2.

60. 2 Sam 15.

61. Myers, *Introduction to Type,* 21.

that envelopes most ENFPs, but the driving force behind that confidence was the wise counsel that he received when he chose to seek the Lord, early and often, regarding his every decision and action.[62]

---

62. See Ps 63:1; Matt 6:33.

18

INFP: Abigail, A Lady, A Queen

ABIGAIL, A LADY AND A QUEEN

ABIGAIL HAD ONLY ONE chapter in the Bible dedicated to her journey, although she is mentioned in other chapters throughout the books of 1 and 2 Samuel. She is discussed in detail in 1 Samuel 25. She epitomizes all of the best traits of an INFP.

Abigail was married to a fool named Nabal. His name actually means "fool," and she was well aware of the metaphorical as well as literal connections with her husband's name.[1] Abigail understood the fact that Nabal was what his name said that he was. She discussed his name and persona during her conversation with King David.

Abigail drew strength from her inner world and was an excellent communicator. She seemed to be a private and reserved person. However, she was also wise beyond her years. Abigail took initiative to rectify a terrible situation to the benefit of everyone when required to do so.[2] She was a sagacious woman who was worth far more than precious jewels.[3] She was a true lady who her husband David, would praise, just as King Solomon wrote in Proverbs 31. Abigail was a strong and wise Introvert.

Abigail followed her iNtuition based on the information available to her. She knew that her first husband Nabal was a fool who did not know

---

1. 1 Sam 25:25 (NIV).
2. 1 Sam 25:14–31.
3. See 1 Sam 25:32–38, Prov 31:10.

how to treat people. She also knew that David was the future king of Judah and Israel. She recognized that when the time and need arose, she would have to spring into action in order to rectify certain situations that were caused by her boorish husband before the people in her household became adversely impacted by his activities. She trusted her inspiration and was wise enough to spring into action in order to rectify issues to the satisfaction of all parties.[4] Abigail used her iNtuition and led her family wisely.

Abigail was deeply empathetic. She expressed this not only through her concern for her husband Nabal, but also through her concern for David, the anointed king of Israel. She decided to spare David from the consequences of his own wrath.[5] She was amazingly gifted with intelligence and wisdom. Abigail used her Feeling preference to inform her wise decisions.

Can you tell that Abigail is my favorite? I love this woman! She was capable of being spontaneous and flexible in her approach to life. She was the epitome of a leader as she led and preserved her and Nabil's household. She had to be that way because she was married to an aptly-named fool.

Yet Abigail demonstrated an ability to become energized by last-minute pressure-filled situations. She was deftly able to work them out to the benefit of all parties. She had a Perceptive preference, among her many laudable INFP qualities.

ABIGAIL'S INTROVERSION PREFERENCE

Abigail demonstrated her abilities as an excellent interpersonal communicator as she saved David from himself. David, while he was on the run from Saul, lived in the southern portion of the land of Judah.[6] David and his men were dedicated Israelites. They protected sheepherders who were in their area without asking the herders for any remuneration for their protective services. David had occasion to guard the herd of a Calebite man from Judah named "fool" or Nabal. Fool lived up to his name.[7]

---

4. 1 Sam 25:14–38.

5. 1 Sam 25:12–13, 32–35.

6. 1 Sam 25:4.

7. 1 Sam 25:1–13.

David found out that Nabal was preparing a feast in celebration of the fact that it was wool-shearing season. David and his men were running low on supplies. David sent his men to speak with Nabal and ask him to give them some supplies and food if he could spare any. They could easily spare some provisions for the future king of Judah and Israel, as well as for his men who protected Nabil's shepherds while they were in the fields. David reminded Nabal that he and his men defended Nabil's herds from those who might rob them without ever asking for payment. Both David and Nabal were from the land of Judah. Nabal, in reply to David's request, insulted David and rebuffed his men. When David heard Nabil's retort, he felt disrespected and told his men to grab their swords.

However, this analysis is about Abigail. The herdsmen ran and told Nabil's wife Abigail how Nabal had insulted David and his men.[8] They told her how kind David and his men were to them while they were herding Nabil's sheep. Abigail knew the nature of her foolish husband, but she was able to draw strength from inside of herself and she sprang into action. She gathered some of the food that was prepared for the feast that Nabal was planning. Abigail had the supplies packed on some donkeys and commanded her men to head out to the place where they knew that David and his men were staying. Abigail was diplomatic and prudent enough to know not to tell Nabal a thing.

She formulated her plan within herself and took the initiative to rectify the situation, while also saving Nabal and all of the men in her household from certain death. David had every right to feel offended and he could justify an attack against Nabal and her household. Nabal was wrong and rude. Nabal should have paid David and his men by giving them some food and supplies. Abigail understood that and went into action in order to fix the problem. Abigail was a strong and wise Introvert.

ABIGAIL'S INTUITIVE PREFERENCE

Abigail knew what would happen if she did not act quickly and appropriately. David would come with all of his warriors and avenge the offense leveled at him by the foolish Nabal.[9] So after Abigail directed her herdsmen to go to David's camp, bearing the supplies that she had taken

---

8. 1 Sam 25:14–22.

9. 1 Sam 25:13.

from the pending feast, she decided not to stop there. Abigail followed her instincts and decided to meet with David herself.

After sending them on their way to meet David, Abigail mounted a donkey and rode out to meet David. She knew that food and supplies alone would not satisfy David's insulted honor. She had to employ all of her creativity and wisdom to try to stem the anger of the future king.[10]

She met David as he descended down the opposite side of a mountain ravine.[11] When she came face to face with the anointed king, she dismounted from her donkey, fell to her knees in reverence to his crown and asked him if she could speak with him. She was inspired to act, and so far, so good. Her iNtuition about the pending calamity was likely correct because coming around the bend of the mountain were David and about 400 armed soldiers, headed straight for her home.

ABIGAIL'S FEELING PREFERENCE

One would think that this woman would have empathy for her husband, Nabal. After all, she married him. But during those times, the marriage could have been arranged. The reality was that she ended up demonstrating a profound level of compassion and empathy for King David.

Guided by her personal and God-inspired ethical and moral value system, she assessed the impact of the potential actions of David that would occur as a result of his proposed retaliation in response to the foolish acts of her husband Nabal. She tried to achieve a conclusion that would satisfy all parties and result in no bloodshed. Her compassion for David was amazing. This compassion and sense of equity was displayed through her subsequent activities and confirmed her Feeling preference.

Abigail demonstrated for David that she could completely empathize with his situation. She showed him that she knew exactly who he was as the future king. She let him know that she understood exactly what he was feeling. She connected with her audience iNtuitively by using common knowledge in order to link with David and convince him of her empathy for him as well as his current plight as the future king. She let him know that she identified with the fact that he was currently on the run from Saul, living in caves instead of living in a palace.[12]

10. 1 Sam 25:14–20.

11. 1 Sam 25:23–24.

12. 1 Sam 25:24–31.

Abigail used two themes to accomplish her goal. She began by stating to David that God would protect him as if he were a precious treasure to God. She used this specific language in order to communicate to David that she understood the type and depth of offense that Nabal had levied at his honor. However, she also did this in order to tap into the emotional pain and discouragement that David surely felt. She knew that he lived in the caves because Saul was trying to kill him. She wanted David to know that it had been God who was protecting him and keeping him as safe as a guarded precious treasure during his entire sojourn in the wilderness.

Abigail followed this statement with a second theme. She said that God was and would continue to keep the future king of Israel as "safe as someone (who) guards a precious treasure"[13] from all of the Nabals and Sauls of the world; she also said that God would throw David's enemies, such as the two mentioned gentlemen as well as all others who opposed him, away as someone hurls stones from a slingshot.

Now not everyone would understand these two metaphorical references employed by the astute Abigail, but both of them would resonate with David. She knew that David had killed the giant Goliath with a stone thrown from his slingshot.[14] This stone was one of five smooth stones that David had collected from a brook and stored in his precious treasure pouch. She wanted David to know that God was involved in his situation, even though at this time he lived in the wilderness. She empathetically let David know that God, as well as Abigail, cared about him and God would soon deliver him safely to the throne.[15] Conversely, anyone who would oppose the future King David would meet with the same ultimate fate as Goliath met with at the hand of David the shepherd.

Meanwhile, David would continue to enjoy God's protection from all of his enemies. Abigail had feelings of empathy and compassion for David, but she also knew that she had to connect with David in order to convince him to allow his anger to subside. She used previously obtained information interwoven with kindness and concern in order to show David that he was not alone and that everything would turn out great if he continued to be obedient to the Lord.

13. 1 Sam. 25:29
14. 1 Sam 17:40, 49.
15. 1 Sam 25:30.

ABIGAIL'S PERCEIVING PREFERENCE

David had been essentially kicked out of the Saul's kingdom.[16] He was Saul's son-in-law as well as Saul's most decorated general. He won many battles in service to the King, including killing the Philistine giant, Goliath of Gath. As reward, and because Saul was insanely jealous of David, David had to flee for his life.

Abigail likely knew that David would not kill King Saul, although God had anointed David as king of Israel.[17] So here we have a king without a kingdom who lived in a cave at Adullam,[18] and Abigail of Judah who wanted to save David's eventual monarchy from the stain of needless though justifiable bloodshed.

She rushed out to meet David, guided by her personal values and ethical code. Abigail was moved with heartfelt compassion for this man, who she knew had to be hurting but who still cared enough about his future subjects the children of Israel, and particularly those from the land of Judah, that he protected everyone he could while he was on the run from Saul. She was a sympathetic and Perceiving decision-maker regarding her ability to organize her world and execute a quickly conceived plan to perfection.

She met David, got off of her donkey, and bowed low to the ground in deference to the king.[19] She demonstrated her wisdom, empathy, and grace as she told him not to pay any attention to Nabal. She said that he was a fool, as his name showed.

She did not prepare a script or an outline as her Judging preference counterparts may have done. No, Abigail played it all by ear. She jumped off of her donkey and just let it fly using her gift for communication to her advantage, which enabled her to achieve her desired outcome of no bloodshed.

She went on to say: King David, you do not need to engage in this act of avenging bloodshed yourself. God has protected and will continue to protect you from all of your enemies. God will keep you as safe as someone under the shadow of his wing.[20] She told David that you will most assuredly become the king of Israel, and when you do, you do not

16. 1 Sam 17–18.

17. 1 Sam 24:1–22; 26:1–25.

18. 1 Sam 22:1.

19. 1 Sam 25:23–31.

20. Ps 91:1, 4.

need to have your rule stained by a needless and avenging act of killing innocent people.[21]

Abigail begged David's forgiveness and asked him to please accept what she had prepared for him and his men. Finally, she asked that when God placed him on the throne that was rightfully his, to please remember her, his humble servant, Abby.

She blew that man's mind! He did not know what to say. He complimented her grace and wisdom.[22] He thanked her for her sage advice and for verbally disarming him, thereby keeping him from a needless act of violence that would be remembered throughout Israel's history after he would eventually become king. He accepted her gifts. He sent her home in peace, and with a piece of his heart that he would never get back.

Abigail was an organized, wise, yet flexible decision-maker. She could spring into action at a moment's notice. She could rectify a situation to the satisfaction of armed men and fools alike. Abigail was perceptive. Abigail was good.

INFP

Eventually Nabal found out what Abigail did for him. Abigail told him everything the following morning. She told him that she saved his life. Nabal learned of these events the morning after passing out drunk from his night of reveling, while Abigail was away interceding for him with King David. When he found out that David and 400 fully-armed soldiers from Judah were on their way to make Nabal answer for the insults he levied at David, he clutched his heart and fell into a coma. Ten days later, Nabal died.[23]

David thanked the Lord for avenging him for Nabal's insults. David was convinced by Abigail to let the Lord fight his battles. David also remembered where that piece of his heart resided, and that Abigail was now free.

So David sent two of his men to extend his proposal of marriage to the recently-widowed Abigail.[24] He offered to take her away from all of the madness that she had endured while living with Nabal. He offered her

21. 1 Sam 25:31.
22. 1 Sam 25:32–39.
23. 1 Sam 25:36–38.
24. 1 Sam 25:39–42.

the opportunity to come with him and live in a cave, but eventually move into a palace in Jerusalem and become the queen of Israel.

She humbly yet gladly accepted his proposal, and in true Abigail fashion, she said that she would be happy to wash the feet of David's servants.[25] Then she said that she would gladly accept the marriage proposal and become his wife and queen!

I personally contend that Abigail was David's first wife of choice. David had been given Michal as his wife by King Saul for defeating Goliath of Gath, as well as for the killing of 200 other random and unfortunate Philistines.[26] Saul later gave Michal to a man named Palti while David was on the run from Saul.[27] David also married Ahinoam. However, according to the order presented in the text, this marriage to Ahinoam occurred after he married Abigail.[28] By virtue of the impact and everlasting impression that Abigail's heart and character made on David, he extended an offer of marriage to Abigail by his choice before any of his other wives, following the death of Nabal.[29] This makes Abigail David's true queen.

Abigail was dedicated to her values. Her wisdom and advice were derived from those godly values. She lived a life that made her able to make decisions that impacted the world around her, such that she could remain steadfastly true to those values while still accomplishing her goals.

Abigail was a quick learner as well as a wise and intelligent woman. She sought to understand David the man, not just David the future king and deposed general who was on the run from King Saul. She was flexible, adaptable, and admirable. Abigail was up to the job of facing any challenge with grace and dignity. Abigail was a lady, a queen, and an INFP.

INFP: THE DEVOTED ONES

APPLICATIONS FOR INFPS

I will begin my discussion on applications for INFPs with two of my favorite people in mind. One of them is Abigail and the other is a friend

---

25. 1 Sam 25:41; 2 Sam 7:1–2.

26. 1 Sam 18:20–27.

27. 1 Sam 25:44.

28. 1 Sam 25:43.

29. 1 Sam 25:40–42.

who I am almost positive is an INFP. I believe that this friend is an INFP for the same reasons that I am sure that Abigail was an INFP; it just fits.

INFPs are resolutely devoted to their values, moral codes, and ethical standards.[30] However, INFPs will not reveal themselves unless something or someone prompts them to do so. They definitely like to work with a larger purpose in mind. This purpose guides many of their life decisions and pursuits.

They have a quick ability to key in on a person's emotional and psychological needs. They can see what is going on with a person in a way that will surprise the other person when the other person discovers exactly how much the INFP actually knows about them. They are almost ninja-like in their ability to insightfully read people.[31]

What I mean by that is an INFP can know someone for a very short period of time, or in Abigail and David's case, not at all, but the INFP is already gathering information about the person while the other person has no idea that this is occurring. The person who just met the INFP are in phase one of the interaction, however, the INFP has already figured them out, including accurately assesing their needs.

If the other party has a need or a troublesome concern, the INFP will use their previously gathered information, which they have also analyzed with their ability to use their keen eye for hidden details, in order to help them. The INFP will iNtuitively know that the person they care about is experiencing a problem. At the same time, they will go through the process of ensuring that the person is able to continue to maintain their peace and dignity, as Abigail did for David. They do this instead of allowing their friend to behave in a rash manner. However, the INFP does not stop there; they are also deciding upon the best way to help their friend resolve the current problem such that their friend and everyone else involved can reach a place of amicable resolution.

This may require the INFP to enter a circumstance where they are uncomfortable yet fully capable.[32] They may have to directly confront the antagonist on behalf of their friend so they can bring about restored order and peace, especially for their friend.

30. Myers, *Introduction to Type*, 27.

31. John 4:16–19, 29.

32. Myers, *Introduction to Type*, 27.

Now the INFP typically does not come off as someone who is ready to grab their sword as King David did when he encountered an offense.[33] Thus, when the INFP takes swift and decisive action in defense of their friend, with the intent of resetting order and ensuring that their friend is taken care of, this action will surprise the antagonist.

If I have to discuss some areas that the INFP can work on, I would say that at times they may underestimate their broad and vast abilities, not to mention their strengths. If they do not believe themselves to be very strong in a specific area, and that area presented a difficult challenge for the INFP, they may begin to withdraw from people or opportunities that they truly desire to maximize or to pursue.[34]

They may withdraw based on a past encounter that directly impacted their Feeling preference in a negative way. In short, they have become gun-shy and fail to trust in their iNtuitive ability to insightfully interpret information. That iNtuitive ability works for the INFP in concert with the rest of their INFP gifts, allowing them to move purposefully forward.

The gifts and talents possessed by the INFPs will put them into position to enter new levels of purpose and the plan of God.[35] But if they become bruised and then allow themselves to stop trusting their gift, meaning their iNtuitive insight, they could become stuck in a very unsatisfying place while their gift inside is dying to get out and grow into that new place of purpose.

Developing As An INFP

In order to continue to properly grow and maintain balance, INFPs need to learn to trust. They can begin by learning to trust the fact that they were wonderfully, specifically, and intricately made to be exactly who God destined them to be and thereby destined to complete all of the things that he has planned for them to accomplish.[36]

Their INFP personality operates as a guiding force. INFPs have an ability to enjoy what and who they are as long as they are in balance. They live on purpose and pursue goals that go well beyond monetary reward.[37]

33. 1 Sam 25:13.

34. Myers, *Introduction to Type*, 27.

35. See Rom 11:29.

36. See Jer 29:11.

37. Myers, *Introduction to Type*, 27.

Their reward and motivation is the ability to live in peace, internally and externally, because they have accomplished all that they set out to accomplish. Their personality type, particularly if they have submitted in their relationship with God, has already positioned them for success in accomplishing their goal of continuously living on purpose.

If I may compare the path of an INFP to my former advising students, INFPs never pick the wrong major. They are not really wired to select the wrong path, because the wrong path or major will result in extreme emotional discomfort for an INFP. If they were purposed to be a nursing major, they cannot sit quietly in accounting classes just because their parents want them to follow in their footsteps. INFPs might be surprised that they are so happy and content with their selections. However, their joy and inner peace is a result of their personality. They are driven to find and achieve their purpose.

At some point the INFP will hopefully come to realize that their personality type positions them to have a unique relationship with God (that is, if they choose that path and worldview) and they can have a very unique place in God's kingdom.

INFPs will usually arrive in the exact place that they were supposed to arrive. They will remain there helping their friends until it is time for them to get up and move to the next place. Their INFP personality (and possibly God) pushes and guides them to move on to the next place of purpose. INFPs are driven by their desire to find and fulfill purpose.

PERSONALITY EXTREMES FOR INFPS

INFPs are sensitive, and highly-attuned to the needs and desires of their connected friends; they are quite complex creatures.[38] However, when they allow their personality to go to extremes they can withdraw, become difficult to understand because they're experiencing uncharacteristic difficulty in expressing themselves, and misjudge certain situations. I sometimes tell clients to "trust yourself" and trust the process. I believe that this is particularly relevant advice for INFPs.

INFPs are Introverts but they are very passionate people. They are especially passionate about advancing toward their purpose and about ensuring that the things which are accomplished in their lives are a direct

38. Myers, *Introduction to Type*, 27.

reflection of their values system.[39] If they are not forcefully advancing to the next place of purpose for themselves, INFPs can become quite verbally expressive and let others know exactly what needs to occur in order to get things back on track.[40]

A situation or circumstance will occasionally occur where their values or their sense of equity becomes violated, or more specifically, where their feelings are very profoundly damaged (in a way that most others would not experience) because of their deeply held values and desire for equity. When this occurs, INFPs may go to an extreme and withdraw. They may also respond to a difficulty from their past by underestimating their present reality and truth.

INFPs are very aware of and in tune with their present realities.[41] However, they may not realize that their (I would say, God-given) personality has been pushing them toward their purpose from the beginning. They will not be able to remain for a very long period of time in a situation or major that makes them feel uncomfortable. Their discomfort appears because their iNtuitive preference is telling them that this experience is not a part of their purpose; it is telling them that they need to move on from this current situation.

However, if the INFP's feelings are damaged as a result of a hurtful encounter, or staying somewhere or with someone for too long, and they don't slow down to seek healing by retracing their steps back to the time and place where they were hurt so they can begin to reapply themselves to the pursuit of purpose, they will begin a slow process of withdrawing. When the next level of purpose presents itself, such as when King David's men came to the widowed Abigail to offer his marriage proposal to her,[42] the INFP will miss the present opportunity to step into the next level of purpose because they've removed themselves from the situation to protect themselves.

My INFP friends can allow themselves to stop trusting, but they need to trust themselves, their personality portrait, and the process. Meaning that, they have arrived where they are in life because they have primarily functioned as a well-balanced INFP, so they need to continue

39. See Matt 11:12.

40. Myers, *Introduction to Type,* 27.

41. Myers, *Introduction to Type,* 27.

42. 1 Sam 25:40–42.

to do the things that have gotten them to this point in every area of their lives: personally, professionally, and relationally.

If they have encountered a harmful situation, they must take the time necessary to understand how it has impacted them. Then they need to open themselves up and seek for emotional healing so that they can get back on track and not miss out on the next level of purpose because they withdrew from people or from institutions.[43]

CONNECTIONS FOR INFPS

The Introverted manner in which the INFPs relate to and interact with their world is connected to the Perceiving preference that they use to organize and make sense of their world. INFPs like to take in information and insightfully as well as instinctively interpret it using their iNtuitive preference. That iNtuitive preference, regarding the storage and retrieval of information within the INFP, is used to inform the INFP's Perceiving preference and decision-making function. We can learn a lot from these connections.

Connections Between The I-P Functions

INFPs like to leave things open-ended without closing the doors on anything. This is based on their Perceiving preference. Their Introvert preference makes them people who can develop fascinatingly complex interpersonal relationships with others.

INFPs can know a person almost inside and out before the other person even notices how or why they have become bonded to the INFP. Their ability to use this gift to disarm people who they care about by gaining a unique understanding of their new friend and their psychological and personal needs makes the INFP invaluable to those they choose to connect with.

Connections Between The N-F Functions

INFPs are highly attuned and excellent at deciphering information. They can extract and interpret information about those people to whom they

43. Myers, *Introduction to Type,* 27.

are connected, and they use that iNtuitively interpreted information to be a consistent and passionate source of assistance. Their Feeling preference is how they form such quick connections, which in the beginning occur in such a stealth manner that they often going unnoticed by their connected friend.

They can at times "wear their feelings on their sleeves," as my grandmother used to say. In that case, they may allow their own bruised emotions, conflated with their Feeling preference, to generate some less-than-positive decisions for the INFP. But the INFP will consistently be pulled back on track because of their internal drive to pursue their purpose.

GROWTH OPPORTUNITIES AND THREATS AS AN INFP

Dealing with hurts from the past is difficult for everyone. One last counseling example: at times I ask the client I am speaking with to stand up. Then I walk over to them, step on their foot, and stay there. My desire is for them to immediately push me off their foot and say, "Ouch!" Unfortunately, most people do not push me off of their foot. They remain there with me standing on their foot while they are in pain. Next, I describe for them, the response that I was looking for when I initially stood on their foot. I will follow that small and slightly painful object lesson up by telling them that "if someone hurts you on the outside, you push them off and say ouch. Why would you do anything less than that when they hurt you on the inside?"

INFPs need to be aware of the point to this example, even if they have never experienced it firsthand. The point is that people get their feelings hurt as a result of living in this world.[44] INFPs can experience deep hurts that no one else may know about. They must seek emotional inner healing because otherwise they begin to allow themselves to withdraw. This in turn causes them to miss opportunities being presented to them, opportunities that are intended to take them to their next level of purpose.

If Abigail had allowed her rocky relationship with her boorish husband Nabal to damage her to the extent that she became withdrawn, then she would not have been able to make her quick decisions that ensured everyone involved in the situation with David would be okay and even

44. See Job 14:1.

remain alive. But Abigail was able to turn a bad situation into a positive one. After her husband insulted David's honor, she told her servants to take some food and supplies to David. She instructed them to take all that the household could spare and all that they could carry. But she did not stop there, as she was in the process of bringing her world back into balance. She went out to personally convince David not to bring down the full weight of his wrath on her household.[45]

In one fell swoop, Abigail fulfilled a part of her purpose, set herself up for the next level, and kept her new friend the future king, whom she had been studying long before she had ever met him, from placing a horrible (though justifiable) black mark on his kingdom's dossier. In the process, she also saved her entire household from calamity, all because she was able to continuously pick herself back up and trust again.

---

45. 1 Sam 25.

19

Concluding Thoughts on Bible MBTIs

HAVE FUN WITH MBTI

MY HOPE IS THAT you had fun with this exercise and that you see yourself in some of the characters and biblical leaders. After you take the short MBTI personality test (it's easy, trust me), my hope is that you not only see yourself in the character with your personality type, but that you see yourself in some of the others.

I mentioned earlier that I can truly identify with the INFJs. One of my most prominent desires in writing this book is that people will be able to see themselves within many of the sixteen personality types. I also hope that we will notice, particularly by this point in the book, that if we take our personality type and switch a letter or two, then we will discover some similarities between our complete personality portrait and those with similar personality preferences. Thus we can visit two related but different preference zone restaurants in one week. We will naturally gravitate to and identify with certain similarly related personality types more than others. My ENTJ is very closely related to the INFJ personality type. As a borderline Introvert, I likely visit my Introverted side as well as, my Feeling side quite often although my preference is to remain most often in the ENTJ restaurant.

No one is a perfect Extrovert. Personally, I am a 51 percent Extrovert, making me a borderline Introvert. Many of my friends who are only allowed to see my stage persona would argue with that analysis, but it is very true of this ENTJ. There are times that I have given out so much energy and allowed so many people to pull on me that I just go back to my room and cry.

Similarly, Joseph didn't spend all of his time on changing the pharaoh's entire governmental structure. There were times that he likely had to get alone by himself with his God or his wife Asenath and recharge. Most people will not test at the extreme end of any of the MBTI personality preferences. Also, everyone needs to learn to achieve balance in each of the areas of their personality traits in order to lead a successful and healthy life.

ADDITIONAL MBTI PROFILES

I matched some additional biblical leaders with their personality profile. I will tell you where I believe that they fit, and you can use the eight MBTI personality preferences to check my work for yourself. I did some of the profiles in long form and a few at the end in short form (a couple of paragraphs or less). Unlike the profiles in the previous chapters, these are presented in no particular order.

ENFJ: NEHEMIAH, THE KING'S CUPBEARER AND ADVISOR

Nehemiah son of Hacaliah of Judah was an ENFJ. Nehemiah was the cupbearer for the king of Persia. He later became both governor and leader of the rebuilding effort in the land of Judah when the Judeans were allowed to return to their homeland.[1] Nehemiah was also a very highly-regarded advisor to King Artaxerxes I around 446–445 BC.

Nehemiah was a valued member of the king's personal leadership staff.[2] He was also very passionate about his Judean homeland. Nehemiah was quite knowledgeable about the inner workings of the Persian kingdom that he served. He was a man who followed the plans and purposes that God placed in his heart to the letter. Nehemiah was an ENFJ.

1. Neh 1.
2. Neh 1:11–2:9.

NEHEMIAH'S EXTROVERSION PREFERENCE

Nehemiah had an Extrovert preference which was demonstrated in the way that he related to: his direct family members; the king and queen; friends that inspected the wall with him; and enemies like Sanballat the Horonite, Tobiah the Ammonite, and Geshem the Arab, all of whom were his fellow officials from the Persian kingdom.[3] He also demonstrated this preference in the manner in which he related to the other Jewish leaders, such as Eliashib the high priest.[4]

Nehemiah was generally surrounded by people. He had no problem providing leadership and direction for Judah as they rebuilt the wall around Jerusalem.[5] He had an easy and comfortable rapport with King Artaxerxes I and his wife the queen of Persia. He was also at ease speaking in front of his people.[6]

He had no problem dealing directly with Sanballat and the other naysayers opposing the rebuilding of the wall around Jerusalem.[7] Nehemiah also set up his brother as the governor of Judah after Nehemiah left to return to serve King Artaxerxes of Persia[8] so that the role would be filledduring the rebuilding efforts. Nehemiah was a well-expressed Extrovert.

NEHEMIAH'S INTUITIVE PREFERENCE

Nehemiah confirmed his iNtuitive preference via the way in which he saw the future possibilities in regards to organizing the information about rebuilding the wall of Jerusalem and its gates. From the conversation with his relatives to his prayer for favor with the king prior to requesting permission to undertake the rebuilding project to his secret information-gathering inspection of the wall and gates, Nehemiah saw the future success of Jerusalem and Judea as being intrinsically linked to the accomplishment of the secret plans that God had placed in his heart.

3. Neh 1:2; 2:1–9; 3; 2:10; 4:1.
4. Neh 1:1–3:32.
5. Neh 3.
6. Neh 2:1–9.
7. Neh 6:1–9.
8. Neh 7:2.

Nehemiah understood how important successfully rebuilding the wall of Jerusalem was to Israel's future prosperity.[9]

NEHEMIAH'S FEELING PREFERENCE

Nehemiah demonstrated his Feeling preference through his decision-making process and the compassion he employed when, with unwavering determination and passion, he decided to implement the plan placed in his heart to rebuild the Jerusalem Wall. He did not let any of the naysayers or oppositional leaders from Persia such as Sanballat, Tobiah, and Geshem dissuade him from his appointed purpose and task.

Nehemiah did all of this because of the passion that he had for rebuilding the wall of Jerusalem. He worked so diligently on the wall because it was God's prophesied desire for them to rebuild the wall and because he had a lot of empathy for the children of Israel and Judah.

At one point, Nehemiah asked his brother Hanani (whom he later made governor of Jerusalem in his stead) for a report about the status of the Judean exiles back in Jerusalem. At this time, Nehemiah served in the palace, located in the fortress city of Susa, as cupbearer and advisor to the king. The group of men traveling to Susa with Hanani had been in Jerusalem and knew of the plight of the Jews who had returned from Babylonian exile. They said that Jerusalem and the wall were in a desperate state. At this news, Nehemiah wept. Then, feeling the pain of his countrymen and his desire to see a rebuilt Jerusalem, Nehemiah fasted and prayed. He asked God for favor with King Artaxerxes I, since it was obviously the petition and desire of his heart to return to Jerusalem himself and help with the rebuilding efforts. His prayers were answered four months later, as the king asked him while Nehemiah was serving his cup why he was so sad, although he was obviously not sick. The king mused that it must be depression or maybe he was just unhappy. King Artaxerxes obviously valued and cared very much for Nehemiah and was concerned about his well-being and his happiness.

Nehemiah told King Artaxerxes that he could not be anything other than sad because his beloved home and people were in tatters. After asking Nehemiah how long he would be gone, King Artaxerxes I, with the queen by his side, approved Nehemiah's request to return to Jerusalem. He also gave him every supply from the royal foundries that Nehemiah

9. Neh 2:11–12.

needed to complete the task of rebuilding the wall. The king also allowed Nehemiah to take a detachment from the king's army along for security purposes. Additionally, King Artaxerxes furnished Nehemiah with permission letters to receive the rebuilding materials and to get through all territories between Susa and Jerusalem. Finally, the king made Nehemiah governor of Jerusalem and Judah for the entire tenure of his stay, as well as giving him the authority to name his successor.[10]

Nehemiah received abundant favor because he felt and then followed the burden on his heart to go and help Jerusalem rebuild, and because he decided to ask God to give him favor with the king as he put the plans in his heart into action.

Nehemiah had a passion for uniting his people and for seeing them return to their homeland. This desire is expressly different from a person with a Thinking preference, such as an ENTJ (an ENTJ would primarily execute their grandiose plans via the decision-making process because they just love "to make miracles happen, baby"). Through these decisions and accomplishments, Nehemiah established his MBTI Feeling preference.

NEHEMIAH'S JUDGING PREFERENCE

Nehemiah demonstrated his Judging preference by how meticulously he organized and executed the rebuilding project.[11] He was both precise in the manner in which he organized the workers to complete the wall as well as in his execution of his plan. He allowed nothing to drag him off of his appointed course. Nehemiah's organizational abilities paid off because the wall was completed in spite of those who said that the rebuilt wall would not hold up under the pressure applied to it by the weight of a fox walking on it.[12] Nehemiah had a Judging preference. Nehemiah was an ENFJ.

ENTJ: HOSEA THE PROPHET

Hosea was both intriguing and difficult for me to assess regarding his MBTI personality profile. However, I am convinced that Hosea was an

10. Neh 1:1–2:10.

11. Neh 3:6.

12. Neh 4:3.

ENTJ. As I formulated this MBTI personality profile, I continuously tried to give him some other assessment profile due to the fact that he had a difficult path in life and because of my personal bias toward our shared ENTJ personality type. In the final analysis, this MBTI personality profile assessment just made the most sense.

HOSEA'S EXTROVERSION PREFERENCE

Hosea had to be an Extrovert. He interacted very comfortably to the prophetic revelations that he was called to share with the children of Israel and Judah.[13] God kicks off the book of Hosea very suddenly by telling Hosea the prophet to "Go and marry a whore"![14]

Why would God place this man in such a precarious and difficult position? God did this because he wanted to illustrate to Israel how irreverently they had behaved toward him by turning their backs on their God and prostituting their worship.[15] They chose to serve other false idols as gods.

However, this is the first indicator to me that Hosea was an Extrovert. This type of command from God to one of his prophets would be much more easily executed by an Extrovert than an Introvert, in my opinion. I believe that Hosea could see the larger picture. He could focus on a goal that transcended the one-on-one interaction required by most Introverts. Hosea could understand that, although he would come to fall in love with Gomer the prostitute whom he was told to marry, there was a larger idea at work than simply their fruitful marriage.

After some time, Hosea also had to go down to the town square and interact with other men, when Gomer left home to ply her former and reinitiated trade of prostitution.[16] However, this time she would also be committing adultery as a married woman serving as a prostitute, one who was apparently owned by another man.

Hosea was told by the Lord not only to go and get her back, but to still love her. The Lord gave Hosea very explicit and detailed instructions on how to handle his wife. Gomer had given Hosea three children, two

13. Hos 1:1.
14. Hos 1:2 (NIV).
15. Hos 1:1–2:1.
16. Hos 3:1–2.

sons and a daughter, by this point.[17] Hosea had to go to the town square to purchase her back for fifteen pieces of silver as well as some barley and wine. He was not allowed to have sexual relations with her for a set period of time. During this same reconciliation timeframe, Gomer had to live in their household and no longer engage in prostitution.[18]

This was all completed to demonstrate the redemption of Israel and reconciliation with God, but it had to be hard on Hosea as a husband and as a father. He likely had to explain to the children where their mother had gone, as well as why she left. He also had to keep his eyes on the higher calling by obediently deciding to endure the humiliation of purchasing his wife the prostitute, knowing that God was also using this situation with the woman that he loved to demonstrate a larger point to Israel.

He was able to endure this difficult and seemingly near impossible trial successfully. It was probably just a little bit easier for Hosea the Extrovert to go to the town square and purchase his wife back (or even marry a prostitute in the first place) and then continue to serve as an interactive prophet in Israel, knowing that his marriage and entire life was always serving a higher purpose.

Hosea had to forego many of the expected comforts of married life, such as faithfulness, unwavering companionship, respect, dedication, and consistency from his wife, who I am sure that he loved. He did this in order to achieve all of God's purposes, not just the calling related to finding a wife and enjoying the "good thing" that a wife should be to her husband.[19]

It may have been more difficult for an Introvert to forgo the comforts associated with the intimate one-on-one relationship shared between spouses. However, God knew that Hosea the Extrovert was the man for this job. Hosea was also very at ease interacting with the children of Israel and Judah as he served them as prophet and delivered God's word to them.[20] He delivered the prophetic word of God to Israel, irrespective of the at times reprimanding and terse nature of the prophecies he had to share.

---

17. Hos 1:3–9.

18. Hos 3:1–3.

19. Prov 18:22.

20. Hos 9:1–14:9.

HOSEA'S INTUITIVE PREFERENCE

Hosea's manner of gathering and assimilating information was interesting to say the least. However, he verified an iNtuitive preference regarding his information-intake process. Hosea had to keep his mind on the larger goal of serving the Lord as prophet and serving the children of Israel and Judah through a living example.[21] He and his domestic life were that living example.

Hosea was profoundly capable of looking for "the thing behind the thing" when it came to his choice in taking Gomer as a mate. He was told by God who to marry and why he should marry her. I am reminded of when Paul prompts the readers to: "Press on to reach the goal of achieving the prize of the higher calling, which is in and is Christ Jesus."[22]

Applying this to Hosea, he had to focus on the higher purpose while simultaneously humbling himself in order to obey God and marry a prostitute. Subsequently he would be required to go and purchase his own wife back. He must have loved her dearly; I believe that God would have definitely put a deep love in his heart for Gomer, since he told Hosea to marry her.

However, Hosea had to be humble enough to lay down his desires to marry the virtuous woman of his childhood dreams in order to espouse Gomer, while also knowing that he was also serving as a living example of God's word to the children of Israel and Judah.[23] Then he had to further humble himself by going to purchase her back from prostitution and bondage, allowing God to provide Israel with another example of their deleterious actions.

Hosea did this with the diligence, faithfulness, iNtuitive insight, and purposeful passion of a prophet. Hosea had a profound ability to maintain his focus on not only what was in front of him, the love for his wife Gomer, but also to attend to "the thing behind the thing": his calling to serve Israel as prophet.

21. See 2 Cor 3:3.
22. Phil 3:14 (NRSV).
23. See Rom 12:1.

HOSEA'S THINKING PREFERENCE

Hosea demonstrated his Thinking preference in his relationship with Gomer, as well as through his ability to provide Israel with the unfiltered prophetic truth revealed to him by God. Hosea made quick decisions to obey the Lord, no matter how strange or difficult these requests may have been for him to endure.

He married Gomer the prostitute at the Lord's behest. He purchased her back after they had been married long enough for her to bear them three children. He followed God's directives to the letter after he repurchased Gomer subsequent to her return to prostitution.

Additionally, Hosea gave Israel and Judah very harsh prophetic words that God spoke through him regarding their disobedience. He did not seem to flinch at God's directives to speak so tersely to the children of Israel and Judah, nor to speak those words directly to the crowds of people. Finally, Hosea also spoke to the children of Israel and Judah about God's love for them and how they would receive healing if they were to become repentant.[24] As a prophet and leader in Israel, Hosea went forth into any and all situations with boldness, declaring and living the word of the Lord as an Extroverted Thinking preference person would.

HOSEA'S JUDGING PREFERENCE

Hosea demonstrated a strong Judging preference regarding the organization of his world. Yes, Hosea was able to go with the flow as many Perceiving preference people are capable of doing; this demonstrates his non-static connection to his Judging preference. However, the plan was laid out for him by God and he followed it without wavering. He eliminated all distractions, any potential confusion, and all other mental dissonance that could have caused him to wonder about the merit of marrying an unfaithful prostitute or going to repurchase her after she had been unfaithful to him.

Hosea clearly demonstrated his organizational preference via the manner in which he explained the new rules to Gomer, following reacquiring her from the town square.[25] He told her that she had to stay in his home for a long period of time without returning to prostitution. He

24. Hos 11, 14.

25. Hos 3:1–3.

also explained to her that they would not have sexual relations for a long period of time.

Regardless of the dual reasons behind Hosea and Gomer's entire relationship over time, Hosea organized his world in such a way that there would be no mistakes or confusion which could hinder his ability to achieve all of the goals that God had set for Hosea. Hosea was an example of an obedient and flexible person with a Judging preference.

ISTP: JOSHUA, THE SERVANT LEADER

I had a far more difficult time coming up with an appropriate and catchy title for this Joshua section than I had actually assessing his MBTI personality type. Joshua represented so many things to so many people. Joshua was a servant to Moses. Initially, he and a man named Caleb entered the promised land with ten other spies from Israel and were the only two men brave and faithful enough to believe that God would deliver the promised land into the hands and possession of the children of Israel.[26] Joshua ultimately led those same people to take full possession of that same promised land as general and leader of his people. Joshua wore many hats and was also an ISTP.

JOSHUA'S INTROVERSION PREFERENCE

Many was the time that Joshua had to get alone with God in order to receive counsel. During these one-on-ones, Joshua received battle strategy, additional instruction, comfort, advice, and direction from God, both via speaking directly with God and by written means of communication through the teachings of Moses.[27] Joshua also spent a lot of time in one-on-one encounters with Moses as Moses led the children of Israel out of Egypt and through the wilderness for forty years.

Joshua did not accompany Moses on his trips to the heights of Mount Sinai, where Moses had direct and intimate fellowship with the Lord.[28] Joshua would usually remain alone at the foot of the mountain waiting for Moses to return. Generally, he would be awaiting Moses's arrival for many days. Joshua was fully capable of speaking to crowds or to

26. Num 13:1–14:10.

27. Josh 1:8.

28. Exod 24:13; 32:15–17.

the entire assembly of the children of Israel, as many Introverts can, but he was likely drained after the experience. Joshua was an Introvert.

JOSHUA'S SENSING PREFERENCE

Joshua seemed to prefer to handle situations, as well as take in and process information, in a straightforward manner. The Lord gave Joshua clear and specific, if at times unconventional, instructions regarding taking the promised land for the children of Israel. In the book of Joshua, the Lord reiterated to Joshua that Moses was dead and that he was now the leader.[29] Joshua was told that he was to lead the Israelites across the Jordan River and to take possession of the entire promised land. They would possess every piece of land that Joshua placed his feet upon, according to the Lord's promise. Joshua was told to be strong and courageous, because all of the promises ascribed to Moses when he was the leader of the Israelites, would be fulfilled under Joshua's leadership and direction.[30]

Joshua also received instruction on how to supernaturally cause the walls of Jericho to fall so the Israelites could defeat the people of Jericho and begin to take possession of the promised land west of the Jericho River.[31] Joshua received many other instructions from the Lord and executed the plans in a flawless and precise manner. He was not one who usually overlooked details in the instructions. Joshua was Sensing in the manner in which he assimilated information.

JOSHUA'S THINKING PREFERENCE

Joshua made decisions in a way that usually provided the most direct route to possessing and securing the promised land for the children of Israel. He would receive instruction in a rather direct manner at times, then provide or reiterate those instructions to the children of Israel in kind. Joshua directed his own set of spies to scout out Jericho.[32] He also told the children of Israel how to cross the Jordan River.[33]

29. Josh 1.
30. Josh 1:1–9.
31. Josh 6:1–27.
32. Josh 2:1.
33. Josh 3:3.

Joshua informed the priests how make the wall of Jericho fall in order for Israel to take possession of the land of Jericho. He did this after having received instruction from the Lord.[34] In all of these situations as well as many others, Joshua was a swift and conclusive decision-maker.

He was also a man of quick obedience. As the Lord provided him with instruction, he would then take decisive and immediate action in deference to the commands of the Lord. He would go to the Lord in prayer at the first sign of a problem, such as with Achan's sin.[35] In that example, when the Lord replied to Joshua's prayer (in a rather terse manner I might add), Joshua took instantaneous action to implement the directives of the Lord which were designed to discover who had broken the Lord's covenant.[36] Joshua was a Thinking, quick, and decisive servant leader.

JOSHUA'S PERCEIVING PREFERENCE

Joshua was a Perceiving person regarding the organization of his world. He wanted everyone to remain in concert and harmony, while also being a man of compassion. Yet Joshua and the other leaders of Israel did not consult the Lord in one instance, when they were approached by the fearful and deceptive Gibeonites.[37]

The Gibeonites were afraid that they would lose their land as well as their lives in a battle with Israel and their God, as the people from Ai and Jericho had. So the Gibeonites decided to trick Joshua and the other Israelite leaders into believing that the Gibeonites had come from a distant land. Because of the mighty power that Jehovah had displayed in defeating the other nations who occupied the promised land, the Gibeonites preferred to make a treaty and become servants to the children of Israel. Joshua and the other leaders questioned them regarding their land of origin, suspecting that they may have in fact lived within the boundaries of the promised land. However, Joshua and the other leaders failed to consult the Lord as was Joshua's normal custom.[38]

34. Josh 1:1–9; 6:2–5.

35. Josh 7:7–9.

36. Josh 7:10–26.

37. Josh 9:3–27.

38. Josh 9:14.

They were ultimately deceived. Joshua and the other Israelite leaders proceeded to make covenant with these people, thus allowing the Gibeonites to become their servants in exchange for not attacking their land. Joshua and the other leaders soon discovered that the true land of these people was the land of Gibeon, which was just north of where they were currently standing. They could not attack because of the covenant, and therefore they did not follow the instructions of the Lord, which stated that Joshua and Israel must completely defeat all people who occupied the promised land.[39]

Unfortunately, they did not consult with the Lord as Joshua had done so many times in the past, prior to making a decision that would impact the taking and occupying of the promised land. This action caused many problems for the succeeding generations of the children of Israel who followed Joshua's generation.

It can be argued that Joshua engaged the treaty with the Gibeonites because he looked at their distressed clothing, believed their lie, had compassion on them, and thought he was doing the right thing by making covenant with people who he thought did not occupy territory within the mandated boundaries of the promised land.[40] Joshua made a decision that lacked his traditional perception and behavioral pattern. However, from the point of view of MBTI, it was a Perceiving preference decision to maintain harmony while still accomplishing the stated goal of conquering the entire promised land. He did not realize, because he did not ask God, that the Gibeonites actually lived in the promised land, thus they should have also been utterly destroyed and removed from the boundaries of that promised land. Joshua was an ISTP with a distinct Perceiving preference.

ISFP: DEBORAH, THE PROPHET AND JUDGE

Deborah, like many in this section, has a personality type that is not as easily assessed as the aforementioned leaders with dedicated chapters. However, Deborah was definitely a leader in her own right and an ISFP.

39. Josh 9:24.
40. Josh 1:4; 9:3–6.

DEBORAH'S INTROVERSION PREFERENCE

Deborah was a prophet and a judge in Israel during the era of the judg-es.[41] She wrote a poetic song which gives some indication relative to her personality type.[42] Introverts, according to MBTI, are more prolific writers, though this particular attribute is not exclusive to Introverts or Extroverts. Writing, as with John the beloved apostle (INFJ), is an at-tributable skill common to many Introverts.

Deborah also rendered her prophetic judgements under an epony-mous palm tree located in the hill country of Ephraim.[43] She obviously served in this capacity in Israel in relative isolation, although she was married to a man named Lappidoth.[44] Deborah transacted her meetings with those who came to her as a judge giving out prophetic advice in one-on-one settings. This indicates her strong preference toward Introversion.

DEBORAH'S SENSING PREFERENCE

Deborah was a straightforward person regarding information-gathering and assimilation. She received prophetic insights from God, but she pro-cessed them in a straightforward manner. She was quick to tell Barak, a general in the Israelite army who had command over the troops from the tribes of Naphtali and Zebulun, specifically how to go into battle.[45] After she sent for him, Deborah informed Barak that if he did not follow the prophetic directive from the Lord and attack exactly as she had told him, which did not include her accompanying him and his troops into battle, then a woman would receive credit for his victory in the battle.[46]

Through the dispensation of this information, Deborah assured him that he would be victorious in battle. She directly told Barak, via another prophecy, that the Lord would win the battle for him and his troops.[47] However, she also informed him that a woman would receive credit for the victory. General Barak likely thought that Deborah, the

41. Judg 4:4.

42. Judg 5:1–31.

43. Judg 4:5.

44. Judg 4:4.

45. Judg 4:6–10.

46. Judg 4:8–10.

47. Judg 4:14.

woman with whom he was currently speaking, would be the woman who would receive credit for the victory instead of him. This apparently did not bother Barak because Deborah ultimately joined him on the trip.[48]

As it turned out, it was a woman named Jael, married to a man named Heber the Kenite, who killed Sisera, the opposing commander of King Jabin of Hazor's army.[49] I initially assumed, as likely did Barak, that Deborah, who uttered to him the prophetic directive via straightforward information received from the Lord, was to be the woman who would receive credit for the victory in this battle if she accompanied him to the battle as he requested.

Jael's husband was friendly with King Jabin and Sisera, as Heber the Kenite moved away from the other Israelites to a town named Zaanannim.[50] Upon seeing Sisera fleeing from Barak and the battle, Jael invited Sisera into her tent. She then covered him under a blanket to hide him from Barak and gave him some milk to drink. When Sisera fell asleep under the blanket after having his milk, Jael killed him by driving a tent peg through his temple and into the ground below where he laid his head. So much for being on the side of King Jabin or the Canaanites!

When our hero General Barak showed up near the tent of Jael, she invited him in to see what she had done to Sisera, the commander who Barak and his men had been pursuing after the main battle.[51] Thus, she was the one who received credit for the victory in this battle with King Jabin of Hazor and the Canaanite armies led by Sisera.

Deborah wrote about all of this in her poetic song.[52] She described the information that she received from the Lord and subsequently provided to Barak, as well as recounting in her poetic song the information about her and Barak's adventure. Deborah wrote all of this in a very straightforward manner, thus indicating her Sensing preference relative to information-gathering, assimilation, and dispensation.

48. Judg 4:10.
49. Judg 4:7.
50. Judg 4:11,17–22.
51. Judg 4:21.
52. Judg 5.

DEBORAH'S FEELING PREFERENCE

Deborah placed herself in Barak's shoes as she told him that a woman would receive credit for his victory over Sisera. She knew that he would not want to share credit for victory in the battle in which he commanded the armies of Israel. But Barak decided to proceed as he saw fit, and had Deborah join him in spite of her warning.

The fact that she was willing to go also indicates her MBTI Feeling preference. One can only speculate that if Deborah did not go, the battle-field would have been the place for Barak to destroy the entire army of King Jabin including Sisera, or that Barak's pursuit of Sisera would have resulted in one of Barak's warriors killing Sisera. As it turned out, as per Deborah's warning, Jael killed Sisera and received credit for the victory in the battle against King Jabin of Hazor's army.

Deborah decided to join him after warning Barak of the pending consequences of his decision to insist that she join him in attending the battle. She preferred that he received the credit for the victory but did not insist. Deborah was flexible, thus also demonstrating her Perceiving pref-erence, as well as willing to accommodate Barak's request. She considered the feelings of Barak by warning him of the results, then acquiesced to his desire to have her accompany him and his warriors. She apparently wanted him to be comfortabl more than than explicitly following the directives of the Lord, which intended for Barak and his troops to go to battle without her. Through these actions, Deborah verified her Feeling preference.

DEBORAH'S PERCEIVING PREFERENCE

Deborah demonstrated the personality traits of a person with a Perceiv-ing preference. She was willing to go with the flow. If Barak wanted her to come to the battle, she would go with him, because the outcome of the battle was already set according to the word of the Lord that was prophetically revealed through her.

If he had followed her initial implicit advice and let her remain be-hind as Barak alone led the armies of Israel into battle, then she would have gladly stayed under the palm of Deborah and Barak would have received all of the glory for the victory achieved in battle. Deborah was flexible and willing to fly by the seat of her pants (or dress as it were) as situations presented themselves within her world as prophet and judge in Israel. Through these actions she confirmed her Perceiving preference.

I guess her personality was more easily discerned that I initially thought!

ISTJ: SAMUEL THE PROPHET

Samuel the prophet and judge was a leader in Israel. Samuel was also an ISTJ.

SAMUEL'S INTROVERSION PREFERENCE

Whether Samuel was speaking one-on-one with King Saul, to Jesse about anointing one of his sons (ultimately King David) as king of Israel to replace Saul, or talking to God, Samuel was generally more comfortable in smaller groups.[53] At times he was required to speak to all of the children of Israel.[54] For example, once Samuel told them not to request a king from God, but rather to allow God to remain their king.[55]

Samuel preferred the one-on-one relationship that Jehovah had with the children of Israel without the third-party intermediary that would occur with the institution of a monarchy in Israel and later in Judah.[56] Samuel demonstrated his Introversion preference in this way as well as through many of his actions and individual interactions with both King Saul and the anointed King David.[57]

SAMUEL'S SENSING PREFERENCE

While Samuel, like all prophets, demonstrated measures of the iNtuitive insight, he appeared to desire information to be presented to him in a straightforward manner, as do most people with a Sensing preference.

He once discussed the rationale behind King Saul's choice to allow King Agag to remain alive, even after God had told Saul to completely

---

53. 1 Sam 16:5–13 8:6–9; 9:15–17; 16:1–4.

54. 1 Sam 10:17–20; 12:1–25.

55. 1 Sam 8:4–22.

56. 1 Sam 8:6–9, 20–22.

57. 1 Sam 9:1–16:13.

decimate the entirety of the Amalekites, including all people, livestock, and property.[58]

When Samuel arrived at Saul's location, he heard the bleating of sheep and mooing cattle. Then, via his preferred pattern of assessing information in a straightforward manner, Samuel knew that Saul had not obeyed the Lord. The Lord told him that Agag was still alive and Saul had been disobedient. Although Samuel the prophet had the prophetic insight which accompanied his mantle and anointing as a prophet, he demonstrated a Sensing preference regarding his ability to process and integrate information.[59]

SAMUEL'S THINKING PREFERENCE

Similar to most with a Thinking preference, Samuel could be rigidly attached to his decisions. God had to talk him out of those Thinking preference positions that he adopted with some regularity. He did not want the children of Israel to name a human king.[60] He also knew that none of the seven sons that Jesse presented to him was the one son that God told him to anoint as king of Israel, but that the future monarch was in fact in Jesse's household.[61] This son was the youngest son of Jesse, who was out in the field serving as shepherd to the sheep and goats: the future King David.

Samuel also lamented the fact that the children of Israel did not listen to him and insisted on God naming and anointing a human king of Israel.[62] Samuel was rigid in his decision-making processes but he was more prone to be totally obedient to the Lord. He followed God's directives and executed each one precisely as God had prescribed, as would a person with his Thinking preference. He preferred things occur as he initially conceived them but would easily acquiesce to the Lord's directives. Samuel did not consider or regard as highly the fleeting desires of the children of Israel as he did the directives from the Lord.

Persons with a Feeling preference would have advocated for consideration of the desires of the children of Israel to have a king, or they may

58. 1 Sam 15:1–3.

59. 1 Sam 15:4–35.

60. 1 Sam 8:4–9, 21–22.

61. 1 Sam 16:1–13.

62. 1 Sam 8:4–9; 8:21–22; 16:1–3.

have been more empathetic to Saul for wanting to keep the best sheep and cattle for himself and allow Agag to remain alive.[63] Samuel corrected that issue immediately and decided to follow the Lord no matter what. Even when he grieved for Saul and the plight of Israel, when God told him to get moving and anoint the new king (David), he immediately obeyed the Lord, even if he was afraid of Saul.[64]

SAMUEL'S JUDGING PREFERENCE

Samuel, demonstrating his Judging preference, desired that things in his world and in the world of the kingdom of Israel remain the same. He wanted God to remain as the exclusive king of Israel. In spite of Samuel's warnings not to name a human king of Israel, the Israelites insisted, and Saul was anointed to rule Israel. When Saul failed to follow the word of God, Samuel mourned the fact that Saul had failed as king, just as he lamented the fact that the children of Israel insisted on making Saul the king in the first place. Samuel the prophet confirmed a Judging preference in regards to how he organized his own world and how he wanted to see the kingdom of Israel organized.

I am not sure why I used Daniel as the person to represent the ISTJs instead of Samuel the prophet. I guess it was just a matter of inspiration. However, Samuel the prophet may garner a more extensive dossier in another possible book on leadership styles.

ENFP: FATHER ABRAHAM

Father Abraham was an ENFP.

ABRAHAM'S EXTROVERSION PREFERENCE

Abraham was not an overly-expressed or extreme Extrovert, but he was an Extrovert. He was comfortable meeting with Melchizedek the king and high priest of Salem.[65]

---

63. 1 Sam 15:4–35.
64. 1 Sam 16:1–4.
65. Gen 14:17–20.

Abram (Abraham's earlier name) shied away from his interactions with the pharaoh of Egypt when it came to his beautiful wife Sarai, but he did speak up when he was required to do so.[66] He also successfully negotiated for a well that he purchased after making a covenant with King Abimelech, a man whom he had deceived into believing that Sarah was not his wife.[67] Sarah was very beautiful and obviously alluring to many kings of the lands that she and Abraham visited. Abraham deceived many of them about Sarah being both his wife and relative in order to avoid conflict.

Abraham led his men into battle to save his nephew Lot. Likewise, Abraham hosted, entertained, interacted comfortably, as well as humbly negotiated with the angels who were going to destroy Sodom and Gomorrah. These same angels heard his wife Sarah laugh at the promise that she would give birth to a son even in her old age.[68] It is the sum total of Abraham's interactions with so many people that indicate his Extroverted personality preference.

ABRAHAM'S INTUITIVE AND FEELING PREFERENCES

Abraham could maintain his focus on God's promises, though many of them were long in coming, because of his ability to organize information and iNtuitively remain focused on the larger goals that God revealed to him. He also begged the aforementioned angels to consider the lives and feelings of not only Lot, but of the residents of Sodom and Gomorrah, before deciding to destroy it. This demonstrated his Feeling preference.[69]

ABRAHAM'S PERCEIVING PREFERENCE

Abraham demonstrated his Perceiving preference working in concert with his Feeling preference as he struggled to completely obey the way that the Lord wanted him to organize his world and travel to the promised land. He did not leave his entire family behind as the Lord had commanded. Rather, Abram (as he was known at that time) brought Lot with

66. Gen 12:10–19.

67. Gen 20; 21:22–34.

68. Gen 18.

69. Gen 18:2; 16–33.

him on his journey from Haran to Canaan.[70] He decided not to completely obey God and leave his entire family behind as he journeyed by faith to a land that God would show him. However, Abram did follow God to a land that was a complete mystery to him.

It is that walk by faith that demonstrates Abram's Perceiving function. Abram wanted to go to the promised land. He did not know exactly where he was going or how he would know when he had arrived. However, Abram trusted God and walked by faith toward a land that had yet to be revealed to him. He was totally comfortable in leaving his journey open-ended and allowing God to fill in the blanks, as is the case with many who share the Perceiving preference.

Abraham also struggled with God's word when it came to letting his son Ishmael leave the home because he desired to maintain his world as is within his version of happy harmony, as opposed to eliminating the contention that existed between Hagar and Sarah.[71] People with a Perceiving Preference are willing to remain flexible and see if the situation improves in regards to contention. They prefer to remain open to change rather than destroy the group dynamic and irrevocably alter the nature of their world by closing the door to the future possibilities of a positive outcome.

Those future possibilities in this case involved Abraham putting his son Ishmael out into the streets or sending Ishmael and his mother into the wilderness, closing the door to a possibility of future accord between his wife Sarah and his son's mother Hagar.[72] In these instances, Abraham, like many Perceiving preference people, preferred to have his world organized in a way that he thought would achieve harmony for all. That could not be accomplished if he was not able to allow the tension between Sarah and Hagar to play out, possibly to a peaceful resolution, via an open-ended extension of the current situation.

One additional instance that clearly demonstrates Abraham's Perceiving preference occurred when God told Abraham to take his son Isaac to a mountain in the land of Moriah and sacrifice Isaac to God. God told Abraham that he would show him on which mountain to offer his son as a sacrifice. Abraham obeyed and left his home, following God in a flexible manner.[73]

---

70. Gen 12:1–5.

71. Gen 21:8–21.

72. Gen 16:1–6; 21:8–21.

73. Gen 24:1–19.

Abraham believed that God would not allow Isaac to remain dead after sacrificing him, because Abraham trusted God as well as the promise that God made regarding Isaac and Abraham's future generations.[74] As it turned out, God stopped Abraham from sacrificing his son Isaac just in the nick of time. However, it was Abraham's faith working in concert with his Perceiving preference that allowed God to tell Abraham to go both to the promised land of Canaan as well as to the mountain in Moriah where he was to offer Isaac as a sacrifice. God did not tell Abraham in either instance exactly where he was going or what would happen in the end. Abraham had to be a very open-minded, and flexible man of great faith. Abraham was an ENFP.

INFP: MOSES, THE DELIVERER AND LAWGIVER

Moses would have made an excellent INFP representative. When I was writing the first draft of this book, my initial thought was that those who know me know that I love Abigail and there was no way that I would choose anyone other than her to write about. Abigail, along with Joseph, might be the prevailing impetus for writing this book.

Subsequently in my attempts to get this book published, I encountered one company's editor who did not find the book a match for their readers. Although of course I disagreed and fully believe that their readers would read this book as distributed by a different publishing house, they asked me an interesting question in their letter. They asked why I did not write more extensively on Moses and David? I knew that I had written expansively on David (in chapter 17 of this book). In the initial draft, I knew that I had written about Moses and described him as an INFP.

As an ENTJ and self-described perfectionist, I love a challenge! Writing about Moses, one of the most recognizable biblical leaders in history, did not present much of a test for me. Also, as I conceived it, Moses would not aid my readers in learning to preliminarily assess some of these characters using the MBTI criteria outlined in the first two chapters of this book. I guess I am always teaching! Finally, I have a pronounced Abigail bias, as I have previously mentioned.

However, upon further review, after considering Moses's importance to so many people, I decided to expand upon his MBTI personality portrait. Moses the deliverer and law-giver, as many have called him,

74. Gen 22:1–19; Heb 11:17–19.

was an Introvert. I base this assessment on many of his personality traits which are on display throughout the Pentateuch section of the Bible.

MOSES'S INTROVERSION PREFERENCE

Moses apparently loved to write, as do many Introverts. Moses also spent most of his time, following the parting of the Red Sea, with Joshua or with God.[75] Moses was willing to take his servant and mentee, Joshua, with him to Mount Sinai. However, Joshua only went so far up the mountain, while Moses was called to meet alone with God. As Moses ascended Sinai, he climbed the rest of the way into the presence of God alone, leaving Joshua at a specific place to wait for forty days or more while Moses had one-on-one fellowship with God, exactly as Introverts prefer it. These one-on-one meetings between God and Moses occurred in full view of Joshua. Moses was an Introvert who was more comfortable interacting in small and intimate group settings.

Initially, Moses had a lot of apprehension regarding going back to Egypt.[76] Aside from the fact that he killed an Egyptian soldier about forty years prior to the burning bush experience and God's subsequent command for him to return and tell pharaoh to let God's people go, Moses wanted no part of taking center stage (unlike his Extroverted brethren), in pharaoh's court to offer the command of the Lord to the pharaoh. He tried to talk God out of using him multiple times.[77] An Extrovert like his brother Aaron would have at least been willing to entertain the idea of going back and telling the pharaoh in front of everyone to let God's people go free from bondage in Egypt.[78]

MOSES'S INTUITIVE PREFERENCE

Moses was also an iNtuitive processor of information. Moses wanted to understand and investigate in-depth why he saw a bush that was burning; but one that was not being consumed by the fire.[79] Many people with a dominant Sensing preference would have just taken in the information,

75. Exod 14; 24:13; 32:15–17; 34:5–28.

76. Exod 2:11–15.

77. Exod 3:11; 13; 4:1, 10, 13.

78. Exod 4:14–17.

79. Exod 3:3.

thinking: "Bush on fire, fire not burning bush, wow, what an anomaly!" and left to continue tending to Jethro's flock. Moses was intent on finding the thing behind the burning, though not consuming, fire.

MOSES'S FEELING PREFERENCE

Moses also made his decisions using his Feeling decision-making preference to follow the Lord's directives in a very cognitively sound manner, yet still inclusive of all of the feelings of the parties involved. After trying to talk God out of sending him back to the pharaoh's court to deliver the command of God to Egypt, partially because he had a murder charge hanging over his head, Moses relented and was obedient and executed the directions of God to the letter. What likely swayed him was the idea or Feeling that he genuinely wanted the children of Israel to remain together as one people under the direction of their God.

Moses relayed God's instructions and told the Hebrews exactly how to conduct the first Passover.[80] Moses also delivered the tablets of the Ten Commandments to the children of Israel, as penned by the finger of God.[81] He later decided to smash those same tablets because he was feeling angry with the children of Israel about their disobedience in deference to their God. Fortunately, God made new ones.[82]

When he and Joshua returned from Sinai, having been given advanced warning by God that the Hebrews had builty a golden calf as an idol because Moses was on Sinai for so long, Moses had to first assuage the anger of God.[83] He employed verbal alacrity and reminded God that he should not be so angry with the children of Israel as to destroy them. Just like Abigail, a fellow INFP, Moses pointed out to God that the Egyptians would question the Hebrew God that was strong enough to deliver Israel from Egypt only to destroy them in the desert. He also called God to remembrance of his promise to Abraham, Isaac, and Jacob regarding the great nation that Israel would become through them, and not through Moses as God suggested. Again, just like Abigail with David, God's anger was assuaged and he relented, deciding not to destroy

80. Exod 12:1–30.

81. Exod 24:12–13; 32:15–19.

82. Exod 34:1–4, 28.

83. Exod 32:9–14, 30–35.

his chosen people.[84] Moses was once again able to keep the entire team together with their God.

However, Moses the Feeling-preferenced deliverer was not finished demonstrating his Feeling decision-making function; as he and Joshua descended Sinai, listening to the sounds of singing in the camp, Moses immediately confronted his brother Aaron the Extrovert. Moses was outraged because of his intimate feelings for God. Moses may have also been close to demonstrating a borderline Thinking function regarding his decision-making preference in his confrontational style. He asked Aaron, in essence, what they had to pay him in order to convince him to build an idol in the form of a golden calf. Aaron the duplicitous priest lied immediately and said that they all threw some gold into a fire . . . and a calf popped out? (I love this story! I should've written about Aaron's (ESFP) personality! Maybe later . . .)

Moses then decided to directly confront the entire congregation of Israel. He temporarily abandoned his empathy for them because their sinful actions were so offensive to God.[85] Although in reality Moses only abandoned those who chose not to side with God; he did not abandon his feelings, affection, or consideration for the entire congregation of Israel, thus displaying his more dominant Feeling preference.

He told them to "choose ye this day" who you will serve! If you will serve Jehovah God, come over to this side where I am standing.

He then told those who came to him to strap on their swords and go throughout the camp, killing everyone who did not choose to serve the Lord: brother to brother, friend to friend, and kill them all. Moses was a swift and decisive as well as confrontational decision-maker, particularly in the face of sin and insurrection. But Moses was dedicated to keeping the camp of Israel together with their God, demonstrating his predominate Feeling preference.

MOSES'S PERCEIVING PREFERENCE

Finally, Moses organized his world in a flexible fashion, notwithstanding that one time when he did not want to return to Egypt.

The reason that he did not want to return to Egypt was evidence of his Perceiving preference regarding the organization of and how he personally

84. Exod 32:11–14.
85. Exod 32:25–29.

made sense of his world. Moses had seen a gross injustice occurring, demonstrating once again his Feeling preference. Moses had witnessed an Egyptian soldier beating one of his Hebrew people while he was down in Goshen, most likely visiting with his family. Moses had been adopted by the pharaoh's daughter, though he subsequently as an adult embraced his Hebrew lineage. When Moses saw this injustice and abuse occurring, he looked around and sprang into action to rectify the wrong. He killed the Egyptian who was beating the Hebrew.[86] After killing the Egyptian, he buried the man in the sand when he thought no one was looking.

Moses once again demonstrated his Feeling preference the next day. He saw two Hebrews fighting and inquired as to why they were at odds. Moses was now trying to maintain the peace among the Hebrews, via various and possibly questionable means. They asked Moses if he were their self-appointed leader? They also asked, "if we do not stop fighting amongst ourselves, will you kill us like you did the Egyptian yesterday?" By that statement from the fighting men, Moses knew that everyone was aware of his rash crime of murder. He decided to reorganize his world, leave his place as adopted grandson to Pharaoh, and flee the kingdom of Egypt.[87]

Moses fled all the way to Midian from Egypt. Through another confluence of circumstances, he chased off some shepherds who were harassing the daughters of Jethro, the sheik of Midian, as they watered his flock at the well. After another display of Feeling-preference compassion, he decided that it was time to exercise his Perceiving preference and reorganize his world once again. Moses was invited to Jethro's home after Jethro learned that an Egyptian had rescued his daughters at the well from the harassing shepherds. Moses ultimately married Jethro's daughter, Zipporah. They had a couple of sons and Moses became a shepherd, watching over Jethro's flock.

Moses worked as a shepherd until it was time to reorganize his world once again and be flexible enough to accommodate the calling of God to deliver the children of Israel from Egyptian slavery and begin to watch over God's flock. God called Moses from the burning bush. God then convinced him to go and deliver the Hebrews from Egyptian bondage. So Moses asked Jethro for permission to leave, packed his wife

86. Exod 2:11–15.

87. Exod 2:16–25.

Zipporah and his sons on donkeys, and went back to Egypt.[88] He had no idea how the entire process would turn out, nor what awaited him in Egypt, other than what God told him from the burning bush. However, after God convinced him to go and told him that the pharaoh would not immediately relent, he reorganized, packed, and left Midian for Egypt. Moses was flexible and adaptable to changing situations with a Perceiving preference. And yes, Moses the INFP was as easy to pen regarding his MBTI personality portrait as I initially thought he would be.

MINI MBTI PROFILES (SAMPSON, SOLOMON, EZRA, JONAH, AND SARAH)

SAMPSON

I believe that Sampson was an ENFP. However, I think that Sampson demonstrated a personality extreme in the area of his decision-making acumen. Thus, Sampson was neither stout in the Feeling preference area, nor in the secondary Thinking preference area.

SOLOMON

King Solomon was an ESFJ. Solomon was definitely an Extrovert: I think he had more wives than anyone in recorded biblical history. He was wisely straightforward in his information-gathering technique as well as being swiftly decisive, though inclusive of the rights and feelings of all parties. He demonstrated these Sensing and Feeling preferences when the issue of the two mothers and the one baby came before his throne.[89]

Solomon was very organized as the one whom God selected to build the temple in Jerusalem.[90] The workers were impressively prearranged. Solomon's kingdom benefited from his Judging preference in regards to how he organized the construction of the temple as well as the expansion of the kingdom.[91] The kingdom of Israel and the influence of King Solo-

88. Exod 3:1–5:5.
89. 1 Kgs 3:16–28.
90. 1 Kgs 5.
91. 1 Kgs 4.

mon's throne extended to greatly exceed that of his father, King David. God selected Solomon for the task of building the temple instead of his father David expressly because he was an ESFJ.[92]

EZRA

Ezra the scribe and priest was an ISTJ. Ezra was an Introvert, based mostly on his penchant for writing. He was a very straightforward information-gatherer as a person with a Sensing preference. He was also a logical and orderly decision-maker, which demonstrated his Thinking preference. He verified this preference through his role in the rebuilding of the wall in Jerusalem.[93] Ezra also played an important role regarding rebuilding the temple in Jerusalem and in the return of Israel and Judah to their dedication to the God of the temple. Ezra was a very well-prepared and clutter-free person regarding the manner in which he organized, the information that he wrote, the prayers that he prayed, and his role during the time of the rebuilding of the wall in Jerusalem, thus displaying his Judging preference.

JONAH

Jonah, as I briefly described him in chapter 2, was likely an ENFJ. Jonah was outspoken and defiant, particularly with God.[94] He also demonstrated his Extroverted preference when he told the sailors on the ship that he almost sunk because of his disobedience to just throw him overboard because he knew that he had been running in the opposite direction from God.[95] Also, Jonah, as with most iNtuitive preference people, could see "the thing behind the thing" fairly clearly.[96] However, he did not always see the right thing![97]

By now, you should be able to find the other preference zones for Jonah. He is not that difficult to assess. Jonah had a tendency to wear his feelings on his sleeve and make some extreme as well as very decisive

92. 2 Sam 7:1–17; 1 Kgs 5:3–5.

93. Ezra 1:1–10:44.

94. Jonah 4:1–3.

95. Jonah 1:12.

96. Jonah 4:1–3.

97. Jonah 1:1–3; 4:4; 6–11.

moves, demonstrating his Judging preference. Although the majority of the time these moves did not produce immediately positive results.

SARAH

I could not decide if Sarah was an Introvert or an Extrovert. But based on her laughter at the angel's proclamation that she was to have a child at 90 years of age, and her desire to persistently confront Hagar her hand-maiden, I believe that she was likely an Extrovert.[98]

You decide on the other three personality zones for Sarah. She was probably an ESFP, though she is not an easily discerned MBTI person-ality type due to the lack of specific, personality-revealing information presented in the Bible.

FINAL ADVICE

One last bit of advice as you begin your journey into the world of person-ality profiles: please do not try to force other people into the preferences that are associated with your personality type. There are sixteen distinct MBTI personality type combinations. All of these personality types oper-ate on a sliding scale; this is why we call them preference zones. There-fore, there are innumerable combinations of personality expressions that occur within one day for one person of one distinctive personality type.

I am an ENTJ. I, at times, will behave as an outsized Extrovert, but the place most comfortable for me under normal circumstances is to behave in a borderline capacity as an Extrovert who enjoys residing very closely related to his Introverted side. To quote the old commercial: "Sometimes I feel like a nut . . . and sometimes I don't!"

This is the case for everyone. Thus, when your spouse or best friend who you have intimately known for years behaves in a way that you may have never experienced and you want them to just act like you would in that situation, they probably never will. I hope we all learn that we are all very dynamic people. We will remain consistent in the expression of our personality type. However, we will never be static creatures.

---

98. Gen 16:1–6; 21:8–21; 18:10–15.

SEE YOURSELF IN MANY PREFERENCES AND LEADERS

I hope that you see yourself, as well as your friends and family members, in many of these characters and leaders. I hope that you also found similarities in the person who was chosen to represent your MBTI.

Finally, I hope that you see yourself in many of them, not just the leader with whom the MBTI test revealed that you shared the strongest preferences in all four preference zones. We all have preferences, but none of us have static personality traits. Take the test and then take your own journey as you find yourself within this group portrait of many different biblical personalities.

20

Appendix

FREE MBTI TEST LINK

http://www.humanmetrics.com/cgi-win/jtypes2.asp

Bibliography

Human Metrics Inc. "*Jung Typology Test.*" http://www.humanmetrics.com/personality

Littauer, *Personality Plus*. Grand Rapids: Revell, 1993.

Myers, Isabel Briggs. *Introduction to Type*. 6th ed. Palo Alto: Consulting Psychologists, 1998.

Rohm, Robert. *Positive Personality Profiles: D-I-S-C-over Personality Insights to Understand Yourself and Others*. Marietta, GA: Personality Insights, 1994.

The Next Generation. "Galaxy's Child." Directed by Winrich Kolby. Written by Maurice Hurley. March 11 1991.

Made in the USA
Columbia, SC
18 October 2020